北京的故事
STORY OF BEIJING

北京九杂谈

Beijing By-talk

张本瀛 著
李有光 译
胡伟雄 金 菊 校
Written by Zhang Benying
Translated by Li Youguang
Proofread by Hu Weixiong, Jin Ju

中国建筑工业出版社
CHINA ARCHITECTURE & BUILDING PRESS

序

舒济

我的几位小友，恕我这样称呼他们。“小”是因为他们都是1950年以后出生的，都比我小上二三十岁，现在都风华正茂，个个有着一个不大不小的职务，负着一定的责任。他们在各自的岗位上，都工作得不错；业余爱好，又都酷爱研究老北京。老北京的“老”，在我心里衡量的标准，至少是有城门城墙的北京。这几位小友，虽没在中华人民共和国成立前生活过，可是不知怎地，他们爱这座大城市中的“老”味儿到了痴迷的程度。业余时间，他们会钻天觅缝地查找旧书本、旧报刊，走访在世的当事人、里手、行家，实地调查；他们肯花钱买自己需要的、喜爱的老玩意儿，多方面地细致了解，认真体味过去，在自己心里营造出“立体”、“真实”的老北京。这样日积月累地增长知识，陶冶了情趣，提高了鉴赏能力，从中得到快乐与满足，使生活过得挺充实，挺有品位。

这几位小友，也是老舍迷。他们熟读过老舍先生的文学作品。对老舍先生本人的事也知道得挺多。谈起老舍先生来，会滔滔不绝，如数家珍。更有甚者，被老舍先生的文学语言感染得手也发痒，动笔写了起来。小友们无论写老北京的人物、事件、地理风情的文章小段，还是改编老舍先生的小说和其他文学形式，都能以北京腔，写出特有的幽默。它们延续着一种老北京特有的文化品格，为当今社会增添着

属于北京应有的文化色彩。

老舍先生在他的抗战话剧《大地龙蛇》序中写道："一人群单位，有它古往今来的精神的与物质的生活方式；假若我们把这方式叫作文化，则教育、伦理、礼仪，与衣食住行，都在其中，所蕴甚广，而且变化多端。"并说："文化亡，必系奴隶。"在当今社会中像他们这样的中青年人并不多，可是他们的爱好，他们的写作，却是社会发展所需要的。旧的东西经过选择、淘汰，在新的社会环境中，用现在的眼光审视再现，就会使美好的文化遗产驻留人间。

张本瀛等几位小友的努力，得到了人们的肯定与尊重。他们利用业余时间写了这套有关"老北京"文化的丛书，其中的每一篇文章都在过去与现在之间穿梭，新的旧的相互交融，让你能看得见、抠得出、闻得着老北京的味儿，从中感觉到北京的美意。虽然文中的个别枝节，可能缺乏更为严格的考证，但这并不影响此套书所要传达出的那种色调和情意。我们品尝美味佳肴，不是讲究色、香、味吗？这套丛书是不是让您也可以品尝一下老北京的色、香、味？

（注：舒济老师是已故著名京味文学家老舍先生的长女，现为老舍纪念馆馆长）

Preface

My several “little friends”(please forgive me to call them this way, the reason is they were all born after 1950 and are twenty to thirty years younger than me) are in their best age now, and they all have some titles. They work pretty well and they also love doing research about old Beijing. Old Beijing, for me, refers to the Beijing with the gate and the wall. These little friends, nobody knows why, are crazy about the “old” charm of old Beijing although they never have life experiences in the period before the People’s Republic of China founded. In spare time, they look for old books and old periodicals everywhere; they visit alive parties and professionals, and do the fieldwork. They would like to spend money to buy some old things they need and like, so that they can get to know the past from many aspects. As a result, a dimensional and true old Beijing is built up in their own mind. Through these experiences, not only has their knowledge increased but also their appeal and ability to appreciate have been improved. Moreover, they get happiness and satisfaction from it, so their lives are more rich and high-standard.

These little friends are also Lao She’s fans. They know Lao She’s literature very well, and know about himself as well. When they talk about Mr. Lao She, they can never stop, just like counting their family treasures. Some people are even influenced by the language of Lao She’s articles that they have started their own writing. The article segments they wrote might be individual, event, or local condition and custom, might be novel that adapted from Lao She’s works or might be articles in other genres. No matter what kind of articles they are, they all keep a typical humor by using Beijing language, which make the Beijing culture characteristics continuing, and also add more culture factors to the modern society that Beijing should has.

In the drama *Dragon and Snake on the Earth* which is about the War Against Japanese, Mr. Lao She wrote, "Every group of people have their own living way on spirit and substance aspects. If we call this culture, nearly everything including education, ethics, and proprieties are included in the culture. The extension of culture is very wide and changeable. " He also said, "When culture is dead, our nation must be slaves." In the present society, there are few such middle aged people, but their hobbies and their writings are needed for the development of the society. The old things remained after selection and elimination will keep the wonderful culture legacy in the world forever when they are reviewed in the present view in the new society environment.

The efforts these little friends have made get confirmed and gain respect. They have written a set of books about "old Beijing" in their spare time. When you read their articles, you will go through past and present, and find new things through old things. You can see, feel, and taste the old Beijing, so that you can feel the goodness of Beijing and be proud of it. Although a few details in the books lack more well-knit proof, it won't influence the keynote and emotion these books have expressed. When we taste a delicious meal, we care about the color, smell, and flavor, don't we? When you read this set of books, is it true that you can also taste the color, smell, and flavor of old Beijing?

Shu Ji

(The Elder Daughter of Famous Writer Lao She)

目录　CONTENTS

古玩与民间艺人
Curio and Handicraftman

大师与国粹
Master and National Legacy

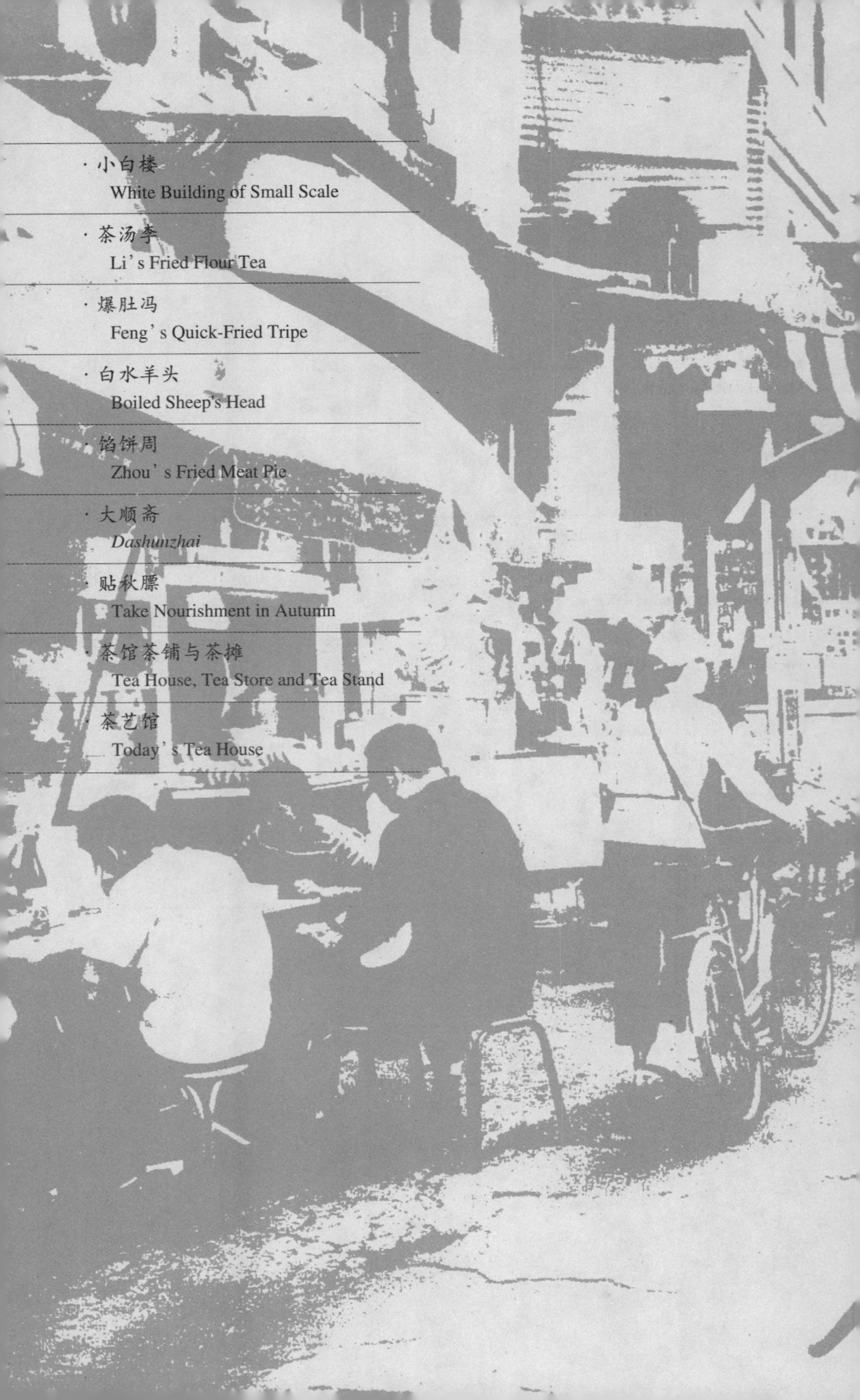

美食与茶

Snack and Tea

小白楼

White Building of Small Scale

□ 通惠河中的仿古船 The Archaized Ship in Tonghui River

几十年前，北京京东通惠河的两岸，垂柳弯弯，曲折纵横的水塘与河流相依。塘内是成片的灌木、茂密的芦苇、地毯似的厚厚水草。水美当然鱼肥，鲤鱼、草鱼、鲇鱼、鲫鱼、黑鱼等都个大肉鲜。

那时北京至通州间的路还是砂石铺就，虽坑坑洼洼，却格外繁华。这里最吸引人就是"小白楼"，一个清真饭铺。所谓"小白楼"其实并不是纯白色，实际上是清一色的灰砖、灰瓦砌制成的一所坐北朝南的四合院，位于通惠河岸边的十字路口。门楼儿附近有两棵百年老榆树，遮天蔽日罩住整所院落，院内宽敞明亮，收拾得干净利落；正房及东西厢房的老式家具摆放错落有致。踏进这

There is a river named Tonghui River in the east of Beijing, along which there were weeping willows several decades ago, and nearby there were many pools filled with shrub, reed and aquatic grass. The water was so rich that fish like carp, grass carp, catfish, crucian and snakehead were very large and their meat was quite fresh.

At that time, although the road between Beijing and Tongzhou built with gravels was rough, it was quite prosperous. The most attracting place along the road was *Xiaobailou* (a small white building of small scale) , an islamic restaurant. As a matter of fact, *Xiaobailou* was not white but grey. It's a quadrangle facing south, made from grey bricks and grey tiles. It was situated at the crossroad near the bank of Tonghui river with

所院落，立刻有人热情打招呼，如沐春风。店老板姓马，慈眉善目，常年戴一顶黑缎子面的瓜皮帽儿，媳妇年轻俊俏，持家有道。最早是马掌柜的爷爷在这块宝地开门立户，信守和气生财，生意一直十分火爆。来“小白楼”的并不都是平民百姓，很多名流显贵也是这里的常客。“京东小白楼”烫金牌就是梁启超先生的墨宝。冬去春来，寒消暑往，“小白楼”就成了京城推杯问盏、谈古论今的“名楼”。

这里每天门庭若市，周围风景如画，店家古道热肠固然重要，关键还是这儿的拿手名菜——“红烧鲇鱼”。这道菜为何叫响京城？说来话长，不过它的成名，从根儿上起，是马掌柜祖上三代潜心琢磨的结果。首先在选料方面，必须严格精选重量为一斤半大小，而且一定是从通惠河现打捞上来的鲜活鲇鱼，并要现场宰杀，去鳞、去五脏，然后在鱼身上切若干个小口儿，撒上少许盐先腌制半个钟头左右，提前进味儿。一切准备完毕后，

□ 位于通惠河岸边的佛舍利塔
Tower Beside Tonghui River

two old elms nearby. The whole yard was shady, spacious and clean, and rooms were decorated with Chinese traditional furniture. When guests arrived there, they would feel at ease. The keeper and chef was a middle-aged man with the last name Ma, who wore a dark skullcap throughout a year. This restaurant was founded by Ma's grandfather and had been always filled with consumers from common people to celebrities and aristocrats. And the restaurant's brand, *Xiaobailou in the East of Beijing,* was, Mr. Liang Qichao's calligraphy. Mr. Liang Qichao was a Chinese scholar, journalist, philosopher and reformist from Qing Dynasty (1644 -1911) to the early of the Republic of China(1911-1949), who inspired Chinese scholars with his writings and reform movements. As the time went on, *Xiaobailou* had become a famous building where people could enjoy delicious food and talk freely.

Everyday, the restaurant was filled with guests because of the beautiful surroundings, warm service and above all, the well-known dish: Braised Catfish with Brown Sauce. It had been developed by three generations from Ma's grandfather. Here's the procedure to make it.

First, choose catfish. The proper fish is about 750 grams and must be just taken from Tonghui River. Kill the fish on the spot, scale and remove the harslet, make several cuts on the body of the fish. Then, sprinkle salt on the fish and wait for half an hour. When everything is ready, the fish can be fried. But how about the temperature of the oil? It's OK just when the fish is put in, the oil splash and a fireball forms. At last, sauce, vinegar, shallot, ginger, garlic, anise, orange peel, wine and other

先放入锅里过油，此时应特别注意“火候”。鱼一入锅，油星四溅、火球升空，才称得上是“火候”到家了。煎完鱼，再配以自己调制的酱油、醋、葱、姜、蒜、大料、陈皮、料酒等佐料，约20分钟的功夫，一盘色、香、味、形俱佳的“红烧鲇鱼”就端上桌儿来了。这其中最关键工序是什么呢？不是店老板精湛的手艺，而是不用当地井里的水！做菜褒汤必须用通惠河新打的河水。这便是“红烧鲇鱼”外焦里嫩、香味醇厚的奥妙所在，也是众食客们常挂在嘴边上的“原汁原味”的首要因素。

以前曾有过有心计的美食家，偷偷观摩马掌柜的烹调手艺，看后感到不过如此，甚至认为无非是“故弄玄虚”的雕虫小技。于是回到家中亲自操练一番，结果味儿差老鼻子了。天长日久，一传十十传百，食客们免费宣传，京东小白楼的“红烧鲇鱼”美名远播。早年京城里一些有头有脸儿的人士，都喜欢在这里小坐，那是“小白楼”风光无限的好时候；解放前后，马掌柜突发暴病撒手归天，“小白楼”饭铺也江河日下，现在只有那些老食客，还在记忆中品尝“红烧鲇鱼”的滋味了。

□ 小白楼原貌 Little Bailou Restaurant in the Past

□ 今日通惠河边的小楼饭店
Bailou Restaurant Now

seasoners are added to the fried fish. It will take about 20 minutes of the whole procession. But what' s the key of the procession? It' s the water used for cooking! The water is not from the local wells, but from Tonghui River! And that' s the reason why the dish is so fragrant with crisp outside and tender inside.

Once there was a gourmet who wanted to make this dish by himself. After secretly watching Chef. Ma how to make it, he felt disappointed because there were nothing special in the procession. Back home, he began to cook catfish. But the taste of his dish was quite different from Chef. Ma' s. Year after year, more and more people knew *Xiaobailou* for its Braised Catfish with Brown Sauce. People from all classes enjoyed consuming here and that' s the uprising time of *Xiaobailou*. After Chef. Ma died of acute disease in 1949, the restaurant had a hard time with fewer guests. Now, only the regular customers come here. For many lovers of *Xiaobailou*, it's a regret that they can only imagine the taste of the Braised Catfish with Brown Sauce in their memories.

茶汤李

Li's Fried Flour Tea

住在皇城根儿下的人有口福。郊区的不算，光是在这城圈儿里历史悠久的大小饭铺就不下上百家。著名北京风味小吃“茶汤李”就是一家很有特色的好去处。总店位于城南天桥儿永安路路北，现在掌柜的是“茶汤李”第二代传人，年已八旬的李秉忠老爷子。“茶汤李”铺面儿开张时值清末民初，地方就选在天桥儿。李秉忠当年不足十岁，人长得还没有条案高，却早随其父李桂林在天桥地面儿上摆摊儿了。那时风光的天桥云集着各地贫苦艺人，个个身怀绝技。天桥声扬四海，山南海北各方来客纷至沓来；那时候“茶汤李”的大棚位于能说会唱的民间艺人绰号“云里飞”的场子旁边。对行儿的诀窍和规矩了如指掌的父子俩，几十年如一日，头顶天上的星星儿，早早将头天晚上封好的炉火打开。不大会儿，炉中的红火苗很快窜出，大铜壶锃光瓦亮，里面的水冒着团团热气腾空而起。然后依次把古色古香的花瓷盆摆上条案，里面装着杏仁茶、菱角粉、油茶、牛骨髓茶等品种，恭候食客的到来。

逛天桥的大多为平头百姓，吃喝讲实惠，“茶汤李”恪守薄利多销的规矩，摊儿前总是人头攒动，多是回头儿客。据说，早年从四九城赶来专门儿逛“天

People who live in the Inner City of Beijing are very lucky because there are hundreds of restaurants with long history there. Among them, *Chatang Li* is very famous with its unique characteristics. *Chatang* is a kind of paste made of millet or sorghum flour. The head restaurant of *Chatang Li* is situated in Tianqiao near the north side of Yongding Road. Now, the keeper is Li Bingzhong at his eighties, the second generation of *Chatang Li*. *Chatang Li* was opened in Tianqiao in the late of Qing Dynasty and the early of the Republic of China. In the early time, although Li Bingzhong was still a child no more than ten years old, he had to deliver *Chatang* with his father Li Guanlin. There had seen many poor handicraftsman, actors and artists from different places with their unique skills in Tianqiao, and the stall of *Chatang Li* was near the place of a folk actor, Yunlifei. Everyday, the father and the son got up very early. They first undrew the door of

□ 云里飞戏班 Yunlifei Theater Groupe

□茶汤李店面 The Storefront of *Chatang Li*

桥儿”找乐子的男女老少，如果不喝上一碗正宗“茶汤李”的喷香茶汤，就不算来过“天桥儿”。此话儿可能有些夸张，但反映出“茶汤李”的茶汤在老北京人心中特殊的位置。过去在鼓楼大街、东四牌楼、西四牌楼、什刹海等繁华地段，以经营茶汤为主业的人并不少，但大都没坚持到最后，而只有“茶汤李”依然不倒。一个重要原因，“茶汤李”尤为注重“信誉”。因为老百姓认了你这块金字招牌，经营者就不能做投机取巧自毁门面的事儿，那可是砸招牌。“茶汤李”原料进货非常严格。如糜子从张家口坝上或内蒙古多伦一带的原产地进，果料、桂花、山楂糕、核桃仁、红、白糖等都要到专供点进货。对原料的再加工工序必不可少，像茶汤的主料糜子粉至少要在加工过后再过三次箩，以手捏不能有小疙瘩为宜。沏茶汤用的铜壶要到专门的厂家定做，且要一水的红铜为主，壶的形状应制成肚膛子大，嘴儿弯尖适度才能受热均匀，只有这种铜壶

the stove and started to boil water. Soon after the water in the big copper kettle was boiling, Li and his father put different traditional porcelain plates on the tables with almond tea, water chestnut powder, *Youcha*, cow marrow tea etc. When everything was ready, customers came one after another.

Most of people who came to visit Tianqiao were common ones. *Chatang Li* had been abiding by the rule of making small profit and selling more, so it attracted numberless customers and most of them were regular ones. It's said that you couldn't count to have visited Tianqiao if you didn't drink a bowl of *Chatang* of *Chatang Li*. It reflected how greatly *Chatang Li* had effected Beijingers. At that time, there were many businessmen who mostly sold *Chatang* at the high streets of Beijing, such as Gulou Avenue, Xisi Pillar, Dongsi Pillar and Shichahai. But most of them couldn't stick to the end and only *Chatang Li* survived up to now. The most important reason is that *Chatang Li* has given special attention to its credit. People believe in this brand, and *Chatang Li* has very strict rules. Their material is all from original producing area, such as millets are from Zhangjiakou or Nei Monggol, and fruit, sweet osmanthus, haw cake, red sugar and white sugar from the exclusive suppliers. It is necessary to reprocess the material. As the major material, millet powder must be screened three times until it's very fine. The kettle used for making *Chatang* are customzied, and they are made of red copper in the shape of men's belly. The mouth of the kettle must have proper curves, so that it can be heated equally. It is only this kind

方可保证茶汤黏稠、口感香味俱佳。

如今京城“茶汤李”的分号遍布北京，东、西、南、北约有200多家，逢每年农历新春佳节举办的龙潭湖、地坛、白云观三大传统庙会，组织者都要请“茶汤李”前去助兴。现在的“茶汤李”早已改变过去手工化、小作坊化的落后制作方法，走上一条工厂化、集团化的现代企业发展的道路。在继承传统风味的基础上，他们不断推陈出新，又创制了不少新品种新风味的茶汤以满足不同人群的需要。茶汤之魅力就在于观其色、闻其香，食之回味悠长，奔波忙碌的都市人，让怀旧在茶汤中萦绕。

of kettle that can ensure the quality of *Chatang*.

Today, there are more than 200 subsidiary companies of *Chatang Li* throughout Beijing. They are invited to three traditional temple fairs in Spring Festival separatedly in Dragon Pond Lake, the Temple of Earth and Baiyun Taoist Temple, and workshop has been replaced by a modern enterprise group. On the basis of adhering to the traditional flavor, they have developed variety of new flavor to meet different people's demands. Watching colours of *Chatang*, smelling its fragrantness and feeling aftertaste, people will find the charm of the *Chatang*, and it may awaken the busy urbanite's reminiscences.

爆肚冯

Feng's Quick-Fried Tripe

爆肚是京城几代老少爷们十分喜食的小吃，早年在北京城里经营爆肚生意的商贩，几乎是清一色的回民，过去仅经营爆肚儿生意的字号在北京就多达20多家，有“爆肚满”、“爆肚石”、“爆肚王”、“爆肚宛”、“爆肚张”、“爆肚冯”等等。其中创业于清代光绪元年（1875年）的“爆肚冯”，历史最为悠久。

第一代“爆肚冯”冯立山从山东陵

□位于大栅栏门框胡同的爆肚冯老店

The Shop of *Baodu Feng* in the Mengkuang Hotong

Quick-Fried Trip has been a kind of favorite snack for several generations of Beijingers. The dealers who ran Quick-Fried Trip business were almost all Muslem. There were over 20 Quick-Fried Trip restaurants in beijing, such as Quick-Fried Trip Man, Quick-Fried Trip Shi, Quick-Fried Trip Wang, Quick-Fried Trip Wan, Quick-Fried Trip Zhang, Quick-Fried Trip Feng. Among them, Quick-fried Tripe Man has a history of more than one hundred years. The old shop of Quick-fried Tripe Man is now located in Caishikou and is still run by the offspring of Man's family. Recently they opened a branch opposite Guiyou Mansion. Same as Quick-fried Tripe Man, Quick-fried Tripe Feng is also a one-hundred-year-old shop. Quick-Fried Trip Feng had the longest history which can be traced back to 1875 when *Baodu Feng* first opened. The first generation owner of Quick-Fried Trip Feng refers to Feng Lishan, the founder of Quick-Fried Trip Feng, who came from Dongling County, Shangdong Province and founded his foothold in Beijing with his skills handed down from his ancestors.

During several decades after he came to Beijing, Feng Lishan ran Quick-Fried Trip Feng painstakingly. As time passed, Quick-Fried Trip Feng became one of the most popular snacks in Beijing. It was Feng Jinhe, the second generation

□ 爆肚冯第三代传人冯广泉 The Third Genenation of *Baodu Feng*(in the middle)

县老家辗转来到京城，用祖传绝技迅速在京都立足。在以后数十年间，冯立山苦心经营。俗话儿讲“人叫人，不如活儿叫人”，久而久之，“爆肚冯”成为旧日老北京的一道著名小吃。在“爆肚冯”百年风光的历史长河中，有一个人可谓居功至伟，这位大爷就是“爆肚冯”第二代传人冯金河。冯金河生于清光绪十三年（1888年），他在清代末年子承父业，成了“爆肚冯”的新掌柜，继续操持传统风味小吃“爆肚”。冯金河多年来随父潜心钻研，最终掌握了一手无人能比的制作“爆肚”的绝佳手艺活儿，爆肚刚一出锅便香气四溢，吃在口中更是味道醇厚，深受当年在紫禁城内当差的官员、画师、太监偏爱。后经太监们大力推荐，“爆肚冯”幸运地成了清宫御膳房的爆肚特供点，这可是件头号露脸的

of Quick-Fried Trip Feng, who had contributed most to the one-hundrend-year brilliant achivements of Quick-Fried Trip Feng. Feng Jinhe was born in 1888, and he became the keeper of Quick-Fried Trip Feng in place of his father in the end of Qing Dynasty. Earlier, Feng Jinhe had learned how to make Quick-Fried Trip from his father for several years and had mastered perfect skills which no one could match. The Quick-Fried Trip he cooked was very fragrant and delicious, and got very popular among officials, painters and eunuches who served in the Forbidden City. Later, recommended by eunuches, Quick-Fried Trip Feng became the exclusive Quick-Fried Trip supplier for the imperial kitchens of Qing Dynasty, and that's one of the most glorious things for businessmen. Later on, Quick-Fried Trip Feng had been fa-

□ 爆肚冯在地坛庙会上
Baodu Feng on Show in the Temple Fair

事儿。从此皇恩浩荡，一直延续到清帝退位。

“肚子”就是牛羊的胃，不过您可千万别小看这些玩艺儿，光一个牛肚就可细分为四个部分，依次为百叶、肚仁、百叶尖、厚头。而羊肚多至可分成九个部位，分别是肚仁、散丹、肚领、蘑菇、蘑菇头、肚板芯、食信、肚板和葫芦。常吃的主儿中有的人愿意吃开锅就捞嫩着点的，也有人喜欢吃略微不烂的感到更过瘾，还有的爷儿们愿吃嘎吱嘎吱的才对口味儿。“爆肚冯”绝就绝在他能根据不同年龄的不同顾客，介绍爆肚哪个部位最适合哪位食客的口味儿。哪位回头客喜欢吃什么火候的“爆肚”，早已熟记于心。每日从天刚擦亮开始迎客，只要打老远儿瞧见哪位主顾来喽，立马儿就在寒暄问候之间，把食客们爱吃的不同“爆肚”端上来。

民国以后，清朝八旗子弟亦从“爆肚冯”店家的常客中间消失了。再加上其他的原因，“爆肚冯”的生意日渐萧条。经过再三权衡，冯金河于民国8年(1919年)将“爆肚冯”的老铺面儿，迁至前门外大栅栏廊坊二条小吃一条街，生意又开始如鱼得水。在过去的北京城

vored in Qing Dynasty until its decline.

Du refered to the stomaches of cows or goats, and the former could be divided into four parts and the latter, nine parts. *Baodu Feng*' s two most famous recipes are boiled goat' s stomach and boiled tripe. Both dishes include meat taken from the rubbery wall of the sach. When the scarfskin and unwanted fat is removed, each cow provides less than 100 grams of meat, so five are needed for each dish. Chefs cut the meat in a special way and cook it for a specific amount of time to guarantee the best tasting dish. Home-made sauces are served with the meat. The sauces are made of sesame paste, soy sauce, vinegar, coriander, fermented bean curd and two kinds of Chinese traditional herb. The goat' s stomach, boiled in water and dipped in the unique sauce, tastes crisp while tripe tastes soft and tender. Some customers would like Quick-Fried Trip to be tender, and others prefers stiffness. And Quick-Fried Trip Feng recommends the most suitable parts to its clients according to their ages and preferences. And that' s one of the reasons why Quick-Fried Trip Feng have been so successful a snack. Every regular customer' preference have been memorized by Quick-Fried Trip Feng. So when they came to the restaurant, they would be given friendly welcome, and before their order, their favourite Quick-Fried Trip would be served on their table soon.

As the foundation of the Republic of China in 1912, the descendant of the Eight Banners of the Man nationality in Qing Dynasty was disappearing among the regular customers. And as well as other reasons, Quick-Fried Trip Feng began go-

流传着“小子不吃十年闲饭”的说法，眨眼间冯金河之子“爆肚冯”第三代传人冯广聚逐渐成长起来。冯广聚自幼随父学习祖传爆肚的制作秘诀，并在实践中更加注意选料、刀功、火候和原材料等，尤其在“爆肚”佐料的配制方面细心钻研、大胆创新，几分耕耘几分收获，“爆肚冯”在继续发扬光大。

解放前后，“爆肚冯”曾接待过鲁迅、巴金、丁玲、老舍、荀慧生、金少山、裘盛戎、尚小云、谭富英、李少春、李万春、白杨、于蓝、韩兰根、侯宝林、刘宝瑞、刘宝全、郭启儒、郭全宝等名人，还有不少是常客。后来门框胡同多家风味小吃在1958年被公私合营，直到1985年，爆肚冯和年糕钱、茶汤李、羊头马等数家老字号，受邀参加春节庙会，老北京的风味小吃才宣告归来。从20世纪80年代初至今，“爆肚冯”在西四小吃胡同中和其他一些地方陆续开业。作为老北京名吃，电视台还为“爆肚冯”制作对象为阿拉伯国家的阿语报导。“爆肚冯”冯老爷子曾两次被请进钓鱼台国宾馆，与羊头马、老月盛斋、豆腐脑儿白等人现场为各国驻华使节现场献艺。“爆肚冯”重现往日的无限风光。

□清真爆肚冯 *Baodu Feng*

ing down. After thoroughly thinking over, Feng Jinhe moved Quick-Fried Trip Feng to the snack street in Langfang 2nd Lane Dashanlan near Qianmen. From then on, the business resumes its thriving. Gradually, the third inheritor Feng Guangju, Feng Jinhe's son, grew up. He also learned from his father the recipe of Quick-Fried Trip handed down from his ancestors, but he attached more attention to material, cut art and *Huohou*(duration), in particular, he had some innovation in the makeup of seasoners. So Quick-Fried Trip Feng continued to be brought to a great height of development.

Around 1949, Quick-Fried Trip Feng have taken in famous writers such as Lu Xun, Ba Jin, Ding Ling, and Lao She; Beijing Opera master performers such as Xun Huisheng, Jin Shaoshan, Qiu Shengrong, Shang Xiaoyun, Tan Fuying, Li Shaochun, and Li Wanchun; movie actresses like Bai Yang and Yu Lan; cross-talk master performers such as Hou Baolin, Liu Baorui, Liu Baoquan, Guo Qiru and Guo Quanbao. Some of them were regular customers here. From 1980s up to now, the subsidiary companies of Quick-Fried Trip Feng have appeared in Snack Hutong of Xisi and other places. As a kind of famous snack of Beijing, Quick-Fried Trip Feng has been introduced to Arabic nations by a TV station. And Feng Guangju, the keeper of Quick-Fried Trip Feng now, has been invited to Diaoyutai State Guesthouse twice, together with Yangtou Ma (Ma's Mutton Head Meat), former Yuesheng Zhai and Jellied Bean Curd Bai, to perform for foreign ambassadors working in China. Quick-Fried Trip Feng has resumed its glory again.

白水羊头

Boiled Sheep's Head

在过去的北京，曾流传着“东四前门西单，王府井大栅栏，小小的门框胡同别有一洞天”之说。这句俚语指的就是旧京七大繁华闹市区。就拿“别有一洞天”的门框胡同风味小吃一条街来说吧，它位于大栅栏以里，同仁堂对过，不过是长30米、宽不足5米的小胡同，可这里却云集了几十种历史悠久的风味小吃。如年糕杨（杨德亮）的年糕，以豆馅儿精细松软、黏度可口适中而备受食客青睐；而豆腐脑儿白（白文清）的豆腐脑儿，吃的就是他用上等口蘑和鲜羊肉片等多种佐料打的卤，清亮透明的卤

□ 羊头马第七代马国义在切肉

Ma Guoyi, the Seventh Generation of Yangtou Ma

In Chinese history, Beijing served as the capital of China in the Kin (1115-1234), Yuan (1279-1368), Ming (1368-1644) and Qing (1644-1911) Dynasties, totaling 700 years or so. And in the past, Xisi, Qingmen, Xidan, Wangfujing, Dashanlan and Menkuang Hutong were the busiest districts. Taking Menkuang Hutong for example. Although it's only 30 meters long and 5 meters wide, there are dozens of snacks such as *Niangao Yang*(Yang Deliang's glutinous rice cake), *Doufunao Bai*(Bai's jullied bean curd), as well as Fushunzhai Pickled Beef, *Yangtou Ma* (Ma's sheep head meat), *Nailao Wei*(Wei's Cheese) and *Xiaochang Chen*. They all have strong local flavor with long history. Mashed red bean is the most common filling for *Niangao*. Glutinous rice, taro, mashed white kidney bean, glutinous millet and buckwheat flour are also used to make the cakes. Yang Deliang's *Niangao* is filled with fine and soft fillings. And It's not too sticky, so it is favored by many people. While Bai Wenqing's jellied bean curd is super tender and smooth, the bean curd jelly is seasoned with thick gravy made of minced mutton and mushrooms. But among all these snacks, Boiled Sheep's Head is the most typical snack.

Boiled Sheep's Head is another Islamic traditional snack food that people loves while drink-

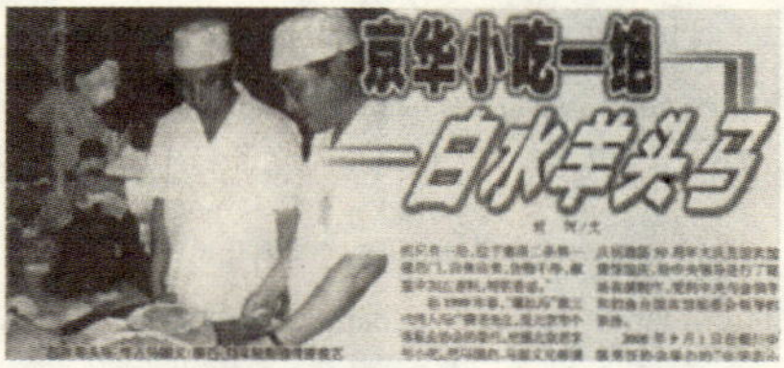

□荣获“中华名小吃” *Yangtou Ma* Titled Chinese Snack

汁再配上乳白色的豆腐脑儿，吃在口中那味道真是鲜嫩爽滑没得挑儿。此外，这里还有与月盛斋酱羊肉齐名的复顺斋酱牛肉、羊头马的白水羊头、奶酪魏的奶酪及小肠陈等多家种类繁多、令人叫绝的京味小吃。其中响誉京华的“白水羊头”是其代表。

“白水羊头”起家于清朝道光年间。回民有制作经营清真食品传统。据介绍，160多年前的马纪元老先生，一般都是头天晚上在家里加工羊头，次日一早便挑着箩筐，带上切肉的刀和菜墩子，沿街串巷叫卖。身为第五代羊头马的马玉昆从其父马元凤手中接过买卖后，在大栅栏廊坊二条门框胡同小吃一条街，由挑筐沿街串巷改为推着独轮车叫卖，到20世纪30年代初，开始在裕兴酒楼门前定点设摊经营。马玉昆老人恪守“宁肯少卖十个人，绝不糊弄一个人”的家训，从开始的原料进货到接下来的加工烹制“白水羊头”全套工序中，几十年如一日讲究货真价实，讲究干净卫生，讲究调味风格，讲究纯正地道的刀法，那时马玉昆一天只加工约20个羊头。马老爷子的独轮车一到，立马儿围满了人，买“白水羊头肉”是其一，欣赏他手持二尺长的大刀片片肉的绝技是其二。行家称马玉昆绝就绝在他操刀切肉姿势优美、

ing some wine. Boiled Sheep’s Head was originated during Emperor Daoguang in Qing Dynasty. And its originator is Ma Jiyuan who belonged to the Hui nationality, which has a tradition of making and running Islamic food. As his descendants told, Mr. Ma processed sheep’s head at home night and next morning,and he would carry his baskets as well as knives and wood block to sell Boiled Sheep’s Head throughout streets and alleyways. As the fifth generation of Sheep’s Head Ma, Ma Yukun began to use a wheelbarrow to sell Boiled Sheep’s Head along Snack Street Menkuang Hutong, Dashanlan instead of carrying baskets. In the early 1930s, he set a stand in front of Yuxing Hotel. As his ancestors, Ma Yukun was very strict in the whole process from choosing material to processing Boiled Sheep’s Head. He sticked to the principle of genuine goods at a fair price, cleanity, unique taste, and skilled cut. At that time, Ma Yukun only processed about 20 sheep’s head a day. Once his wheelbarrow arrived, the stand would be surrounded by people who came to buy his Boiled Sheep’s Head and watch his cutting skill. Cooking experts had appraised he had elegant gesture and fast speed when he cut Boiled Sheep’s Head. The sliced meat was very thin and half transparent but not broken. But later on, Ma Yukun gave up his skill and became a transport worker. He resumed his business until Nanlaishun Restaurant opened again in the early 1960s.

The sheep head must be from the Inner Mongolia Autonomous Region with white fur and within two years old. Further more, it must have been castrated. The processings of the sheep’s head

动作麻利，刀起刀落，那肉片儿薄而不碎，弹性强却呈半透明状。老爷子现切现卖成为街头一景。后来马玉昆改行当了运输工人，直到60年代初“南来顺”饭庄在菜市口重新开张之际，他又重操旧业并干到退休。

白水羊头所需羊头必用内蒙古的两岁以内白毛山羊头，且必须阉割过。买回来后，首先要放入凉水中浸泡约两个小时，用刷子反复洗刷羊头，以清洁白净为宜，但又不能用力过大以避免刷破头皮。接着掰开羊嘴，来回刷舌根，将口、鼻、耳依次洗净，再放入大盆中用净水反复冲洗多次，然后放在箧子上晾干。约半小时左右，将羊头皮正中至鼻腔处划一长口，按老嫩程度逐个放入锅中，再倒入凉水，漫过羊头10厘米为好。用旺火约煮一个半钟头待七成熟时

are as follows. First, soak it in cool water for two hours, then brush the sheep' s head thoroughly until it' s clean. Don' t brush it too hard, or the skin of the head will be torn. Next, open the mouth and brush the tongue. Clean the mouth, nose and ears in turn. Then put it into a bigger basin and wash it with clean water for several times. Dry it by airing for half an hour. Then cut a slot from the middle to the nose, put the sheep' s heads into a boiler according to their tenderness. Pour cool water into the boiler until it is 10cm. higher than the heads. Boil the heads with quick fire for one and a half hours. When they are seven-tenths cooked, take them out, push the mutton aside from the slot. Meanwhile, remove the hair of nose and earwax, cut off the lips and raze the eyebrow. Sheep' s faces and tongues are cut off and put into cool water for another one hour, so that they will be crisp, tender and easy to

□ 前门大栅栏内 Inner Dashanlan,Qianmen

取出，趁热从头皮划口处将羊头肉扒向左右两边，与此同时还须除净鼻须，清净耳垢，割去唇边，刮去眼眉，去掉鼻孔、草芽、抹头胰子等。再将每个羊头剔下的两块羊脸子、羊舌，全部放入凉水中浸泡1小时，使肉脆嫩、色白、筋道、好切。随之取大盐若干放入砂锅，靠微火慢慢将老汤耗干，佐以花椒研成的碎末与丁香粉、砂仁粉混合而成的椒盐，装入特制的牛角做成的容器内，食客吃时现切、现洒，防止羊头肉软塌不筋道。其他还讲究夏天用冰镇，冬天带冰花等。

梁实秋、侯宝林、马连良、谭富英、尚小云，张君秋等人均是这里的常客。有这么一档子事儿，2001年夏天，一个老太太领着一个小女孩来到“羊头马”的店堂上，开口就向服务员提出要求买半斤去皮羊头肉。羊头马第七代传人马国义正好看见，“有！请稍等”。很快，马国义左手托着一盘去掉皮儿的薄片羊头肉走了出来，老太太凝视片刻：“这确实是老羊头马的绝活儿。”老太太说在半个多世纪前，当她长得还没有八仙桌儿高的时候，就由父亲带着来门框胡同吃羊头马的“白水羊头”。如今几十年过后旧地重游，细细品尝仍然感觉风味依旧如初。饭毕，老太太自报家门，原来她俩是梁实秋先生的女儿梁文茜和孙女。第七代传人马国启、马国义兄弟子承父业，在保留传统风味小吃“白水羊头”之外，加大开发新的品牌，现已推出五香酱羊蹄、爆牛肉浇面、炸肉松等不同的品种。

cut. Put salt into the earthen pot, boil with tiny fire until there is no original soup in the pot. With salt and pepper in tailor-made containers, people can scatter them over the mutton once they begin to eat. The Boiled Sheep' s Head will be more delicious if it is cooled.

The regular customers of Boiled Sheep's Head Ma included Liang Shiqiu(writer, translator, and literary critic), Hou Baolin(master cross-talk performer) and Beijing Opera master performers such as Ma Lianliang, Tan Fuying, Shang Xiaoyun and Zhang Junqiu. In the summer of 2001, an old woman came here with a little girl and asked for 250 grams of peeled Boiled Sheep' s Head. Ma Guoyi, the owner of Boiled Sheep' s Head Ma at that time, happened to be there and he said, "Ok, wait a moment please!" After a while, Ma Guoyi came out with a plate of sliced and peeled sheep' s head mutton on his left hand. The old woman gazed at it for a moment and said,"it' s really Ma' s Boiled Sheep' s Head." She recalled that her father often took her to Mengkuang Hutong to have Boiled Sheep's Head when she was still a little girl more than half a century ago. And she thought Ma' s Boiled Sheep' s Head remained its flavor for so many years. Who' s she? Liang Wenqian, the well-known essayist Liang Shiqiu's daughter. And the little girl was her granddaughter. The seventh generation of Boiled Sheep's Head Ma are Ma Guoqi and Ma Guoyi who both remain the traditional flavor of Boiled Sheep' s Head and have developed new varieties such as pickled lamb hoof, noodle with griddle-fried beef, fried meat floss and so on.

馅饼周

Zhou's Fried Meat Pie

老北京风味小吃大多以家庭小作坊为主。小吃店从一大早开门，全家男女老少齐动手，一天到晚的忙活，店主一般不雇佣外人，生怕别人偷偷学走手艺。现在年龄六旬以上的老北京人，尤其是老戏迷大概都记得20世纪40年代前后，前门外粮食店街东有一家专营馅饼的小饭铺，在当时京城著名的中和戏园子斜对过。掌柜的约40多岁，早年跟着爷爷从山东德州辗转而来，姓周，食客们习惯称之为“馅饼周”。此公纯朴厚道，烙的馅饼主料有五花肉、大葱、姜等，水灵灵的全是鲜货。馅饼外皮儿焦黄，里面馅儿倍儿嫩，馅儿大皮儿薄是其特色之一，肉馅儿拌得肥而不腻，瘦

□ 中和戏园 Zhonghe Theater

Most Beijing snacks were made in family workshop in the past. Snack restaurants were opened very early in the morning and every one of the familes was very busy in the whole day. There was no need to hire anyone out families in order to prevent the skills from being learned secretly. The Beijingers over sixty years old, especially the old theatergoers, would remember there was a small restaurant mostly selling *Xian'rbing* at Liangshidian Steet near Qianmen in 1940s in the opposite of Zhonghe Theater. The keeper of the restaurant was a man at his forties from Dezhou, Shandong Province,whose family name was Zhou. The customers prefered to call him *Xian'rbing Zhou* as his nickname. *Xian'rbing Zhou* was honest and kind, and the main material of his *Xian'rbing*, such as meat, scallion and ginger, were all fresh. His *Xian'rbing* was characterized by its rich delicate stuffing and thin skin,crisp outside and tender inside. There was neither too much fat nor too much muscle in the stuffings, and they had a strong fragrant scent. The key of why it was so delicious lay in the material. The main materials were from 75-kilograms pigs produced in Daxing and Tongzhou District, and must be the best part of the pork. Scallion must be from Shangdong Province or the east part of Beijing where they were irrigated by sweet well

而不柴，喷香扑鼻。其味道与众不同关键在选料，主料肉需选用大兴、通州一带产的约150斤左右猪的五花肉，出高价取其最好部位，大葱则要山东或京东的甜井水浇灌种植的。此外，肉馅的调拌自有一套，剁馅之前仔细检查，将不宜做馅筋头巴脑的一律剔除，切忌用酱油，在精心备好的肉馅里，再放入精盐、香油、五香面、姜、味精、黄酒及晾凉的白开水等，人工搅拌半个小时，将馅儿打出白浆来才算大功告成。另外，面和得不用擀面杖就能成型，用文火烙。

“馅饼周”的生意红红火火，与斜对面中和戏园有很大关系。该戏园子是当时京城家喻户晓的大戏园子，京剧界四大名旦梅兰芳、程砚秋、尚小云、荀慧生，还有“活曹操”侯喜瑞，梨园名净萧长华、钱金福等都是中和戏园的名角儿。平常日子的晌午和晚间的饭口上，“馅饼周”忙得不可开交，两个特大的饼铛左右开弓地烙，仍然供不应求。看完戏，兴致未消，戏迷们围坐在八仙桌旁，仍沉浸在剧中，不时有人即兴来上段京剧对白，不闲着，以细竹筷子夹上馅饼，再蘸着红红的辣椒油，佐以盘子中的山西老陈醋，边吃边擦汗，吃得那个香！小伙计们总会悄没声儿地及时把一碗碗不凉不热、稀稠适度的绿豆粥端到客人面前，花个三瓜俩枣儿便让戏迷们感到吃得甭提有多滋润。这一切为“馅饼周”的小饭铺带来了浓郁的文化氛围，也成全了“馅饼周”这个与票友、戏迷百姓息息相关的小小饭铺。

water. Besides, there are some tips in mingling all the material. First, check carefully before chop the pork, remove the veins and membrane unsuitable for stuffing. Secondly, do not use sauce as seasoner. Then, put in the stuffing salt, sesame oil, ginger, gourner powder, Shaoxing wine and boiled water cooled by airing. Mix round by hand for half an hour until white liquid emerged. Besides, the *Xian' rbing* should be baked with gentle heat.

The business of *Xian'rbing Zhou* was thriving, which had a close link to Zhonghe Theater. The theater was well known in Beijing for its celebrated Peking Opera actors ranging from the Four Famous *Dans* — Mei Lanfang, Cheng Yanqiu, Shang Xiaoyun and Xun Huisheng—to Live Cao Cao, Hou Xirui, Xiao Changhua and Qian Jinfu. *Xian' rbing Zhou* usually was very busy at noon and during supper. Although they had two extra big roasting pans, their *Xian'rbing* still weren' t enough when the performance in Zhonghe Theatre was over. The Peking Opera fans, who still immersed in the opera, would sing some segments while having *Xian'rbings*. And hot pepper made them sweat but the taste of *Xian'rbing* would be more strong and delicious! Waiters would serve bowls of mung bean porridge in time. Without too much money, clients can eat very well. All of that had made the small restaurant have a cultural atmosphere because it had so strong links with the *Piaoyou* of Peking Opera.

大顺斋

Dashunzhai

□ 大顺斋 *Dashunzhai*

北京京东的通州城，京杭大运河的起点处，有一座驰名中外约300余年的回民糕点铺面——大顺斋，其精心制作的传统清真糕点“大顺斋糖火烧”声名远播。刘大顺是大顺斋的创始人，是来自江苏南京的回民。刘大顺于明崇祯十三年（1640年）携家带口来到有“一京、二卫、三通州”之称的大运河源头落脚谋生。最初的几年，以走街串巷、沿街叫卖的经营方式为主，手中有了一些积蓄后，遂在毗邻闹市的回民胡同买下五间临街的铺面房，并正式以自己的名字“大顺斋”为铺面字号。在隆重开张以前，刘大顺还特地托人请当时名噪京城的书法家吴春鸿老先生专门题写“大顺斋南果铺”的烫金大字牌匾，挂在铺面儿的醒目位置。

到刘大顺的第六代孙刘九爸，先后开了四个分号。设在通州城里的大来

There is an Islamic pastry shop named *Dashunzhai* with 300 years history at the starting point of Jing-Hang Grand Canal in Tongzhou District, Beijing. It is famous for its traditional Islamic *Dashunzhai Tang Huoshao*, a baked sweet cake. The founder of *Dashunzhai* was Liu Dashun, the Hui from Nanjing. In 1640, he came to the headstream of Grand Canal to make a living with his families. During the early years, he peddled his baked cakes along streets and began to save money. Later, he bought a shop at Huimin Hutong near the busy area and named it *Dashunzhai*. Before the grand opening celebration, Liu Dashun asked Wu Chunhong, the wellknown calligrapher in Beijing, to write for him the brand *Dashunzhai South Candied Fruit*, and hang it on a striking position.

Up to the sixth generation of Liu Dashun, four subsidiary shops have been opened one after another and they all have their own charateristics. *Dalai Hao* sold raw material used for making baked cakes such as oil and flour in Tongzhou County (today' s Tongzhou District) ; *Dasheng Hao, Daxin Hao* and *Daxing Hao* sold sweet baked cakes most and other necessities in old Beijing city. The three typical snack in Tongzhou County refered to *Dashunzhai* Baked cakes, *Xiaobailou* Braised Catfish and *Wangtong* Sauced

号，专门提供油、面等制作糕点的原材料；设在北京四九城里的有大生号、大新号、大兴号，则以出售糖火烧为主，同时兼营一些老百姓日常生活离不开的柴米油盐酱醋茶等。它很早就与“小白楼烧鲇鱼”、“万通酱豆腐”，并列为通州城三大招牌性的风味食品。“大顺斋糖火烧”的风味特点可概括为香甜、松软，回味悠长。据记载：20世纪20年代初，北京牛街回民阿訇张迁前往伊斯兰教圣地麦加朝觐。中东地区地处沙漠，酷暑难耐，当时许多教徒所带食品大都变质和馊坏，惟独张迁随身所带的“大顺斋糖火烧”历经两个月，仍然松软如初，香甜可口，令众多朝觐的信徒们对中国食品的制作绝活赞叹不已。1960年印度总理尼赫鲁应邀来中国，曾点名要吃“大顺斋糖火烧”。

“大顺斋糖火烧”，主要原料面粉一直坚持用自家精磨的细白粉，不能有一丝半点的马虎；香油要用本地盛产的小磨香油；桂花采用江南张长丰字号的；红糖要台湾产的“赤娄”糖；麻酱，则一律用经过筛选的白芝麻细细研磨而成的。制作工序虽非常复杂，但每个环节均丝丝相扣，这就是老字号经久不衰的成功真谛。

Bean Curd respectively. *Dashunzhai* Sweet Baked cake was characterized by its softness and sweetness. According to a record, at the first of 1920s, Imam Zhang Qian living in Niu Street, Beijing, went on a pilgrimge to Mecca, Saudi Arabia where was extremely hot and dry. Most of the food that pilgrims took spoiled or became too sour to eat, only Zhang Qian' s *Dashunzhai* Sweet Baked Cakes remained soft and sweet as fresh as they were made two months ago. The making skills of Chinese food gained highly praises among numerous pilgrims. Jawaharlal Nehru, the first Premier of India, who was invited to China in 1960, particularly ordered *Dashunzhai Tang Huoshao.*

The flour, main material of *Dashunzhai Tang Huoshao*, is ground finely by *Dashunzhai* themselves; sesame oil is the local one produced by small stone mill. Osmanthus flowers are from Zhang Changfeng in the south of the lower reaches of the Yangzi River; Brown sugar, *Chilou* sugar produced in Taiwan. The processing of Sesame paste is very complicated with many trivial details, but there lies the secret of why *Dashunzhai* Sweet Baked cakes has been so successful for so long.

贴秋膘

Take Nourishment in Autumn

什么时节玩什么，什么时候吃什么。每年的“立秋”过后，一向讲究的北京人，自然不会忘记了祖祖辈辈延续下来的“贴秋膘”这一老规矩。何谓“贴秋膘”呢？北京盛夏的高温少雨和炎热天气，让人极其难耐。人的身体消耗会很大，出汗多，饭量相应减少，所以，在立秋过后，要适当地吃一些肉食，用以补充三伏天带来的损耗。老北京人管这种很有针对性的进食方式，为“贴秋膘”。

“贴秋膘”汉人多以传统的猪肉为主，也有喜食牛羊肉的，譬如“东来顺”、“西来顺”、“南来顺”等几家老字号的清真涮羊肉，多年来深受百姓们欢迎。据说，这些餐馆“涮羊肉”的羊肉，均来源于张家口以外优质绵羊，配以店家各自调制的不同风味的传统佐料，辅以粉丝、冻豆腐、卤虾油、酸菜、糖蒜、芥末、白菜等，老远就能闻见随风而来的肉香。在秋风送爽、丹桂飘香的好时节，一家老少、亲朋好友围在火锅旁“贴秋膘”，是不是一件美事呢？

此外，在京城还有以经营烤肉为主的两家老字号，那就是“烤肉宛”和“烤肉季”，这里也是“贴秋膘”的上佳去处。老百姓习惯地称之为“南宛”、“北季”。“烤肉季”的烤肉可归纳为八个字——“自成一体，名不虚传”。“烤肉季”历史

□ 贴秋膘 Taking Nourishment in Autumn

As far as eating is concerned, Beijingers think it should be suitable to the season. Every year, after the day of Liqiu, the Beginning of Autumn (the 13th solar term in lunar calendar), Beijingers will never miss the convention of *Tieqiubiao*. But what is *Tieqiubiao*? In mid-summer in Beijing, people eat too little and sweat too much from the high temprature and little rain, and the energy will be consumed greatly. Therefore, after the Beginning of Autumn, people will take in some meat to compensate their energy. Old Beijingers called this *Tieqiubiao*.

The Hans mostly have pork to *Tieqiubiao*, and others perfer mutton and beef. So instant-boiled mutton of Donglaishun, Xilaishun and Nanlaishun are very popular among common people. It's said that their mutton is all high-quality from Zhangjiakou, Hebei Province. Seasoned with bean vermicelli, iced bean curd, shrimp sauce, pickle, preserved garlic, mustard, Chinese cab-

悠久，它始创于清道光二十八年（1848年）。当时一个名叫季德彩的通州人，每年阴历五至七月来到内城什刹海赶“荷花市场”，在银锭桥东侧摆摊，挂着“烤肉季”的牌子，专门烤羊肉。季德彩去世后，他的子孙继续经营，生意越做越好，便在这里买下了一座小楼，由从前的饭摊变成了固定饭铺。

“烤肉季”百年老饭铺的拿手菜“烤羊肉”，从选肉到刀功到烤制，都有其传统与独到之处。吃起来鲜嫩润口，具有不膻、不柴、含浆滑美等特点。约上几位老友，围坐在八仙桌旁吃烤肉，呷美酒，凭窗远眺，小舟在湖水中轻轻荡漾，水鸟在蓝天下嬉戏，酒不醉人人自醉，岂不美哉？

□ 京城名店烤肉季　Ji′s BBQ Restaurant

bage and so on, it has a strong scent which can be smell at a long distance. It's very agreeable and harmonious that all family members sit around the pot to take nourishment in autumn.

In addition, Beijing has a large Muslim population whose presence in the city is marked by the men in white caps, veiled women, and numerous Muslim restaurants. There're two traditional *Kaorou* restaurants in Beijing: *Kaorou Wan* and *Kaorou Ji*, or South Wan and North Ji as common people call them. *Kaorou Ji* (Ji's BBQ Restaurant) has its own unique characteristics with long history. It was created by Ji Decai from Tongzhou in 1848. Every year, from the fifth to seventh month in lunar calendar, Ji Decai came to Water Lily Market, Shichahai to sell grilled mutton. After Ji Decai died, his children and grandchildren continued his business. Because the business was so thriving, they bought a small building as their restaurant in place of previous stand. The processings are traditional and original, from choosing mutton to cut skill. The mutton is fresh and soft without any bad odor. *Kaorou Ji* may not be the best place for a vegetarian meal, however, its lentils and potatoes are tasty. If you are a carnivore, the self-cook, meat kebabs will be the tastiest you have had. While you sit around old-fashioned square table with friends and enjoy your grilled mutton and good wine, you can also watch little boats rocking gently on the lake and water fowl frolicking. Isn't it a great dining experience?

茶馆茶铺与茶摊

Tea House, Tea Store and Tea Stand

□ 老舍茶馆外景
The Outer Scene of Lao She Tea House

上了些年纪的人大都很留恋老式茶馆，它是过去皇城颇具特色的一景。比较有名的有位于前门外大栅栏的老字号“张一元茶庄”，珠市口附近的“永安茶庄”，以及东城的“吴裕泰茶庄”等。这些有着百年历史的老字号，大都在南方定点收购原茶，运至京城，自家薰制加工茶叶，在店堂中专设茶馆，供南来北往的客人在买茶叶前先行品尝。

老茶馆在清末、民国时期人气最旺。就拿位于繁华闹市大栅栏、花市、琉

Most elders have been deeply empressed by the old-fashioned tea house which was a unique landscape in Beijing in the past. The most famous tea houses include Zhang Yiyuan Tea Store at Dashanlan' r, Yong' an Tea Store near Zhoushikou, Xuanwu District, and Wu Yutai Tea Store in Dongcheng District. These teashops are all hundred years old. They purchase raw tea from Southern China and transport them to Beijing. Then, they process the raw tea by themselves and set tea house in their shop. So the client can taste the tea before they decide to buy them.

The prime time of old-fashioned tea houses was during the Republican period or the first half of the twentith century. Taking Dashanlan, Huashi and Liulichang for example, the old-fashioned tea houses were all decorated with traditional wood furniture, and their waiters wore white towels on their shoulders. Every festival, there were a great deal of guests. The furnishings and their lay-outs embodied a traditional culture atmosphere. Wood screen with faint scent, snowwhite walls, calligraphy from Zhang Daqian, Huang Binhong and Qi Baishi, as well as rare flowers, all of these have given great vitality to tea houses.

Tea is originated from China and the history of

璃厂一带的老茶馆来说吧，老式硬木家具古色古香陈设其中，几位伙计肩搭白毛巾，忙里忙外招呼客人。每逢年节更是高朋满座。茶室内的陈设与布局，体现的是一种浓浓的传统文化的氛围。材质为黄花梨的影壁散发着一股幽幽的清香，墙壁雪白，挂着名家如张大千、黄宾虹、齐白石的墨宝，一盆盆奇花异草平添了几分生气。

茶叶源于中国，有关茶文化的历史可追溯至上古时期。而作为茶文化一部分的茶馆，又以老北京的茶馆最有代表性，老舍先生的名作《茶馆》，使人加深了对老北京茶馆的了解。茶叶乃国饮之第一品，讲究很多。上好的花茶、绿茶应分别选用造型别致、典雅古朴专门用于泡茶的紫砂壶、小瓷壶来泡，水切忌不要滚开，以温水为最好，慢慢小呷最佳。旧时北京，世代居住在什刹海、东四、西四一带的，有相当一部分人是有些名望的官宦人家的后人，他们是茶馆中的常客。不论春夏秋冬，只要天刚亮，他们就从各自的宅院中出来开始遛弯儿，然后来到就近的茶馆里。由早茶开始，吃着店家备好的精美茶点，谈古论今，乐在其中悠哉悠哉。

相识的茶友间见面双手抱拳问候，这是老北京多年来养成的习惯。老友们话题投机，闲谈神侃的以京城的一些名人趣事为主。兴头上，不时有喜欢操着京腔、京味、京韵唱上两口的梅派票友、余派戏迷挺身而出。只见他们拉开架势，在悠扬的京胡伴奏下，奉献《贵妃醉酒》和《珠帘寨》等传统名段，功夫达到一定水准的，还会博得众茶客们阵

tea culture can be dated back to ancient times. Tea drinking originally appeared in Southern China, and until the mid-Tang Dynasty it started to gain favor with Northern Chinese. Tea house plays an important role in tea culture and among all kinds of tea houses, Peking's is most typical. Thanks to *Tea House*, a play witten by Lao She, Peking's tea house became well known all over China. Tea is the most preferred drink in China, and there are many details which one should pay attention to. Top-grade scented tea and green tea should be matched with purple sand pot or small porcelain pot which has simple and novel shape. The water is by no means too hot and lukewarm water is fit for making tea. It's proper behavior to drink tea in sips. The regular customers were noble persons living in Shichahai, Dongsi or Xisi. For them, it had become a routine to stroll about at dawn, then come to tea houses nearby to have morning tea.

Acquanited tea-drinkers used to greet each other with one clenched fist in the other hand. And their gambit during drinking tea were mostly involved with celebrities and their anecdotes. Some Peking Opera fans would sing parts of a play with enthusiasm. After the founding of the

□ 老舍茶馆内砖雕
The Brick Carving in Lao She Tea House

阵喝彩。新中国成立后，许多大名鼎鼎的文人雅士，如老舍、曹禺、焦菊隐、吴祖光、赵树理等先生，都喜欢选择老茶馆作为会友的理想场所。

上述所谈的只是京味儿茶馆中档次较高的一类。还有一种边听评书边喝茶歇脚儿的“书茶铺”，更适合平民的口味。书茶铺中播讲评书的，大多为这一行当的走红名角儿。像当年以擅长说大部头评书的关顺鹏，拿手叫彩的有《三下南唐》、《前后七国》等，他的表演声情并茂，广大书迷们听得如醉如痴。特别当一句“欲知后事如何，且听下回分解”说出时，他微微一笑，这次也就暂告一段落。

还有一种喝茶的地方，就是老百姓称之的“茶摊”。它是小本儿生意，基本上没有固定的场所，大都选择在交通便利的路口、公园、庙会附近。临时搭顶扎棚子，支几个方桌，配几条长凳，一把沏茶用的大铁壶，一个煤球火炉子，十几个粗瓷大碗摞在桌子上，老百姓俗称“大碗茶”。来这儿的清一色是生活在社会最底层的劳苦大众，有以拉洋车为生计的车夫，拉脚的脚夫，穿街走巷焊铁壶补锅底的铁匠，磨刀磨剪子的师傅等。如今，网络遍布全球，抚今追昔自会浮想联翩。现实生活中的每个人，不管你从事何种职业，年长年少，信仰如何，在茶馆中，返璞归真的情感能拉近彼此间的距离，这也是怀旧的原因。

People's Republic of China, many famous men of letters took old-fashioned tea houses as idle places to meet friends, such as Lao She(writer and playwright), Cao Yu(playwright), Jiao Juyin (director, drama theorist and translator), Wu Zuguang(playwright) and Zhao Shuli(a novelist and a leading figure of modern Chinese literature).

These tea houses belonged to the high level ones. Others were Pingshu Tea Store where common people could enjoy storytelling show and take a break while drinking tea. Pingshu is a kind of folk art which also can be called "storytelling". Most of the storytellers were the most popular ones at their time, for example, Mr. Guang Shunpeng, who were expert at telling long stories and enjoyed great reputation among his fans.

There were another kind of place to drink tea, which was called tea stand. Without fixed site and much capital, they could mostly be seen near crossroads, parks and temple fairs. And they were made up of a shelter set up temporarily, several square tables and benches, a kettle, a coalball stove and dozens of big-sized coarse porcelain bowls. People called them *Dawancha* which means drinking tea with big bowls. They met the needs of poor people such as blacksmiths, stevedores, cart-drivers and so on. Although today is a internet world, it is easy to communicate with each other if people have tea together in a tea house whatever occupation,age and belief are.

茶艺馆

Today's Tea House

□ 茶艺馆一景　Today's Tea House

没用几年的功夫，集休闲、文化和品茶于一身的"茶艺馆"，纷纷在京城繁华的地区安营扎寨，且经济效益还相当可观。越是到晚上或双休日客人则越多，特别受有一定文化素养人士的青睐。不过这类"茶艺馆"，您可千万别跟旧京黎民百姓乐意泡的"老茶馆"混为一谈。"茶艺馆"的适时涌现，在很大程度上是应现在生活节奏快、压力大、时尚化等特点而出现的。时至今日，人们在观念上有很大变化，其中有相当一部

Just in a few years, Beijing has seen tea house mushrooming in its busy areas. And they have become quite profitable business which concentrate recreation, culture, sipping and tasting tea on themselves. More guests go there at night or on holidays. Intellectual people particularly favor this kind of tea house. But tea houses are by no means equal to previous old-fashioned tea houses. They emerge as life pace is so fast, and pressure is so intense and lifestyle becomes fashionable. Up to now, people's concept has

□ 说书茶馆内部布置（20 世纪）
The Inner Display of Tea House(20th Century)

分人，厌倦了生意事宜一定选在饭局子上谈的陈规。不少人把目光投到集清静、雅气、休闲诸功能于一身的“茶艺馆”。另外，当仪表堂堂、言行举止均很得体的先生小姐们忙碌一整天下班以后，很需要一个环境休闲别致的地方来放松一下，既时尚又休闲的“茶艺馆”，便和京城这一阶层亲密接触了。

金受申先生曾对北京过去的茶馆有过这样一番精彩的描述：“茶馆是以幽静清雅为主，矮矮的几间土房，支着苇箔的天棚，荆条花障上生着牵牛花儿，砌土为桌凳，砂包的茶壶，黄沙的茶碗，沏出紫黑色的浓苦茶，与乡村野姥谈一谈年成，话一话桑麻，眼所见的天际白云，耳所听的蛙鼓蛩吟，才是野茶馆的本色。”过去休闲的地方是到乡村古镇去享受大自然，如今在城里同样可使身心放松。野茶馆现在已经难寻其踪了，“茶艺馆”可以说是传承它的衣钵而出现的。

位于西单的五福、东四的御茗楼等几家茶艺馆都较有特色。信步进入五福茶艺馆内，仿佛置身于生机勃勃的大自然中；怒放的粉红色杜鹃花，油黑葱绿的君子兰，纤细的文竹，令人感到十分

shifted greatly. Most of them are tired of negotiating business at restaurants, and tea houses become the first alternative because people can relax themselves at a quiet atmosphere at the end of a busy day. In conclusion, the teahouse has become a place for people to not only sip tea and relax, but also to experience Chinese culture, hold social activities, host private parties and conduct business negotiations.

Mr. Jin Shoushen described the old-time tea houses as below: “The tea house is characteristic of quietness and elegance. It is made up of several low earthen rooms with its ceiling covered by reed matting. Tables and benches, tea pot and tea bowls are made of earth and sand respectively. At the tea house, you can chat with the peasants while drinking your tea.” In the past, people must go out to countryside to enjoy the nature, but now, they can relax themselves thoroughly in town. Tea house is the heritage of the old-time tea house.

Wufu Tea House at Xidan and Yuminglou Tea House at Dongsi are very famous. Wufu Tea House was the first teahouse to introduce the Chinese tea ceremony to Beijing, showing the public the ancient ritual for the preparation, serving and drinking of tea.As well as providing a tea

□ 春华茶馆门脸（20 世纪初）
The Gate of Chunhua Tea House(Early in 20th Century)

惬意。墙壁上镶嵌着茶圣陆羽的画像，以及文人雅士撰写有关“茶文化”的论述，洋洋洒洒，多则几百字，少则十几行。茶叶的飘香，古乐的悠扬，与室内古色古香的硬木家具相得益彰，无限度接近自然。茶客落坐后，身着传统旗袍的小姐，按客人的不同需求，将散发着淡淡幽香的茶具分别准备好。茶客们在品茶聊天时，几位靓丽姑娘们又非常适时地出现在茶客们中间，娴熟地操起扬琴、二胡、古筝等乐器，演奏一首首民族声乐的经典之作，如《春江花月夜》、《喜洋洋》、《雨打芭蕉》等，客人们一边品着茶，一边陶醉于传统乐曲的美妙之中。

“茶艺馆”是京城闹中取静的一方净土，与朋友相约一块到“茶艺馆”中一边饮茶、一边欣赏动听的音乐，管保让您工作的疲惫顿时一扫而光。现在人们生活讲究的是“质量”，工作和休闲都是不能缺少的。不久的将来，除了“茶艺馆”以外，北京还会陆续出现更多更新的休闲生活方式来供大家选择。到那个时候，身为现代人的您，会深深感觉自己活得可比上几代人舒坦多了，那才叫滋润。

service, Wufu offers high-quality tea, hand-made tea sets and books. There even organizes tea forums and lectures. Wufu now has 12 outlets, 11 in Beijing and one in Northeast China's Changchun, capital of Jilin Province. When you walk into Wufu Tea House, you will feel like in nature. Verdant plants and beautiful flowers make the house full of life. There is the portrait of tea sage Lu Yu and writings of literature men about tea culture. Fragrant tea, melodious music and the wood old-styled furniture, make you feel very close to nature. When guests are seated, waitress dressed in traditional *Qipao* will prepare tea set for the guests according to their needs. During tasting tea and chatting, several beautiful ladies will perform classical folk music for the guests.

So tea house can refresh oneself if you drink tea with your friends and enjoy wonderful music there after work. It is an invaluable quiet place in a noisy city. Today, people seek for the quality of their life, so that work and recreation both are necessary. Besides tea house, in the future, there will be more new recreation style in Beijing soon. And you will feel that life is much more comfortable than the elder generations.

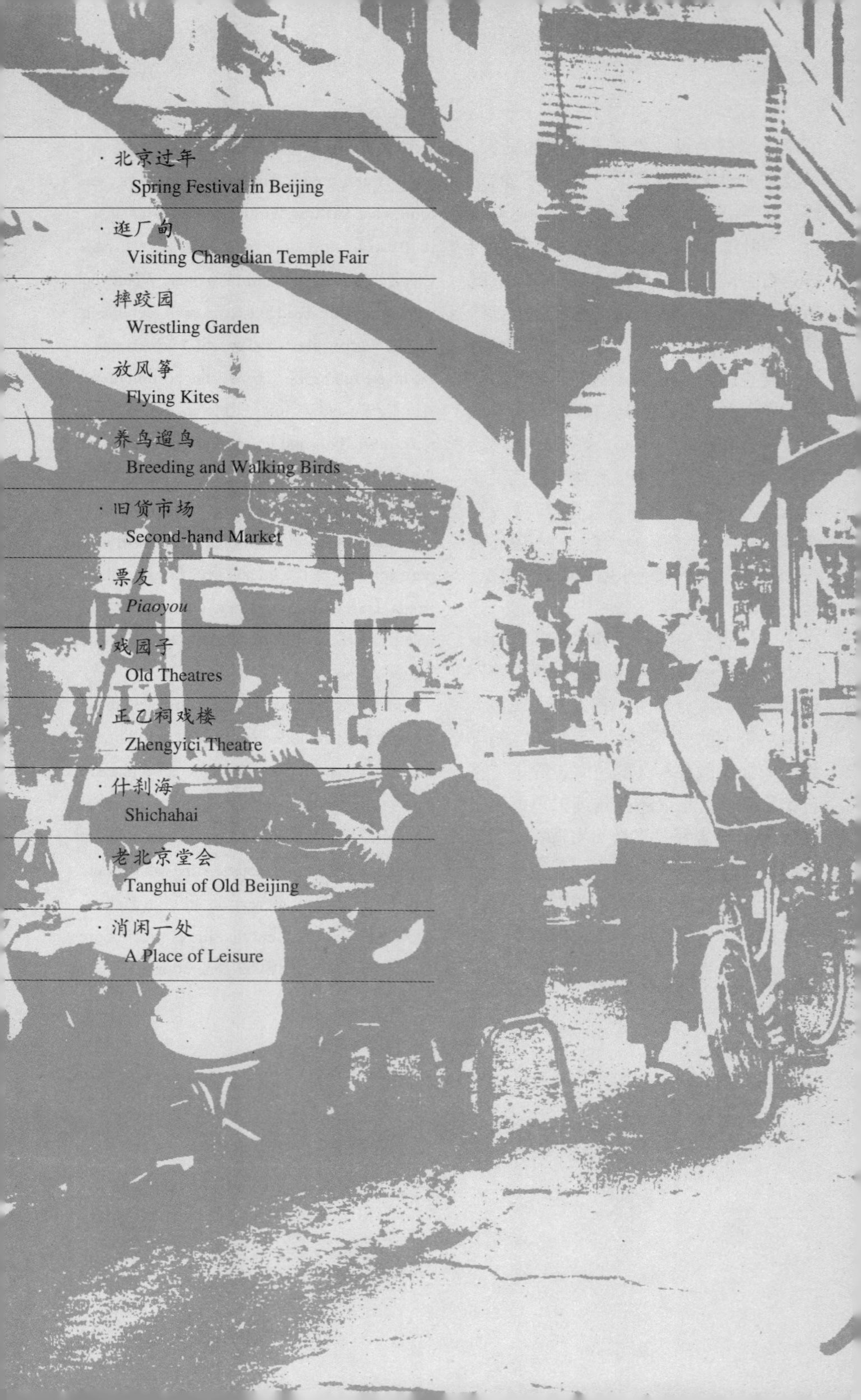

「古都与民俗」

Ancient Capital and Custom

北京过年

Spring Festival in Beijing

汉民族四大传统节日中最为隆重的还是“春节”。每年农历腊月三十为除夕之夜，又称大年三十，讲究多多的北京人辞旧迎新的主要礼仪大多集中在这一天进行。过年亦是一年当中最为热闹、最为欢快、最为喜庆的一天。以往老北京人过年，和如今可不大一样。刚进腊月，家家户户的心里就惦着“阴历年”的来临，并开始掐着指头盼望合家团圆、五谷丰登的美好年景。如果此时与亲朋好友相约一块来到景山公园雅聚，然后

□过年逛庙会 Visiting Temple Fair in Spring Festival

The Spring Festival is the most important festival in China, just like Christmas in the West. All people living away would return their hometown to reunite with other family members. The Spring Festival originated in the Shang Dynasty (c. 1600 BC-c. 1100 BC) from the people’s sacrifice to gods and ancestors at the end of the Lunar year and the beginning of a new one. Strictly speaking, the Spring Festival is the Han’s most grand and important traditional festival. Minorities celebrate their Spring Festival almost the same day as the Han people, and they have different customs. The Spring Festival falls on the 1st day of the 1st lunar month, often one month later than the Gregorian calendar. Actually, it starts every year in the early days of the 12th lunar month and will last till the mid first lunar month of the next year. Of them, the most important days are Spring Festival Eve and the first three days.

The thirtieth day of the twelfth month in lunar calendar is the eve of the Spring Festival. Most ceremonies are held on that day. It is the most lively and joyful day throughout the whole year, and every one expects the family reunion on Spring Festival. At that time, if you and your relatives or friends gathered in Jingshan Park and stood at the peak of Jingshan, the Wanchun

站在景山主峰的万春亭上远眺北京，便可将京城美丽的风光尽收眼底，一座座错落有致的青砖小院，遍布在皇城胡同里，炊烟袅袅，成群的鸽子带着阵阵清脆的哨声在古城楼上边自由飞翔，蓝天白云下的皇城显得是那样的和谐幽静。

旧时京都年时的装饰性点缀，各家各户也不完全一样。一部分出身于买卖地儿的商贾人家，因家境殷实，自然出手大方阔绰，很有气派地在自家老宅门的门楼上挂上一对大红灯笼，一幅幅招财进宝的春联，有序地贴在朱红色的柱子上面，与一左一右两个抱鼓形门礅相互衬托，凸显出深宅大院的辉煌。然而更多的是寻常百姓人家，他们用自己特有的方式"过年"。如书香门第人家往往亲自动手，书写春联和剪贴窗花，希望将一家人对新年的美好祈盼，通过春联的形式尽善尽美地抒发出来。还有一些没有什么文化的人家，就采取到街头去买春联的方式来解决。这时，头戴瓜皮帽、鼻子上架着一副老花镜、专门为人代写春联的老先生稍稍看看来客，不用详细问客人的具体意思，便可因人而异，将不同内容的喜庆春联呈献给顾客。

除夕晚上吃"团圆饭"和"守岁"，是"过年"最重要的内容。饭菜质量的高低，尤其应了过去京城那句老话儿，"吃喝量家当儿"。家境好一些的，自然要讲究一下排场，首先要冷荤搭配，还要以"八"作为吉祥数，像八大件：扣肉、米粉肉、红烧肘条、四喜丸子、红白丸子、冷炖鲤鱼、鲫鱼、酱牛肉，这些都需要在数天以前做成半成品，以备随时食用。青菜更是必须要准备的，过

Pavilion, you could overlook the beautiful scenery of Beijing: rows of yards, flocks of pigeons, and so on. The city seems very harmonious and peaceful against blue sky and white cloud.

In the old days, different family had different ornament for spring festival. Rich family would hang a pair of big red lanterns on the door. Spring Festival couplets, with the words of praying for more fortune, were stuck on vermeil poles. The exquisite drum piers were on both sides. All of these added splendid elements for the grand yard. Common family had their own way of celebrating Spring Festival. Literate family would wrote Spring Festival couplets and made paper-cut for window decoration by themselves. And they also expressed their pray for the next in the Spring Festival couplets. Because Spring Festival couplets acted so important a role in celebrating the festival, illiterate family who was incapable of writing by themselves would buy them at street.

The climax of celebrating Spring Festival is eating reunion dinner and *Shousui* which means waiting for the lunar new year day to come. Chinese People attach great importance to Spring Festival Eve. At that time, all family members eat dinner together. The meal is more luxurious than usual. Dishes such as chicken, fish and bean curd cannot be excluded, for in Chinese, their pronunciations, respectively *ji, yu* and *doufu*, mean auspiciousness, abundance and richness. In the past, reunion meal included 8 cold dishes and meat dishes, and they were respectively Steamed Pork, Steamed Pork Slices with Glutinous Rice Flour, Braised Elbow with Brown Sauce, Sixi Balls, Hongbai Balls, Cold Braised

□过年卖春联 Selling Couplet in Spring Festival

年时菜肴往往都油腻大，适当佐以清新的新鲜蔬菜和瓜果，有增进食欲与爽口的效果。汉民主食一般以水饺为主，品种有羊肉白菜馅的、猪肉韭菜馅的、三鲜馅的等，这些就是“家庭团圆饭”。饭菜丰盛，美酒佐之，祈盼着来年丰衣足食、升官发财、皆大欢喜。团圆饭，一般都要讲究吃到掌灯时分或者深夜。按中国人传统的习惯，年夜饭后至夜间为接神的时间，在初一正式拜年以前通宵达旦不能休息，这就是大家习惯的“守岁”。其意义亦是非同寻常：对年长的人标志着辞旧岁、珍惜时光之意，对年轻的儿女来说，有为父母延年益寿的良好祝福。一般父母健在的人，还有一条不成文的规矩，即儿女都必须在过“大年”时，提前赶到家中为父母守岁。

从正月初一开始到正月初十这些天里，亲朋好友都要到各家相互拜年，范围和形式也多种多样。像初一这天，首先应到岳父、岳母家去拜年。拜年时还需带上一些礼物，以示孝顺，岳父母一般都要留女儿、女婿在家中吃饭。礼节

Carp and Crucian, Pickled Beef. The number 8 is a lucky one for Chinese people which means making good fortune because it has similar pronunciation with the Chinese word *Fortune*. People usually had to prepare these eight kinds of half-made food several days ago. Vegetable and fruit are absolutely necessary because they can increase one's appetite. The staple food of the Hans was dumpling with different stuffings, such as mutton and Chinese cabbage, pork and leek, and so on. People eat them and wish for money and treasure as they think dumpling in sound means bidding farewell to the old and ushering in the new. Also, the shape of the dumplings is like gold ingot from ancient China. Good wine often appeares to match rich reunion meal. The meal usually lasts late at night. According to the tradtion, after the meal, every one should stay awake throughout the night to meet the lunar new year, which is so-called *Shousui*. And it had very important meaning for different people. It reminds elder people to cherish time and offered a chance for young children to bless their parents. There is also a unwritten rule that as children, you should get to your parents house to *Shousui* for them if they are still alive. Southern Chinese eat *Nian gao*, (New Year Cake) on this occasion, because as a homophone, *Niangao* means higher and higher one year after another.

From the first day to tenth day of the first month on lunar calendar, relatives, friends, and classmates as well as colleagues exchange their greetings, gifts and chat leisurely. In Chinese, this is paying a call in New Year. On the first day, they go to the parents-in-law's home with gifts

性拜访指同行、同事、朋友之间的互相拜年，一般情况下不宜久坐，寒暄客套一番，随即就该告辞。感谢性的拜访，指对在刚过去的一年当中对自己或家庭有过帮助的人，借新春佳节之际，带上礼品登门去致谢，以表补欠人情的意思。串门式的拜年，则主要指过去北京人大多都住在同一座院子中，而且有部分人家是世世代代为邻的老街坊。平常来来往往就比较多，老话说，远亲不如近邻，到了年禧，一定要到其家中拜年，说些“恭喜发财”之类的吉祥话，多年的交情随着岁月的延续而与日俱增。

“过年、拜年、守岁、贴春联、吃年夜饭、逛庙会”等风俗习惯，一直保留到今天。不过现在它已被时髦的年轻人赋予了全新的内容。不少高收入的年轻白领已不满足于像父辈母辈那样，在家中按传统习俗来“过年守岁”，而是利用春节公休长假的机会，到北国冰城哈尔滨、海南三亚的热带椰林，甚至与朋友一块携手到更远的新、马、泰等国家一游，更具有时尚特色。不过这话儿还得说回来，这还不是京城大多数平头百姓所能享受得起的。更多的京城百姓，还是要在大年以前赶到家中，与父母兄弟姐妹，一块吃上一顿团圆饭，共同“守岁”。这种传统形式的“过年”，就像一张张皇历，伴随着一代代的北京人就这么一年一年走过来。

to wish them a happy new year and have dinner with them. Children will get money wrapped up in red paper. This is called *Yasuiqian* with adults' wishing growing up healthily for their children. Then Chinese people go to visit their colleagues or friends. But it doesn't last too long. They also express their thanks to the people who helped them or their family during the last year. Neighbors extend their greetings to each other during Spring Festival, too.

Many customs has remained today such as celebrating Spring Festival, exchanging a New Year greeting, staying up for the lunar new year, pasting Spring Festival couplets, having a big dinner together on the Eve and going to visit traditional temple fairs. But they have been endowed with new contents by modern young people. Young white collars with high salary would rather travel far away during the holidays than stay home to celebrate Spring Festival. However, most common people can not afford traveling overseas. Or they would rather try to come back hometown to reunite their parents, sisters and brothers for the family reunion dinner. After the dinner, the whole family will sit together, chatting and watching TV. In recent years, the Spring Festival party broadcast on China Central Television Station (CCTV) is an essential entertainment for the Chinese both at home and abroad. This is new content of *Shousui* in the last two decades.

逛厂甸

Visiting Changdian Temple Fair

☐ 琉璃厂文化古街 The Old Culture Street in *Liulichang*

“生活在北京，没逛过厂甸，根本谈不上算是北京人”。您瞧瞧，这厂甸儿在过去北京百姓心里的位置有多么重要。旧时的厂甸，在春节期间有庙会，为过年助兴。庙会北边从和平门开始，南到虎坊桥路口，整整一条街。开市时逢过大年这一喜庆日子，大清早儿，天还没亮，四九城的人准备来逛厂甸的，就开始熙熙攘攘地行走在路上，场景好不热闹。此时街两边的食品大棚里，厨艺高超的厨师们正“八仙过海、各显神通”，现做现卖，将各式各样的北京风味小吃提前摆上自家台面，煎、炸、炒、涮，扑鼻撩人的香味，吸引着四面八方的食客。像造型别致的盆糕儿，以及油酥火烧、麻酱烧饼、江米炸糕、灌肠儿、炸春卷、豆汁、茶汤、豆腐脑、白水羊头、杂碎汤，各具特色；正宗、色香、味美、花样齐全，是厂甸庙会小吃的特色。特

In the old days, Beijingers had a choice of eight temple fairs to attend, but Changdian Temple Fair, as the oldest and best known temple fair in Beijing, was always the most popular. It was originally held on open ground outside Liulichang, now a pedestrian shopping street full of curio and antique shops.

“If you have never been to Changdian, you can not count to be a real Beijinger at all even if you live in Beijing. ” From this old saying, you can see how important Changdian was for Beijing common people. In the past, Changdian held temple fairs during Spring Festival. And the Temple fairs usually occured from the first to the seventh day of the first month on the lunar year. And it covered the whole street from Hepingmen in the north to Hufangqiao in the south. At dawn, people began to flock there. Along the street, there were all kinds of snacks. Some were made on the spot. Chefs’ skill and the strong fragrant scent would attract many customers to their stands. There are various snacks with their own characteristics at Changdian Temple Fair: unique-shaped *Pengao* (a kind of cake), *Yousu Huoshao* (Crisp Baked Cakes), *Majiang Shaobing* (Baked Cakes with Sauce), *Jiangmi Zhagao* (Fried Cakes with Glutinous Rice Flour), *Guanchang* (Filled Sausage), *Zhachunjuan* (Fried Spring Roll),

□ 琉璃厂老店荣宝斋
Old Store *Rongbaozhai*

□ 东琉璃厂街的老店铺
Curio Store in East *Liulichang* Street

大糖葫芦迎着寒风矗立着，红玛瑙似的，外表包裹着晶莹剔透的上好糖汁，还有极具挑逗性的吆喝：“刚蘸好的冰糖葫芦，又大又脆呀，吃上一串甜掉牙哟。”随之人群一拥而上，更是乐坏了那些得了机会撒欢儿的孩子们，只见他们一块唧唧喳喳，如小鸟儿闹林。

接近海王村的地界，有一处专给舞文弄墨的人找乐子的地方，可称之为“文化市场”。其中有文房四宝、线装古书、戴月轩狼毫笔，以及不同材质和造型的古玩字画，来此寻觅的文化人一般不会空手而归，多多少少会有收获。如果运气不错，说不定在哪会儿淘到位曾经的皇亲国戚迫于应急而低价出手的值钱古董。来到厂甸一条街，如同步入老

Douchi (Mung Bean Milk), *Chatang* (Tea paste or custard made of millet or sorghum flour), *Doufunao* (Jellied Bean Curd), *Baishui Yangtou* (Boiled Sheep’s Head), and *Zasuitang* (Lamb Gizzard Soup). All kinds of snacks at Changdian Temple Fair are genuine and delicious with fascinating color. Extra-sized *Bingtang Hulu* (Sugar-Coated Haws on a stick) are especially favored by children. Hearing the hawk of the vendor, “newly made Sugar-Coated Haws, big crisp, and sweet ”, and seeing the transparent red Sugar-Coated Haws, people will come towards the vendor at once. Children are so happy that they laugh and romp around the vendor.

There is a so-called culture market near Haiwang Village where literate people like to go. They can find the four treasures of the study, i.e. writing brush, ink stick, ink slab and paper as well as traditional thread binding ancient books, wolf hair writing brush of Daiyuexuan, antique and calligraphy and painting of different quality and shape. Every one who comes here to seek the things they like most won’t come back home with empty hands. If you are lucky enough, you can come across some relative of the emperor who is forced to sell antique to meet an urgent need. Walking into the street of Changdian is as if stepping into a folk custom museum. You can see kites flying in the sky which are made by handicraft men and controlled by themselves, too. Among the colorful kites, there are two to three *zhang* (or: 6.6-9.9 meters)big centipede-shaped ones with moveable joints and eyeballs as well as vivid red dragonfly kites which are flying in the wind. Suddenly, children’s laugh divert

北京的一座民俗博物馆。人还没来到跟前儿，就能瞧见手艺精湛的艺人，放着自己亲手制作的风筝在天空中飞翔。五颜六色的风筝中，有两、三丈长关节儿会动、眼珠会转的大蜈蚣，还有正在飞舞之中的栩栩如生的红蜻蜓。忽然孩子们的嬉笑声又将人们的目光吸引过去，民间艺人娴熟地将柔软的一团团黄泥儿变戏法似的，就在围观者的眼皮子底下，转眼间捏成钟馗、包公、刘罗锅子、铁拐李、孙悟空，虽然手中忙得早已滴儿溜转，但仍供不应求。孩子们眼睛中露出渴望与企盼的目光，一双双小手早早地伸开着，都希望快点拿上自己希望得到的那个可心的小泥人。

老北京的厂甸始于清末，兴于民初。一些文人雅士鲁迅、齐白石、徐悲

□ 海王村旧址大门（20 世纪初）
The Relic of Haiwang Village(Early in 20th Century)

people's attention to a handicraft man who is kneading mud dough into different figures such as Zhong Kui (a figure of Chinese mythology, an expert in seizing ghosts), Bao Gong (999-1062, a much-praised judge in Song Dynasty), Liu Luoguo (a legendary prime minister known as "Hunch-backed Liu" and for his sense of humour and justice), Tieguai Li (one of the eight Taoist immortals in Chinese mythology) and Monkey King. Although quite fast, demand still exceeds supply. Children are expecting clay figures with their hands stretching out and they nearly can not wait.

At the temple fair people can also experience or purchase many New Year celebration items such as wind wheel. It is basically made of wood or bamboo. Once the wheel is powered by wind, the connector will trigger a stick beat on its base producing exciting sound. Another funny toy is candy figurine, and it's definitely children's favorite item. Then there are many others attracting children and adults. Just watching the process of making a toy is very enjoyable. It brings out the spirit of New Year celebration. Performances include martial arts, acrobatics, Peking Opera, pop music and folk dancing. Vendors from come to set up shop and sell books, magazines, paintings, toys, tasty snacks, and dried or fresh fruit. There's plenty of food to tempt you including *Bingtang Hulu* (sugar-coated haw berries speared onto sticks), *Kaohongshu* (Roast sweet potatoes) , *Aiwowo* (Sticky Rice with Sweet Fillings) and *Ludagun* (pastry made of steamed glutinous millet flour or soy bean flour mixed with sugar) . You can also find traditional Chinese crafts such as kites and painted

□ 西琉璃厂老街 Old *Liulichang* Street

鸿、老舍、余叔岩、马连良等，也多次光临这块风水宝地。厂甸丰富多彩的民俗文化养育了京都子民，年复一年地伴随着北京人一代又一代，甭管您是家境殷实富裕一些的爷也好，还是贫寒一些的小户人家也罢，都能在这儿找到一份真正属于自己的乐子。当您的手里拿上一个随风摇动的小小风车，听着一阵阵脆响，边走边逛，观赏绚丽多姿的民俗风景画时，未尝不是一件很爽的事。

masks taken from Peking Opera characters to buy. Acrobats and other performers are on hand to keep the crowds entertained throughout the day.

Changdian originated from the end of Qing Dynasty and reached its height at the early years of the Republic period (1912-1949). Changdian is the oldest and most renowned street in Beijing. It is the center stage for New Year parade and temple fair that has started 400 years ago. Rich and colorful folk custom and culture foster and accompany generations of Beijingers years after years. Some famous literate men often visited this place such as Lu Xun, Qi Baishi, Xu Beihong, Lao She, Yu Shuyan and Ma Lianliang. Whether you are from well-to-do family or poor family, you can have a lot of fun outdoors during the Spring Festival if you attend Changdian Temple Fair. Isn’t it a cool thing to saunter about with a mini wind wheel in your hand and enjoy the splendid folk custom pictures!

摔跤园

Wrestling Garden

□ 著名跤手双德全在指导徒弟

The Famous Wrestler Shuang is Teaching

在北京的地面儿上，提起摔跤名宿双德全先生，北京的跤迷们没有不知道的。双德全，满族，1938年生于北京，自幼练习中国式摔跤。早在1957年，双德全便正式拜京城著名跤手王茂林先生为师，四十多年如一日，练功不辍，多次在市、区级的比赛中取得好名次。前几年，老双最早在德胜门外滨河公园开办了20年来北京第一个“中国式掼跤”园地，红红火火；特别是双休日，老双带着二十几位弟子，早早地先把场子支应好，沙堆堆平，再洒上一层清水，喜好跤行儿的老少跤迷们此时已陆续围坐在场子四周，为的是一睹老双和众跤手们的掼跤绝技。

在北京喜欢掼跤的爷们儿当中自胡同里出道的为多，这是因为过去从京城胡同中长大的孩子没有几个不会“掼

In Beijing, when speaking of wrestler Shuang Dequan, none of wrestling fans doesn't know him. Shuang Dequan, the Mans, was born in 1938 in Beijing and learned Chinese wrestling when he was still a little boy. As early as 1957, Shuang Dequan formally acknowledged the famous wrestler Wang Maolin as his teacher. He kept practising for forty years and made good achievement in the municipal and district competitions. Several years ago, he founded Beijing's first Chinese Wrestling Field in Binhe Park near Deshengmen for the last 20 years. The field was very flourishing especially on weekends. Early in the morning, Mr. Shuang with his two dozens of disciples began to prepare his field for wrestling. While weekends Mr.Shuang and his prentices level up the sandpile and sprinkle some water on it, and wrestling fans began to sit around the field one after another to witness the skills of Mr. Shuang and other wrestlers.

Beijing wrestlers most came from Hutong because most of the children growing up in Hutong could wrestle. Actually, wrestling is Manchu's patent. Manchu lived among Mt.Changbaishan and the Heilongjiang River, northeast of China for generations. They worshiped Wushu, the Chinese martial arts, and wrestling was the basic skill of Wushu. During Manchu ruled China in Qing Dynasty, they vigorously advocated

跤”的。提起掼跤，它其实是满族人的专利，世代生活在东北“白山黑水”之间的满族男人，一直延袭尚武之风，掼跤又是习武的基本功。满族入关统治中国后，在民间大力提倡掼跤，不但一般的老百姓玩跤，就连清朝的皇帝、王爷、贝勒在年幼时也要练跤，所以掼跤长期以来在北京不仅受到皇室的重视，更在民间得到极为广泛的普及。如今上了点年纪的人都知道，过去在四九城圈里圈外早就流传这样的老话儿：“三年的把式，不如当年的跤手。”这话儿是什么个意思呢?“把式”，这是指人们对练武术人称呼的专业术语。就是练了三年武术的人，真要上阵与对方交起手来，未必如一个练了只有一年掼跤的人。

双德全自20世纪90年代初退休之后，眼瞅着中国式掼跤这一民间体育活动逐渐走下坡路，跤行有失传的危险，感觉不是个滋味儿，于是他决定身体力行，为恢复传统的掼跤这一老玩艺做一些实实在在的工作。双德全找到弟弟双德禄和几个徒弟，齐心协力办起了滨河

wrestling. Not only common people practised wrestling, but the emperor and other royal members began to practise wrestling at childhood. So over a long period of time, wrestling has been given great attention by royal family and become very popular among common people. Elder people still remember an old saying, “ A *Bashi* for three years can not hold a candle to a wrestler who engages in wrestling just one year.” What’s the meaning? *Bashi* is a professional term referring to Wushu learners here. And the saying means in a real fight against strong opponent, a person who has learned Wushu for three years may not stand comparison with a person who has learned wrestling only one year.

Shuang Dequan retired in early 1990s. When he noticed Chinese wrestling were going downhills gradually and this folk sport may be not handed down, he felt very upset. He decided to do some material work to resume the traditional wrestling. Shuang Dequan called his younger brother Shuang Delu and his disciples together and they founded a Wrestling Garden in Binhe

□ 双德全在跤场向观众表演老天桥的撂跤技艺 Wrestler Shuang is Perfoming

公园摔跤场。随后在酷爱老天桥民俗文化的画家王树生先生的鼎力支持下，跤场从北城的滨河公园移师到京南潘家园，定名为“潘家园华生老天桥演武场”。搬到这里后，双德泉和弟子们风雨无阻，在这个场子里为观众奉献“掼跤”的精彩表演。

每次正式演出之前，作为垫场儿节目，先要进行一节耍中幡表演，只见高大沉重的中幡在舞幡者手中左右盘旋，显得格外轻盈得心应手。一会儿“乌龙搅水”，接着又来个“苏秦背剑”，紧跟着又来一个更绝的，用小姆指单独将中幡轻轻勾住，好一个“封侯挂印”，观众的叫好之声连成一片。稍歇片刻，伴着锣鼓声，压轴戏掼跤表演开始，跤手们甩去汗衫，麻利地换上跤衣，脚蹬青黑色的跤靴。只见跤手们拱手施礼后，单手交臂，另一手伺机捕捉对方的空档儿。几番试探之后，一方迅速来个大跨步儿，紧接着轻身弯腰，漂漂亮亮地摔翻对方，全场顿时报以一片热烈掌声。接下来跤手们又两人为一对儿，纷纷登场献艺，他们各自表演自己的拿手绝技，如跤行的“倒口袋”、“穿腿”、“小德合勒”、“掸手”等一系列跤行中的绝

□天桥把式显身手 Wrestlers' Performance

Park. And Mr. Wang Shusheng, a painter who are keen on old Tianqiao folk custom and culture, gave great support to them. So the wrestling field moved from Binhe Park in the north city to Panjiayuan in the south and had a formal name of Panjiayuan Huasheng Old Tianqiao Wrestling Performing Field. Rainy or sunny, Shuang Dequan and his disciples would perform wrestling for their spectators.

Before formal performance, there is a Zhongfan juggling, Flag Balancing performance. The heavy and long flag pole seems very light under performers' perfect control. And spectators gave them ardent applause continuously. After a while, the wrestling performance begins accompanied by the beat of gong and drum. Wrestler put off their shirts, and wear their wrestling clothes and dark wrestling boots promptly. Wrestlers first make an obeisance by cupping one hand in the other before chest to each other. Then they begin to seek for any mistake their opponents will make. Through several rounds of trying, a wrestler quickly makes a big step and bends over, throwing the other wrestler down at ease. Spectators give him ardent applaude. Then two persons as a pair, the wrestlers perform their tour de force in turns. Their motions are very neat and so prompt that spectators have no time to understand what has happened before the result comes out. Over sixty years old Coach Shuang Dequan and Wang Dongchuan put on wrestling clothes and step into the field with high spirit to add to the fun. Of course, young disciples won't admit defeat so easily. They wrestle with their master in turn. Shuang Dequan throws his disciples down

活儿，动作干净利落，瞬间一气呵成，甚至连观众还没看清楚，跤手们却已分出输赢。年过六旬的双德全、王东川两位老教练，为了给大伙儿助兴，也立马儿换上跤衣，斗志昂扬地走进场子，真有雄风不减当年的架势。年轻的徒弟们自然不肯轻易服输，轮番上前和师傅过招儿。只见双德全步履轻捷，跤法和招术儿灵活多变，左一勾又一拽，前一拉，紧接着向后一推，借助巧劲儿，毫不费力，将几个徒弟们摔得人仰马翻，心服口服。

“掼跤”是我国民间百姓爱好的体育项目之一，而且在过去还曾产生过广泛的影响，但与其他体育项目相比，如今喜欢中国式摔跤的人还是显得太少了。

□ 潘家园的摺跤表演　Wrestling in Panjiayuan Garden

easily with spry step, agile and varied movement. These disciples are all sincerely convinced by their master' s skills.

Chinese wrestling is one of most popular sports in China. In the past, it had great comprehensive influence on common people. However, nowadays, there are few people who like Chinese wrestling as compared with other sports.

放风筝
Flying Kites

中国是风筝的故乡，古代哲学家墨翟曾“斫木为鹞，三年而成，飞一日而败”。这是世界上较早有关“风筝”的文字记载，距现如今至少已有两千年的历史。木工行当的鼻祖鲁班，经过一番去粗取精制成“竹鹊”，能在天空中飞行三日而不落。

风筝作为一门充满魅力的传统民间艺术，在我国流行很广。而在古都北京，糊风筝、放风筝，更是辈辈儿相传，扎、绘、糊、放四艺俱佳的风筝艺人数不胜数。如早在民国年间即名声大振的哈长英，人们戏称其“风筝哈”，他制作的大沙雁在扎糊、造型、绘画、飞行诸方面都堪称一绝。其首次代表中国参加1915年巴拿马万国博览会，凭着高超的技艺荣获银质奖章，为中国赢得了荣誉。这一时期还出现了以善做孙悟空、哪吒、

□放风筝 Flying Kites

China is the birthplace of kites and more than two thousand years ago, a great philosopher in Warring States of China Mo Di, also known as Mo Tzu, once cut wood to make harrier, and it took him three years to achieve, but the kite only flew one day. This is the early record about kite in written words. Lu Ban, the originator of carpenter profession in China, philosopher, military thinker, stateman, born in the State of Lu, made a bamboo magpie after discarding the dross and selecting the essential of wood kite, which could fly in the sky for three days.

As a kind of charming traditional folk art, kites are very popular across China. The skills of making kites and flying kites have been passed down from fathers to sons in Beijing which served as the capital of six dynasties. There are numerous kite handicraft men who are expert at binding, painting, pasting and flying kites. For example, during the period of the Repbulic of China, Ha Changying had a great reputation in binding, pasting, modeling, painting and flying big swan goose kites and people gave him a nickname Kite Ha. In 1915, Ha Changying won a silver medal in the International Panama Fair. Meanwhile, there was another kite handicraft man who was good at making mythological figures like Monkey King, Nezha (a deity in

□ 艺人扎糊风筝　Making Kites

猪八戒等神话人物风筝而著称的“猴儿常”。猴儿常制作的风筝，造型十分精巧别致，栩栩如生，其绰号“猴儿常”广为人知，大名儿反倒无人知晓。只见三四个手持金箍棒儿火眼金睛的齐天大圣由细绳连在一起，在湛蓝的天空中随风飘扬。“蜈蚣金”是另一位善做“蜈蚣”风筝的女艺人，学名金淑琴，她扎制、糊成的大蜈蚣共三十八节，串成一串儿，足有二十多米长。令人感到极为奇特的是，蜈蚣的茸毛都跃然在上，远远望去如同一只活灵活现的真蜈蚣在蓝天与白云中欢快飞舞。旧时在老北京城风筝圈内外，这几个风筝艺人的大名可以说无人不知。

每个风筝都是一幅美丽的图画，是形式技巧的结晶，它把我们伟大的民族文化巧妙地体现在平凡的作品中。主人寄托的情感在放飞中得到更美好的升华。风筝种类繁多，千姿百态。在春日的天安门广场，夏日的天坛公园，金秋

Chinese mythology) and Zhu Bajie(one of the three helpers of Xuanzang in the classic Chinese novel *Journey to the West*). No one knew his name, but he had a well-known nickname, Monkey Chang. His kites are delicate and unique and true to life, e.g., his monkey kites are made up of three to four Monkey Kings with penetrating eyesight and golden cudgels in their hands. They are linked by a fine thread. Centipede Jin was a handicraft woman named Jin Shuqin. She was adept at making centipede kites. Her centipede kites had 38 joints altogether, more than 20 meters long. To one’s great surprise, the centipede kite was covered by fine hair, so it seemed a real centipede flying in the blue sky. In the past kite circle of Beijing, everyone knew these kite handicraft men.

Each kite is both a beautilful picture and a crystal of form and skills. They embody Chinese great national culture from ordinary works. The owner’s emtion has been sublimated during flying kites. There are different types of kites. You can see all kinds of kites flying at Tian’anmen Square in spring, or at Temple of Heaven in

□ 卖风筝　Selling Kites

的陶然亭公园，随处可见各种各样的风筝在天空中竞相飞翔。造型别致的一只只“雄鹰”在盘旋，一对对小“燕子”在嬉戏，五颜六色的“花蝴蝶”在飞舞，一件件逼真的“沙雁”睁着又大又亮的眼睛在俯视大地，而寂寞多情的嫦娥仿佛在月宫里独舞。风筝传友谊，银线连五洲，多少年来皇城根儿下的京城百姓就是这样父一辈子一辈，将老北京的民俗文化通过风筝这种艺术形式，奉献给国内外的朋友们。

summer, or at Taoranting Park in autumn. Hawks are hovering overhead; Swallows are romping; multicolored butterfly are dancing; vivid swan goose are looking down at the earth with their big and bright eyes while lonely and solitary Chang'e, Chinese mythical goddess of the moon, is dancing lonely. Kites can pass friendship and their silver thread links all the continents. Generations after generations, Beijingers present folk custom and culture of old Beijing to domestic and overseas friends through the art form of kites.

养鸟遛鸟

Breeding and Walking Birds

□ 鸟市一景　A Scene of Bird Market

养鸟、遛鸟一直是京城老百姓的一项传统爱好。这也是部分游手好闲的八旗子弟十分爱好的活动。在明、清以前，北京就有了提笼架鸟一族，出没于皇城脚下的街头巷尾。其中一些人最大的嗜好，就是特别喜欢到茶馆中坐坐。名义上为品茶，倒不如说是意在大家面前亮亮自家养的鸟，具备哪种令人叫好儿的绝活儿，以博得众茶客们的喝彩之声。

观赏鸟的种类很多，而北京人尤好“画眉”。画眉羽毛通体为黄褐色，头顶

Breeding birds and walking birds is a tradtional hobby of Beijingers. Walking birds means going for a walk in a quiet place with birds. Walking birds was particularly favored by the descendants of the Eight Banners. Before Qing Dynasty (1644-1912) or even Ming Dynasty(1368-1644), there appeared people walking birds in the street or lanes of Beijing. Some of them were interested in staying in teahouses. They intended to show their birds and the latter’s skills to evoke cheerings of the guests in the name of tasting tea.

至背部有黑色的纹线，眼圈及眉毛均为白色，腹部呈灰褐色。画眉顾名思义，其眉如画，因而取名画眉。其以善哨见长，优美动听。它嗓音圆润而高亢，歌声甜美又极富韵律，仅这两个很重要的优点就博得许多养鸟人的厚爱。清末文人张潮曾著有一篇《画眉笔谈辞》，文中对画眉鸟有一精辟准确的描述："鸟语之佳音，当以画眉第一。"几百年以来，画眉一直就是皇城老少爷们儿的优选。要想驯好、养好画眉，能让它开好口儿，婉转歌唱，哨声还要抑扬顿挫，绝非易事。

养鸟的行家里手说："画眉中黄眼儿、黄腿儿、黄羽毛的为佳。"接着又说："红眼的画眉当然更妙，但十之八九难以遇到，万里挑一极为稀少。"看一只鸟的好坏，首先要瞧它眼睛是否有精气神儿，这就是养鸟人挂在嘴边儿上的双目一定要放光，眉毛要像月牙儿似的往上挑。和所有的鸣禽一样，应首选"原毛儿"即雄鸟为最棒，行话讲"最叫口儿"。其最大的乐趣还在于，如果调教有方，能将猫、狗、鸡、鸭、喜鹊、八哥儿的声音，摹仿得惟妙惟肖。

要想养好鸟还得先学会遛鸟，也就是养鸟人常说的"遛功"。单说一个"遛"字，便很有讲究。养鸟人不紧不慢地踱着四方步，手臂轻携鸟笼前后有节奏地摆动，闲情逸致涌上心头。养鸟人多年以来习惯于每天的一早一晚，提着鸟笼子到环境优美的树林和护城河岸边，尽情享受着大自然的恩赐，将笼子挂在树枝上，让鸟适应周围的环境，让它在明媚的晨光和落日的余辉中放声吟唱。时

Among various birds which can be enjoyed, Beijingers espcially love a kind of thrush. The thrush has brownish feather with black lines from head to back, white eye socket and eyebrow and taupe belly. Because its eyebrows seems to be painted, it has its name Huamei Bird. In Chinese, *hua* means to paint or draw, and *mei* means eyebrow. Noted for its mellow, resounding, sweet and melodious songs, Huamei Bird has been appreciated by many breeding birders. In an essay *Huamei* written by Zhang Chao(publisher, writer and poet in Qing Dynasty), there were concise and accurate describing about Huamei Bird, and he praised Huamei Bird as the bird with the most melodious sound. For several centuries, Huamei Bird has been the first choice for breeding, watching and walking. Huamei Bird is able to sing melodious songs depended on the training of the owner. The whistling of the owner must have rhythm too, so it is not a easy job to tame a Huamei Bird into the one with impressing voice.

People who are expert at breeding bird think Huamei Bird with yellow eyes and yellow legs covered with yellow feather is better than others. And the best Huamei Bird has red eyes, but they are so rare that very few people can get them. The quality of a bird lies on its eyes. The brighter their eyes are, the more valuable they are. As all the other songbirds, male bird or cock is recommended. Under proper instruct, Huamei Bird can imitate the sound of cat, dog, duck, magpie and myna vividly.

To breed the birds you can learn to walk them first. But how to walk the birds? It demands you

□ 清晨遛鸟　Walking Birds in the Morning

下社会讲人与动物应和谐生活在同一片蓝天白云下，或许让小鸟回归大自然也是一种趋势。如果真有那么一天，京城满院子的树梢上迎来野生画眉前来做客的情景，那北京就可能成为了最适合人类生活的城市。

have enough leisure time and relaxing mood. People walking birds are never anxious. Instead, they will walk lazily with swinging cages to a quiet place such as a wood or bank of the moat. They are used to going outdoors twice in the morning and afternoon. As soon as arriving, they will hang their cage on the surroundings and sing songs in the bright light of morning sun or in the dusk. Today, more and more people realize that human being should live with animals harmoniously,so perhaps it' s a trend to let the birds return to nature.One day when wild Huamei Bird fly to visit the yards of Beijing, Beijing will be the city which is most suitable for living.

旧货市场

Second-hand Market

近些年来，北京的旧货市场冒出了不少，多数在地地道道的老北京民俗风格上作文章，吸引了数以万计的人，双休日里从早到晚人头攒动，都希望在这里撞上好运儿，没准儿就遇上老祖宗留下的“宝贝”。

有人把北京的旧货市场与旧时的“鬼市”相提并论，不无道理。现在潘家园的旧货市场，只有双休日营业，延用了“鬼市”的一些运作方式。有人说由于旧货市场的东西难辨真伪，所以才称

□ 旧货市场淘金　Bargaining in the Second-hand Market

□ 旧市景观　Scene of the Second-hand Market

In recent years, many second-hand markets emerged in Beijing. Some of them focus their eyes on old Beijing’ s genuine custom. Such second-hand markets attract tens of thousands of people who are expecting to hit good luck and encounter some antique of ancestors. So this kind of market is always filled with people on weekends.

Some people like to compare second-hand market with ghost market in the old day in Beijing because they have common things. Today’ s Panjiayuan Second-hand Market only opens on weekends and in a sense, operates in the way of ghost market. Maybe the second-hand market is called ghost market just because you can not tell whether the goods there are counterfeit or not. Before the liberation (1949), the curio stalls in Hongqiao were set to run business before the watchman beat drum for the fifth time or before dawn. Once daybreak, they would dissapear just like the behavior of the ghosts, so they were called ghost market by common people. According to elder people, each seller used to hold a headlight in hand. But an unwitten rule stipulated that the light can not be used to brighten people but goods. It was a taboo to greet your acquaintance when you met them there. Otherwise you would violate the taboo. Normally,

□ 旧货市场上专注的老先生
The Old Man Absorbed by the Curio Stall

"鬼市"；在解放以前红桥，今龙须沟东晓市附近的古玩地摊，就定在每天五更前开市，天一亮踪迹全无，老百姓为此称它为"鬼市"。听老辈人讲那时卖货的人习惯手里提着一盏桅灯，行规为只许照货不兴照人，在这块地面上如果遇上熟人您可千万别打招呼，那是犯忌的事。一般情况下，治安队的根本不在这里抓人办案。买卖双方都心知肚明，来这里交易的货多是来路不明的，卖主中既有贵族落破子弟，又有沿街串巷摇着拨楞鼓收旧货的（老百姓称打鼓的），还掺有偷鸡摸狗的梁上君子。来找宝的人中呢，淘珍稀宝物者有之，而出于自家赏玩，凑凑热闹的同样不乏其人。"鬼市"中瓷器、字画、玉石、鼻烟壶、紫檀笔筒、线装古籍等应有尽有。在这些不起眼儿的各式各样的旧货里，还真有名人的手迹、照片、书札之类的稀罕物品，等着慧眼淘金者发现。

police ignored this kind of market intendedly and hadn't arrested anyone there at all. Both sellers and buyers were all aware that most of the goods had dubious background. Among the sellers, there were aristocrats in distress as well as second-hand collectors who were nicknamed as *Da Gu De* by Beijingers. And the other sellers were actually thieves. But how about the buyers? Either antique and curio collectors or ordinary people who came here just for fan or purchased some antique and came back home to appreciate it. On the list of the articles, nearly everything is available ranging from porcelain, uncarved jade, snuff bottle to calligraphy and paintings, rosewood brush pot, and traditional thread binding books. Celebraties' original handwritings or paintings, pictures and letters may hide among the unstriking second-hand goods and they are waiting to be discovered by gold diggers with accurate insight.

As one of the biggest second-hand markets in China, Panjiayuan second-hand market, has attracted people from all over the world. It is located in the southeast corner of Beijing's Third Ring Road. People from overseas come here for cultural relics, paintings and calligraphy, the traditional four treasures of study (writing brush, ink stick, ink slab, paper), porcelain even furniture. A number of well-known people have visited the market, including former American First Lady Hilary Clinton, Princess Shilintong of Thailand, and the prime ministers of Romania and Greece.

票友

Piaoyou

票友是随着国粹京剧在皇城根儿下的全面走红而发展起来的。在这块地面儿上，以此为乐儿唱了一辈子的老票友为数众多，对京戏不同行当、各个流派的在行程度，是中国其他任何一座城市所不及的。旧时的北京，能到前门外各大戏园子里听名角儿唱戏，既风光体面，又标明了一个人的身价。“京戏”在京城的红红火火，更是离不开广大戏迷和票友。

京戏“票友”相约一块儿唱戏吊嗓子的地方，官称为“票房”。当年在老北京四九城里遍布着各种“票房”、规模大小不等，其中知名度较高的有齐化门（今朝阳门）外大街的“关帝庙票房”、位于西城西四附近的“松筠庵票房”。值得一提的是，昔日梨园界相当一部分名角儿都是票友出身。譬如当年以唱须生行当红遍京津的孙菊仙、许荫棠，擅演武二花、且嗓子特亮堂而名噪四方的黄润

□京戏票友一展风姿　Piaoyou is Singing

What is *Piaoyou*? Actually, *Piaoyou* means Peking Opera fans. Since Peking Opera enjoys a higher reputation than other local operas, almost every province of China has more than one Peking Opera troupe, which is called *Piaoyou* in Chinese. *Piaoyou* who were developed as the nation opera, Peking opera, became very popular in Beijing. There are many social celebrities among Peking opera fans, and *Piaoyou* of Beijing are more expert at different roles and schools of Peking Opera than those of any other cities in China. In the past, it's a very graceful thing and the symbol of the social status to watch and listen to famous actors of Peking Opera at opera houses near Qianmen. And the flourishing of the opera in Beijing owes greatly to the fans or *Piaoyou*.

But what is *Piaofang*? *Piaofang* means the place where *Piaoyou* meet to amuse themselves. When you come across with a small group of Peking Opera fans singing in a street corner, that corner can be considered a street *Piaofang*. In the old days, there were all kinds of *Piaofang* in the inner city of Beijing according to their scale. *Piaofang* which enjoyed higher reputation were Guangdi Temple Piaofang near Qihuamen (today' s Chaoyangmen) and Songyun Nunnery *Piaofang*. Remarkablely, quite a few fa-

甫、何桂山、金少山等，最初均是票友。此外，还有一部分由社会名流组成的票友大军，像逊清贝勒爷载涛，佛学名士卧云居士，以及张伯驹、红豆馆主溥侗等知名人士，个个是对京剧艺术有很深造诣的“名票”。

而现如今的“票友”，则是来自各个行业的平头儿百姓，他们一般以唱会友，三五成群，在一起自娱自乐。每当晨光映照着京城大地的时候，“票友”们便在一阵阵京胡、月琴、三弦及锣鼓声中，在天坛祈年殿下的长廊里，故宫筒子河边等地方拉开架势，尽情展示。一曲荡气回肠的《空城计》选段，便将马（连良）派诸葛亮运筹帷幄的精彩声腔儿唱得够滋够味；张（君秋）派的女票友将其代表作《望江亭》中的女主人谭记儿的唱段更是学唱得圆润贴切，入木三分。“票友”虽说全国各地都有，但是能像北京城的“票友”这样将京剧艺术诠释得如此精到，对京剧各种流派研究得如此深入的，实不多见。“票友”名副其实是“京味文化”的一块金字招牌，是几代北京人用大量心血辛勤铸就的。

mous actors came from *Piaoyou*, for instance, Sun Juxian , Xu Yintang, Huang Runpu, He Guishan and Jin Shaoshan. In addition, the army of Piaoyou also included many celebrities such as Zai Tao, Zhang Boju and Pu Tong.

Today, *Piaoyou* are made up of common people. Generally, several of them meet together and enjoy themselves. At dawn, *Piaoyou* begin to perform at the corridor of the Hall of Prayer for Good Harvests, the Temple of Heaven (Tiantan Park), or on the bank of the moat, the Imperial Palace, accompanied by music instruments such as jinghu, yueqin, sanxian, gong, drum and so on. The selections of *Empty-city Stratagem* are favored by Ma Lianliang school fans, while the selections of *Wangjiang Pavilion* are favored by Piaoyou of Zhang Junqiu school. Although Piaoyou are across all of China, fewer can annotate this art more thoroughly and study the different Peking Opera schools more further than Beijing *Piaoyou*. *Piaoyou*, literally, is a golden brand for Beijing traditional culture, and it is cast by generations of Beijingers painstakingly.

戏园子
Old Theatres

□ 恭王府大戏楼内 Grand Theatre in the Mansion of Prince Yixin

北京是享誉海内外的世界文化名城，其颇具地方特色的“京味儿文化”，熏陶和影响了一代又一代在皇城脚下繁衍生息的京城子民。而提到京味文化，就不能不提及长达几百年的老北京“戏园子”。

京戏在京城的迅速传播发展以及为北京人喜爱和痴迷，离不开一个人，就是乾隆的功劳。清初，徽调在南方深受欢迎，有许多著名的徽班艺人在各地演出。乾隆五十五年（1790年）是乾隆的八旬大寿。清王朝从前一年就开始筹办庆典的事宜，各省官员竞相献礼。浙江盐务大臣约集了久享盛名的徽班之一“三庆班”入京祝寿。继三庆班以后，徽班陆续进入北京的还有很多，其中最著名的是四喜、春台、和春，加上三庆世

Beijing is a famous culture city known by the world. Its jingwei’r culture with strong local characteristics has natured people’s spirit greatly. Peking Opera and theaters are an important part of the culture. Some of the opera theatres in Beijing are several centuries old.

The widespreading of Peking Opera throughout Beijing and beloved by several generations of Beijingers owed greatly to a person, the Qing Dynasty Emperor Qianlong (1736-1795). Beijing opera has an over-200-year history.The main melodies originated from Xipi and Erhuang, in Anhui and Hubei Province respectively and over time techniques from many other local operas were incorporated. At the beginning of Qing Dynasty (1644 - 1911), Anhui Opera were so popular in south China that many well-known

人称之"四大徽班"。四大徽班在艺术表演方面各具特色，当时对其有这样的赞誉：三庆的轴子、四喜的曲子、春台的孩子、和春的把子。"轴"是指三庆班擅长演有头有尾的整本大戏。"曲子"，指的是昆曲，意思是说四喜班擅演昆腔为主的剧目。"孩子"即童伶，意思是说春台班的演员多以少年为主，在表演上生气勃勃。"把子"指的是武戏，意思是和春班的武戏十分火爆，深受京城百姓的喜爱。四大徽班进京后，逐渐取代了昆曲和弋腔在北京舞台的位置。随之而来，一批具有相当规模和特色的戏园子应运而生。据《道咸以来朝野杂记》一书中所载："戏园，当年内城禁止，惟有正阳门外最盛。属于大栅栏内者五处：曰庆乐、曰庆和、曰广德、曰三庆、曰同乐轩。"以后数年，陆续在不同地区又建成了吉祥、中和、长安、开明、哈尔飞等戏园子。名噪中外的前门大栅栏胡同里，云集着同仁堂、瑞蚨祥、张一元、步瀛斋、马聚源等一批久负盛名的老字号，这里从早到晚商贾云集，人头攒动，几百年中一直是京城有名的繁华地，因

□20世纪30年代的北京戏楼　A Theatre in Beijing(1930's)

Anhui Opera players had performance everywhere. In 1790, to celebrate Qianlong's 80th birthday, the minister of salt affairs from Zhejiang Province summoned a prestigious opera troupe to perform for Qinglong in the capital. On his frequent hunting expeditions or inspection tours in south China, Emperor Qianlong developed an interest in the local operas. This troupe was "anqing Anhui Opera Troupe" and this was the first time for them to perform on the stage in Beijing. Before long, other troupes from different localities followed suit. Among them, four local opera troupes were most well-known, and they are "Sanqing Anhui Opera Troupe", "Sixi Opera Anhui Troupe", "Chuntai Anhui Opera Troupe", and "Hechun Anhui Opera Troupe" respectively, which were the renowned " Four Anhui Opera Opera Troupes". The four troupes all had their own specialties. As a result, Sanqing's scripts, Sixi's melody, Chuntai's boy actors and Hechun's acrobatic skill became common catchwords among their fans. After the birthday celebrations, the four troupes remained in the capital and began to perform for ordinary audiences. Gradually, Anhui opear overwhelmed Kun Opera and Yiyang Opera on the stages. As time required, many opera theatres in big scale with striking features emerged. According to records, opera theatres were forbidden to set up in inner city of Beijing. They were flourishing in the area near Zhengyangmen. There were five Opera theatres at Dashanlan, i.e. Qirgle Opera Theatre, Qinghe Opera Theatre, Guangde Opera Theatre, Sanqing Opera Theatre and Tonglexuan Opera Theatre. During later years, Jixiang Opera

此各种戏园子也纷纷在这块地面上安营扎寨。

四大名旦之首梅兰芳先生早年表演的主要剧目，几乎无一不是在三庆戏园子演出的。1912年6月，梅先生首次登台与谭鑫培联袂演出谭派剧目《桑园寄子》，当天就见诸京都各大报纸，大获成功，成为家喻户晓的一段梨园佳话。到解放初，梅兰芳和武丑名家叶盛章共同在西单路口东侧的长安大戏院，分别将各自的代表剧目《霸王别姬》、《三岔口》等名剧名段儿，献给人民领袖毛泽东，据说毛主席很少亲临剧场看戏，这是很难得的一次。以往京都四九城各大戏园子邀请谁来，挑台演出大轴戏，不论红角儿还是名伶，演出并没有那么多的讲究。到后来，才各自互相攀比，纷纷出高价或者彼此挖墙角，将有高票保证的红角儿拉入自家戏园子，分红数额相当可观。天长日久，不同的角儿，就有了

□ 故宫畅音阁戏楼

Changyinge Theatre in the Forbidden City

Theatre, Zhonghe Opera Theatre, Chang' an Opera Theatre, Kaiming Opera Theatre and Haerfei Opera Theatre were founded one by one. The famous Dashanlan Hutong was known by the world as a prosperous place with so many *laozihao* here, for example, Tongrentang Drugstore, Ruifuxiang Silk Store, Zhang Yiyuan Tea Store, Buyingzhai and Ma Juyuan. There were so many businessmen and customers here from morning to night that different kinds of opera theatres were attracted here.

As a great master of Peking Opera and the leading one of the Four Famous *Dan*-players, Mei Lanfang (1894-1961), made outstanding contributions to the development of the opera and the spread of the charm of Chinese Opera all over the world. Nearly all his plays were performed on the stage of Sanqing Opera Theatre. Remarkably, in June, 1912, Mr. Mei made a overwhelming victory after he cooperated with Tan Xinpei, performing a Tan school opera for the first time. From that time, his name was remembered by almost every household. In 1950, Mei Lanfang and Ye Shengzhang, a famous acrobatic clown player, performed their representative works of the Mei Lanfang School *Conqueror Bids Farewell to His Concubine* and *At the Crossroads* respectively for Chairman Mao Zedong at Chang' an Theatre, Xidan crossroad east side. It is said that Chairman Mao seldom went to theatres to watch performance, so this time was a rare opportunity. According to senior beijingers, originally, the theatres were not fussy about players leading the performance. Until later, profit led them to invite the most popular players to

□ 东苑戏楼　Dongyuan theatre

分属于各自范围的戏园子，每人都有自己的一方领地。

作为特例，在一些带有官办色彩的比较盛大的公益性演出活动中，那些不同流派的名生、名旦、名丑、名净等人应主办方邀请聚集一堂，共同登台表演。像当时很有影响的唱工老旦龚云甫、黑头金少山等人就专门到庆乐戏园子去演出。而春仙茶园则是清末老生新三杰孙菊仙、许荫棠、金仲仁等一批名角展示艺术的天地。开明戏院，就定为一代名丑萧长华、名净郝寿臣等艺术大师施展表演才华的固定舞台。

不过以上所谈，都是猴年马月的老黄历了。早年那些老戏迷见面三句话不离本行，互道有关“泡戏园子”，“听名角儿”一类的话儿。现在怕是再也听不到了。经济发展，三天两头的城市市容

their theatre because they can ensure their box office. As time went on, different jue'r were affiliated with different theatres.

It is only on special occasions that different schools from *Sheng*(leading male role), *Dan* (leading female role), *Chou*(clown) and *Jing* (supporting male role) would performed together, such as the performance for public welfare sponsored by the authority. *Laodan* player Gong Yunpu and Black Head Jin Shaoshan were fixed to perform at Qingle Theatre, while the new outstanding Three *Laosheng* at the end of Qing Dynasty performed at Chunxian Teahouse, and Kaiming Theatre was the fixed stage for famous crown player Xiao Changhua and *Jing* player Hao Shouchen. At that time, the opera fans were lucky enough as they could enjoy the performance of so many Peking Opera artists.

However, all of these mentioned above have been lost in history. And the opera fans' catchwords can not be heard now. Because of its booming economy and reconstruction, Beijing city has changed greatly. Few of the theatres survived now although they had brought endless happiness to our forefathers. But in recent years, as tour culture is given more and more attentions, several tradtional opera theatres remains as historical sites. They are the Theatre in Huguang Assembly Hall at Hufangqiao, the Little Theater in Qianmen Hotel, the theatre in the Mansion of Prince Yixin, Xicheng District, and the grand theater in Summer Palace, Haidian District. It's the fans' luck that these theaters can be preserved. As a member of Beijingers, we should cherish these theatres because they are the epitome of

改造，北京城已经变了个大模样，那为老辈人带来乐子的戏园子已不再容易寻找。不过这些年来随着旅游文化的发展，作为能代表老北京特点的旧迹之一，还保留了几处老戏园子，在这些地方，依稀还能找回过去那份美好的情感。眼不前儿的有位于虎坊桥路口的湖广会馆，前门饭店的小戏园子，还有西城区柳荫街的恭王府花园戏楼，远点的还有海淀的颐和园大戏楼等，这几处可称得上老化石级别的戏楼，现在能够得以完好保存，也是老北京戏迷的福分。

□ 安徽会馆戏楼外景 Theatre in Anhui Assembly Hall

traditonal Beijing culture which incorperates *jing qiang, jingwei* and *jingyun* or the native accent and tune.

正乙祠戏楼

Zhengyici Theatre

□ 正乙祠戏楼大门
Gate of *Zhengyi* Ancestral Temple Theatre

到如今有三百多年历史的正乙祠戏楼，位于和平门烤鸭店的后边，它东临古都北京中轴线上的前门楼子，南边依托琉璃厂古文化街，地处繁华之地。这座纯木结构的古戏楼，秉承中国正宗传统建筑风格建造，相传在明代曾是一处香火极盛的寺庙。清兵入关定都北京之后，酷爱汉文化的清圣祖康熙顺应民意，下圣旨在这里改建了一座宏伟华丽的大戏楼。

正乙祠戏楼坐北朝南，建国后由于政治运动，现有的占地面积只有一千平

Zhengyici Opera Theatre with a history of more than three hundred years was situated at the prosperous area, Hepingmen Roast Duck Restaurant in the front, Qianmen in the east and Liulichang in the south. Zhengyici was built in a typical traditional Chinese style with wood structure completely. It is said that Zhengyici once served as a temple in Ming Dynasty. But during Qing Dynasty, Zhengyici was rebuilt into a splendid theatre at the order of Emperor Kangxi, who was very interested in the Hans' culture.

Zhengyici Peking Opera Theatre is one of the best-known Beijing opera theatres. It is also one of the oldest wooden theatres in China. It has a rich history that includes performances by the grandmaster of Peking Opera, Mei Lanfang. Located in a Hutong in Xuanwu District of Beijing, Zhengyici Peking Opera Theatre covers an area of more than one thousand square meters now. It remains its traditional layout with three sides of the stage are opened. There are two-storey balconys and a pool which can contain more than two hundred opera fans. Although three centuries old, this wooden theatre is still in a good state basically because of the preservation work. It is called as the milestone in the history of Chinese theatres by experts and is praised as the living fossil of Chinese theatre culture with high

方米左右，但遵循老式戏园子的传统格局始终未变。戏台为三面开放式，戏台正前方和两侧开辟为上下两层的高级敞开式包厢，另外面对戏台前边约有百余平方米的看池，可容纳二百余位戏迷一边品茗一边看戏。虽历经三个多世纪的岁月沧桑，该所木质戏楼至今仍基本保存完好。它被专家称为中国戏楼发展史上的里程碑，还有不少学者赞誉为“中华戏楼文化史上的活化石”，具有极高的历史文化研究价值。

聊起老“戏园子”那话题可就长了，过去供老辈儿北京人娱乐休闲的场所少之又少，而且比较单一。赶上年节及可喜可庆的事，也不过相约几位朋友到饭铺，来瓶二锅头，点上几个菜吃顿便饭意思一下，然后去“戏园子”里找找乐子，也就这个样子了。

清王朝统治期间，凡是满族人，生下来享受国家俸禄，他们可以一年365天锦衣玉食，吃喝不愁养尊处优。当年这些公子哥儿们每每酒足饭饱后，就喜欢到茶园里品茶聊天，消遣打磨时光，众伶人们也就专门来到茶园为这些腰缠万贯的八旗子弟们唱戏献艺以养家糊口，双方各有所求，互有所需。这就是过去不少戏园子均是在茶园基础上发展而来的主要原因。具体到正乙祠戏楼，同样也是照此模式走过来的，但值得浓墨重彩书写一笔的，还源于它是国粹“京剧表演艺术”诞生、发展和进一步繁荣辉煌的历史见证。在清末民初，京剧很风光，那时老北京还是四九城，许多梨园界的老前辈，堪称泰斗级的几位表演艺术家都曾在这里登台献艺一展风彩。近代当代的许多京剧名

research value by many scholars. In the past, there were few places for entertainment. So on festivals or to celebrate for something, people would invite several friends to restaurant, then go to theatres for fan. Basically, no other entertainment was available.

During Qing Dynasty, all Manchus were born with salary and they had no need to work. So they liked drinking tea and chatting at tea houses to kill time. So the opera players came to these tea houses and performed for the wealthy descendants of the Eight Banners to make a living. And here lies the main reason why many theatres were developed on the basis of tea houses. As far as Zhengyici Theater is concerned, it has followed this pattern. Notably, it witnessed the birth and development of Peking Opera performance art. Between the end of Qing Dynasty and the beginning of the Republican, Peking Opera enjoyed high social status. Many eminent Peking Opera artists performed on the stage of Zhengyici. During moderm times and the contemporary era, many artists frequently visited Zhengjici Theatre, devoting their school’s selections and stunt to the audience.

When you enjoy youself at this ancient theatre, you will feel contented and proud of the consummate art achievments our ancestors made. Meanwhile, a sense of responsibility will haunt in your mind. That is, how we protect and carry forward the traditional culture. Whether the splendid old theatres with uique style or the Peking Opera with singing, dialogue, acting and martial arts as its basic performing forms, they are all the repesentives of Chinese vast and intensive his-

家也经常光临该戏楼，将不同流派的名戏名段儿奉献给观众，平日难得一见的各派名家群英荟萃，抖搂出各自绝活让戏迷们大饱眼福过足戏瘾。

追忆过去风光无限的岁月，让人觉得置身于这座历史悠久的老戏楼里，看戏、品茗，票友悠闲地自娱自乐，都会有一种满足之感，都为我们祖先取得如此高妙的艺术成就而感到自豪和骄傲。同时陶醉之余又有一股厚重的历史责任感萦绕于心，那就是怎样弘扬和保护好传统文化，因为不论是古色古香、流光溢彩、风格独特的老戏楼，还是在唱、做、念、打方面已自成艺术体系的京戏，都是我们几千年博大精深的历史文化的代表性缩影之一，应给予足够的重视和爱护。

值得欣慰的是，现如今的正乙祠戏楼如一棵蟠虬老树，虽饱经风雨又再发新枝，它沐浴着明媚的春光和丰沛的雨露，仍然顽强地焕发着第二个艺术青春。其经营者在保留传统风格基础上又为老戏楼注入新的内容，请一些京剧、昆曲、曲艺、河北梆子等剧种的演员加盟，每天晚上定时上演优秀的折子戏节目助兴，给各界观众带来美好的艺术享受。如今，这座老戏楼又以它独具特色的文化景观，古朴典雅的艺术风姿及魅力，为生活在现代化的大都市中抱有怀旧情结的京城老百姓和热爱中国历史文化的国际友人，营造了一个举办中式古典结婚、祝寿、办生日等活动的温馨殿堂。此外，它还成为近些年来外宾来北京城游览时值得一游的景观，同时亦是一处弘扬展示传统民族文化，了解中国和老北京民俗生活的一个很有意义的窗口。

□ 正乙祠戏楼内部 Inner of Zhengyici Theater

torical culture. Great attentions should be given to them to make them everlasting.

To our great relief, today's Zhengyici is experiencing its second high time after the hardship of its life, like an old tree, which has suffered from voilent wind and the cold in winter, and resumes its spirit in the bright sunshine and the showering of spring rain. The operators of Zhengyici has added new items into it as well as kept its traditonal style. To meet the new need of the audience, they also invite some other opera players to join them, such as Kun Opera, Qu Yi, Bangzi and so on. Every night, there is outstanding opera highlights show at Zhengyici as scheduled. This old opera theatre has taken on extra roles. Traditional Chinese-style wedding ceremony and birthday celebration can also be held at this ancient theatre with exquisite culture sight and elegant art charm for urbanite with reminiscent complex or foreigners who love Chinese history and culture. In addition, Zhengyici has been both a deserving sight when foreigners visit beijing and a window for the world to understand Beijing tradtional custom, life and culture.

什刹海
Shichahai

□ 初秋时节的什刹海风光 Shichahai in Autumn

什刹海位于北京地安门外，北海后门对过，由于它自然地理位置适中，又与以往的皇家禁地保持一定的距离，因此在旧时的北京，什刹海成为繁华闹市中一块难得的清闲之地。什刹海共由前、后、西三海组成，西海又称积水潭。整体中的“三海”形状各异，它像一对宝葫芦束在中段的腰上。在老北京人的眼中，什刹海至今保存了京城最为完整、最为优美的胡同和四合院，这里的胡同纵横交错，几百年来建筑格局并无太大的变化。所以要想了解原汁原味的北京胡同和四合院，什刹海应成为首选。因为在这里，你能仔细观赏许多古色古香的胡同四合院和雍荣华贵的王府花园，品味流淌其中的市井文化、士大夫文化和皇家文化。

半个多世纪以前，寓居京城什刹海一带的人家，都会很留恋它那杨柳轻

Shichahai is a majestic lake situated in downtown Beijing near Di'anmen, opposite Beihai. For the moderate locality and the distance away from the imperial Forbidden City, it provided local residents with a sanctuary from the hustle and bustle of the day in the past. Shichahai is composed of three man-made lakes, Qianhai (Front Sea Lake), Houhai (Rear Sea Lake) and Xihai or Jishuitan (West Sea Lake). And it once formed part of a system of waterways that fed into the Imperial Capital. For centuries wooden boats carrying produce from the south would make the journey up the Grand Canal and enter the city via these waterways. The best preserved and most graceful *Hutong* and quadrangles can be found in Shichahai area. And its *Hutong* has remained the crisscross pattern for centuries. If you want to understand original *Hutong* and quadrangles in Beijing, Shichahai is the best place. Here, you can find many old *Hutong* and quadrangles as well as splendid imperal mansions and gardens. Besides, you can understand folk culture, scholar-bureaucrat culture and imperial culture in details.

The local residents will recall the scene of old Beijing half a century ago with nostalgia sometimes. The overhanging willows ling its banks, the elegant old Wanning Bridge and the

拂、古桥依旧、蝉鸣夏日的旧京小景。当年，这里成为许多人及周边百姓参观、游览、休闲、纳凉的上佳场所。昔日的什刹海还被世人盛赞为“北方的水乡”，每当春风拂面的时候，百鸟齐声高歌、鱼儿在碧水中尽情穿梭，洋溢着丰厚浓郁的生活气息。盛夏时节，湖中一株株粉红色的荷花在绿伞似的叶子映衬下，透着如年轻姑娘一样的万般妩媚。如果深入其中，十分惬意的感觉会不由自主地涌上心间。

放眼远眺，沿湖岸边的老茶馆、酒肆、杂耍场子等尽收眼帘。步入中间，一阵阵抑扬顿挫、时高时低的吆喝声传入耳中，游人们的食欲大振，对各色风味特色小吃“垂涎三尺”。清末至新中国成立，什刹海作为吃喝玩乐、品味民俗的好地方一直深受好几代人的青睐。精于此道的人介绍，每年自清明前后人开始多起来，等到了盛夏和金秋时节，什刹海岸边的茶馆和酒肆里几乎是座无虚席。每个人的嗜好各不相同，在这处供平民百姓尽情开心的地方，三教九流五行八作，教书的行武的，都能在一天忙忙碌碌的劳作过后，在这里得到休息和放松。稍微讲究一些的茶馆里，小伙计热情地为客人沏好茶。两鬓斑白的老翁一边慢慢地品着茶，一边手摇着扇子，聚精会神听着评书艺人绘声绘色地说书表演。亦有一部分中下层劳动者里三层外三层地围着唱大鼓词的、唐山落子的、变戏法的、掼跤的，争睹不同行当艺人的技艺。总之，过去前来什刹海开心找乐子的男女老少，都不同程度地把它当作北京第二个“老天桥”。

song of the cicada in summer are all long gone. At that time, Shichahai was the prime destination for visit, recreation and enjoying the cool. So was praised as an oasis by the world. In spring, it was flourishing with life. Birds were singing and fish was swimming happily in the lake. While in hot summer, pink lotus in full blossom seemed very charming against the green umbrella-like leaves. Boating among them, an easy feeling would hit you.

Looking farther, visitors would see old tea house, pub and vaudeville field along the banks. Walking inside, they would hear different hawk which attracted them to snacks with strong flavor. From the end of Qing Dynasty to the founding of People's Republic of China in 1949, Shichahai had been a favorite recreation destination for local residents in Beijing, especially in midsummer and autumn. Most visitors were common people. Although they had different hobbies, they could all enjoy themselves there, because Shichahai provided a tranquil escape to stressed workers seeking relexing. At more decent teahouses, customers could sip their tea and enjoy the vivid storytelling performance. Story-

□ 什刹海前的荷花市场　Lotus Market by *Shichahai*

此外，便是高声吆喝的人，多为卖牛肝、卖羊杂碎汤、卖豆汁、卖卤煮火烧、卖年糕、卖驴打滚的小商小贩。他们当中有的推着手推车沿湖岸叫卖，还有的随便支上个芦席棚，几张桌子摆在中间，旁边放着几个长条板凳，食客们则一个个低着头尽情品尝京城历史悠久的传统风味小吃。昔日，京城人民在吃上很喜欢这种形式。逛了大半天什刹海后，已饥肠辘辘，这时来上一碗热气腾腾连汤带水的羊杂碎汤，外加两三个芝麻酱火烧，也可称得上惬意极了。当年几乎所有的风味小吃摊位前，一天到晚总是门庭若市，人头攒动。

来什刹海放松休闲的游人们中间，也不乏有一些文化层次较高的人，与亲朋好友划着小木船儿，在湖水中轻柔地荡漾，或在湖中间的人工小岛上漫步，周围被满目绿色所环绕，不知不觉已心旷神怡，那种美好感觉让人抚今追昔，感慨万分。

telling with drum accompaniment, Tangshan *Laozi* (a kind of local opera), magic, Chinese wreslting were also available, and the fields were surrounded by many common labors. In short, Shichahai had been regarded as the second recreation destination by old Beijingers, which was only inferior to Tianqiao.

In addition, people who hawked were vendors selling snacks such as Cow Liver, Lamb Gizzard Soup, Mung Bean Milk, Glutinous Rice Cake and Pastry Made-of Soy Bean Flour. Some of them peddled along the bank of the lake with a barrow, others sold their snacks under a reed shed with several tables and benches. These traditional snacks with long history were very popular among customers. In the past, it was a high enjoyment to have a bowl of hot Lamb Gizzard Soup and two or three Baked Wheaten Cake with Sesame Sauce (*Zhimajiang Huoshao*) after a tired visit. And all of the snack were never lack of customers.

□ 烟袋斜街上有特色的店铺
Distinctive Store in *Yandai* Diagonal Street

□ 银锭观山 Mountain Vision from Yinding Bridge

□ 湖面宽阔的什刹海 *Shichahai with Widen Water*

1992年市政府将什刹海定为历史文化风景区。在2000年批准的北京25片历史文化保护区中，什刹海地区的面积是其中最大的。景区历史文化积淀深厚，共有文物保护单位40余处，国家级保护单位3处。远至郭守敬、纳兰性德、张之洞，近至鲁迅、宋庆龄、郭沫若等都在此留有足迹。在历史上很多文人墨客纷纷为什刹海题诗赋词，古代的僧人们在这里修寺建庙，而皇亲国戚则在岸边选址筑府造园，名人雅士也先后迁居湖畔。这样，什刹海地区经过长期的历史积淀，已逐渐成为一个名人贤士聚集的宝地。

如今北京市已经从诸多方面对什刹海的周边环境、绿化、水源做了许多工作，使其恢复了往日的风貌。

Among visitors, there were also literate people who boated in the lake with their friends or strolled on the man-made island which was located in the centre of the lake. Surrounded by green trees, a sense of peace, carefree and pleasure would hit them. The desirable feeling was never forgotten in one' s life.

In 1992, Shichahai was classified as a Historical Cultural Beauty Spot by Beijing Municipal Government. And it covered the most area among the 25 historical and cultural beauty spots authorized by the government. There were more than 40 cultural relics and three of them were national preservation of cultural relics. Many celebraties once lived here from Guo Shoujing(1231 - 1316, a Chinese astronomer, engineer, and mathematician), Nalan Xingde(1655-1685, poet) and Zhang Zhidong(1837-1909, classicist and one of the foremost reformers in Qing Dynasty) to Lu Xun(1881-1936), Song Qingling and Guo Moruo. A lot of men wrote poems for Shichahai. In ancient times, monks built temples here while the imperial relatives chosen here to set up mansions and gardens. Later, many celebraties moved to the lake district. Over time, Shichahai had become a place for celebraties to gather.

Today, due to a great deal of improvement worked on the surrounding environment, including afforesting and waterhead by Beijing municipal government, Shichahai is resuming its old historical scene. This prestigious historical and cutural beauty spot will serve not only as a paradise for common people but also a window for the world to understand Beijng.

老北京堂会

Tanghui of Old Beijing

往日老北京的“堂会”，对现在的年轻人来说，已经是个非常陌生和遥远的词，知道的人微乎其微。但对于老北京来说，“堂会”曾经的荣耀是怎样令他们怀念啊！那可是风光的一件大事情，不是真正有头有脸的人家，是绝对摆不起这个谱儿的。旧时老北京人讲究很多，像买卖开张、乔迁新宅、孩子过生日、办满月、红白喜事等，除了招待亲朋好友、置办酒席以外，还要专门办喜庆的“堂会”，演出一些戏曲、杂耍、八角鼓、皮影戏之类的节目，老北京人习惯管“堂会”上演出的节目叫作“玩艺儿”。玩艺儿规模的大小，戏曲中角儿的知名度高低，演出时间的长短等，则因人而异，但图的都是个“吉祥”。

For young man, Tanghui of old Beijing is quite a strange and remote thing, and few of them know about them. But old Beijingers were very familiar with it. Once a time,Tanghui, the Opera performing in home, is a glory event which is deeply bearn by heart. However, only wealthy or upper-class household could afford to hold Tanghui at that time. The host not only treated his friends and relatives with feast, but also held Tanghui on some occasions like business opening ceremony, moving into new house, children' s birthday or one month old celebration, wedding ceremony as well as funeral. The contents of Tanghui included opera, sideshow, octagon drum and shadow play. Old Beijingers used to call the programmes performed on Tanghui as *wanyi 'r*.

□早年“堂会”的缩影
The Relic of Tanghui in Beijing

就拿昔日皇亲国戚举办的家庭“堂会”为例，一般情况下都是演唱整出的京戏剧目，不惜重金邀请的都是当时走红梨园的各个流派的腕儿级名家，不光富贵华丽的王爷府内，就连附近的街巷也要提前张灯结彩，烘托气氛。演员的包银往往是他们在戏园子中挑台唱戏的数倍，但有与办堂会的王爷本人私交很深的名角儿则是分文不取，此种情况属于特例，另当别论。一出大轴戏正式演唱以前，总要先由几位不太知名的配角儿，扮成福、禄、寿、喜一类的笑星给办堂会的老王爷、福晋一家人添喜儿，表示祝贺。紧随其后以《报喜》、《赐福》、《拜寿》等小戏儿作为“堂会”中正宗大戏的垫场，又称“帽儿戏”。王爷根据当时的心情，给数量不等的赏钱，这些老理儿都属家庭“堂会”的基本定式。最叫彩儿的重头节目，当然是以吉祥如意为表演内容的压轴大戏。如著名的京剧传统剧目《麻姑献寿》、《打金枝》、《状元印》等，都是众多戏迷百看不厌的梨园佳作。

据有关书籍记载，早年一些京剧名流儿、名票儿家中一旦喜事临门，同样要按照老传统举办家庭“堂会”以示庆贺。“堂会”的风光无限和演出质量之高，堪比群英荟萃的梨园盛会。就拿四大名旦之首，梅兰芳先生家的一次堂会就可得到印证。据京剧史学家介绍，当时有梨园界祖师爷之美誉的王瑶卿老先生大驾光临。一出传统名剧《艳阳楼》，竟分别由那个时代很多名角儿反串成不同行当的角色，像有铁嗓子之称的著名余派老生创始人余叔岩饰高登，王瑶卿

According to diffenent hosts, the scale of *wanyi 'r*, the popularity of the opera players and the duration of the performance differed, but they all had one same goal, that is, to pray for propitiousness.

Taking Tanghui held by the relatives of the emperor in the past for example. Generally, the performance was a whole Peking Opera play, and players were most popular who belonged to different schools. Not only the gorgeous imperial mansion but the neighbourhood were decorated with lanterns and colored streamers in advance. And the actors's salary was several times higher than that of the leading player at the opera theatres. There was exception. If the actor had deep personal friendship with the host, he would ask for no payment. Before formal performance, some less well-known supporting players were dressed up as clown like *fu*(blessing), *lu*(salary), *shou* (longevity) and *xi*(happiness), expressing celebration to the host. Then, some playlets (also called *Mao 'r* Opera) followed, such as *Report Good News*, *Bestow Blessing* and *Celebrate Birthday*. Then the host would give the players tips. The amount of the tips depended on the host's mood at that time, but whatever more or less, it was a Tanghui routine. The most wonderful part of Tanghui, of course, was the opera play expressing the idea of good luck. Among them, there were well-known traditional Peking Opera plays such as *Ma Gu's Birthday Present to Queen Mother of the West, Beat Princess Jinzhi, The Seal of Number One Scholar*.

According to records, some renowned Peking Opera players and *Piaoyou* also held Tanghui to

之弟王风卿饰花逢春，梅兰芳饰呼延豹，贯大元饰贾斯文。这个标新立异的家庭“京剧堂会”，被当年北京各界人士赞誉为一段难得的梨园佳话传颂至今。

还有一部分办堂会的京城人家，平常就喜欢唱上两口儿京腔京味的小曲儿，这回适逢办“堂会”，好似如鱼得水。托圈里人将曲艺演员请到青砖灰瓦的四合院家中，与家人、亲友逐一欣赏相声、五音大鼓、京韵大鼓、梅花大鼓、河南坠子、西河大鼓、太平歌词等。说书唱曲儿这种艺术符合黎民百姓的欣赏水平。在过去，有不少家庭“堂会”上，均以说书唱曲出现。

上述所谈的“喜庆堂会”，基本是过去上层社会中的王爷府、大宅门、买卖人家“堂会”上所展示的内容。大多数当时在经济上并不富裕的小门小户人家，有时也要办一些与自家情况相适宜的“堂会”，只不过从规模、演艺的形式上都不能与有钱人家相比。“富人有富人的一套活法，穷人有穷人的生活路

□ 清末北京堂会
Beijing Tanghui in the Late of Qing Dynasty

celebrate once they had happy event. Tanghui's quality was so high that it could be compared to a big pear garden event. This could be verified by a Tanghui held in Mei Lanfang' s house. According to Peking Opera historian, Wang Yaoqing — the so-called " Founder of Theater Garden" — jioned the Tanghui. In the traditional play *Yanyang Pavilion*, many outstanding perform artists acted different roles reversely to make the fans and audience feel excited. For example, Yu Shuyan, the founder of Yu school, acted as Gao Deng; Wang Fengqing(the famous performer and educationist of Peking Opera Wang Yaoqing's brother) acted as Hua Fengchun; Mei Lanfang acted as Hu Yanbao; and Guang Dayuan as Jia Siwen. And this unconventional household Tanghui has become a much-told tale.

Some households who were very fond of folk art could not miss the opportunity of holding Tanghui. Through insiders, they invited folk art actors to their house and enjoyed cross talk, Wuyin Drum, Jingyun Drum, Meihua Drum, one by one with their friends and relatives. Story-telling suited the taste of most common people. So in the past, many household Tanghui were composed of story-tellings.

All of above were the upper-class household Tanghui such as the princes, nobilities and the businessmen. To most of less-wealthy households, they sometimes held Tanghui which of course, could not compare with that of the rich in scale and form. However, everyone had their own style of life. Common poor people could not afford luxury feast but they had their own way to entertain themselves. They would invite some

数。"普通老百姓，虽然没有能力置办酒席大庆大贺，但穷人也同样应有自己开心的形式。他们把一些在天桥撂地的艺人朋友请至家中，一壶清茶，艺人们分别以唐山落子、杂耍等，把对穷哥们的真诚祝福送到他们的心坎上。

总之，不管往日讲究排场的富人"堂会"也好，还是简朴寒酸的贫苦人家的"堂会"也罢，它都曾是皇城根下几代老少爷们儿追求幸福生活的一种形式。尽管还远远谈不上多高级，但"知足者常乐"这句老话儿，不是一直伴随人们好几辈子吗?

obscure Tianqiao actors to their house with little money. And the actors expressed their sincere blessing to the poor. through Tangshan *Laozi*, sideshow and so on.

In a word, whether extravagant or simple, Tanghui is just a form that generations of old Beijingers seeking happiness. As an old saying goes, "people who are contented with their lot are always happy", generations of people has gained a lot of happiness from Tanghui.

消闲一处

A Place of Leisure

□ "老澡堂子"的延续——"浴池"
The Relic of old Bath House

这才几年的光景，北京洗浴业就脱胎换骨，旧貌换新颜，而且越换花样越翻新，什么"桑拿浴"、"芬兰浴"、"土耳其浴"、蒸汽浴，形式多多、五花八门，此举还真让一部分人产生跟不上时代的感觉。可话儿说白了，不就是"洗个澡"吗？在过去，老辈北京人想搞搞个人卫生无非就是到澡堂子去洗洗，目的很明确，图个清洁干净爽利就得活。可眼下，洗浴却注入了几分休闲味道在里边，什么泡脚聊天啦，养颜洗面啦，按摩保健啦……两者间的最大区别，那就是过去平民百姓可没那么多的讲究，花个毛儿八七的到澡堂子洗个澡，把全身洗干净就是最终目的，而现在名副其实地成为一种休闲与享受，洗澡倒退而求其次了。

但是，不少老北京还是对过去的洗澡极为留恋，不断回味解放前后的那些

Bathing industry in Beijing has growing up and changed a lot in the recent years, and there are more and more new names to it, such as Sauna, Finland Bath and Turkish Bath. Types are so various and garish that some people find it hard to catch up with the fashion. But to speak directly and bluntly, isn't it nothing but to have a bath? In the past, Beijing natives would go to bathhouse if they wanted to do some body-cleaning. The purpose was simple just to keep cleanliness and neatness. But now, bath also has a meaning of leisure. The business includes foot-relaxing bath and chatting, skin-caring and face washing, massage healthcare and so on. The biggest difference was that the common people in the past didn't demand so much as people now. They paid some *jiaos* to enter a bath house, and the purpose was simply to take a bath, cleaning themselves. While today, bath was endowed a meaning of leisure and self-indulgency, and cleaning was only the second.

But for many people, the old bathhouses before and after liberation, such as Qinghuayuan, Yuhuayuan, Baoquantang and Chunqing in Beijing, were more interesting and meaningful. Although the facilities in old bathhouse in the past was much inferior to bath places nowadays, it's actually open for common people, and

老式澡堂子，如京城的清华园、裕花园、宝泉堂、春庆等。虽然这些老洗澡堂子，各方面条件远远比不上时下兴起的洗浴场所设施那么优越，但那可是名副其实的为一般老百姓开的，真正拿平民当“爷”侍候的“消闲一处”。

过去的澡堂子一般淋浴、盆浴、池塘三者俱全，每个人可根据自己的喜好分别选择不同的洗浴方式。泡澡的大池子上面的房顶中间有并列的天窗供通气之用，热水一律都用燃煤的锅炉来烧，热气腾腾的，温度很理想。想泡澡的客人刚一进澡堂子的门，店小二就满脸微笑地迎上前来，紧接着一整套甜话儿便脱口而出：“大爷，您往里请，里面儿有闲位子，地儿清静还不吵。”这廖廖数语，顿时让浴客感到来这儿心情倍儿好，有一种宾至如归的亲切。客人开始更衣之时，店小二儿又适时来到身边：“大爷！您看您想喝点什么，我们这儿有五分一两的高末儿，一毛一两的茉莉花茶……”

老澡堂子除洗澡的主业以外，还有专门为客人搓澡、拔罐子、修脚、推拿按摩一类的服务。对那些因劳累或者着凉什么的导致腰酸腿痛的主儿来说，经大池子中热水这么一泡，马上会大汗淋淋，头疼脑热的小毛病一下子全都除了，是一剂花钱少、见效快的天然良药。当时京城大大小小的洗澡堂子，几乎都是从上午开始就恭候客人的到来，一直要开到深更半夜才打烊，深受中下层平民百姓的欢迎。泡澡儿曾是当年老北京人最津津乐道的一件事儿，其实您还甭说，不论从事何种营生的人只要泡上俩

really a leisure place treating customer as milord, just as it had alleged.

Bathhouses in the past often offered all three types of bath: shower bath, tubbing and pond, and every one could make a choice according to his preference. Above the big bath pool, there were paralled skylights for breath in the middle of roof. Water was heated by boiler burning coal exclusively and the temperature was moderate. No sooner had a customer entered into a bath-house than the waiter came to welcome him with a big smile on his face, followed by a complete set of flattering words, “come in please, sir. There are spare room inside and not noisy at all.” A few words like that would make customers happy and feel at home. When the customer began to take on clothes, the waiter would come along in good time and said, “Sir, Would you like to drink something? We have cheap tea, five *fens* per *liang*, and Jasmine Tea, one *mao* per *liang*……”

Bath was the main business of old bathhouse, but they also offered some special service such as rubdown, cupping, pedicure and massage. For those who got tired or caught a cold and suffered hurt in waist and legs, all the slight illnesses would go away as soon as they come into the big pool and had a great sweatiness in the hot water. It’s really a good natural medicine which was cheap and took effect quickly. At that time, almost all the bathhouses in Beijing opened from morning until midnight and were popular with the middle and lower classes. Bath was one of the biggest pleasure of Beijing natives in those years. In fact, people from all classes would eliminate

钟头，一天的累和乏，顿时神奇般地全泡没了。代之而来的就是全身的轻松，容光焕发。这些特别舒服的感受，只有身临其境才能够体会得到。

旧时北京人的生活节奏比较慢。天子脚下的子民们，多年来追求的是一种闲适、轻松的生活方式。在洗澡方面也是如此，这一洗一泡就是半天的功夫，很少有半个钟头左右就走出来的。尤为值得一提的是，一些老主顾多年来养成的习惯是澡儿洗上一会以后，先走出池子躺在一排排专门安置好的硬木板床上，有滋有味地喝着茶房提前沏好的不凉不热的茶水歇会儿回头再接着洗。其间，粗通文墨的主儿，手里拿着两份报纸，一边看一边品着茶香。从事手工业的体力劳动者，凑在一块，更爱侃一些

□一品香浴池遗址 Relic of the Yipinxiang Bath House

their tiredness and fatigue magically if only they had a bath in the pool for a couple of hours. Then they would feel relaxed and comfortable, and be aglow of health. And only these person who ever came here could experience all these pleasing feelings.

In the past, life rhythm of Beijing natives was very slow. The people living under the foot of Forbidden City pursued a kind of quiet and leisure life in many years. So did they do in the aspect of bath. They would spend almost half day in the pool and rarely come out after half an hour. It' s worth mentioning that some old customers had got a habit in the years. They would wash for a while, then walk out of the pool and lie on the rows of hardwood beds which were set there especially, and have some tea racily which was made in advanced by the waiter, neither too hot nor too cool. Someone knew a little literature would take a piece of newspaper and read it while drinking the tea. When the handicraft producers got together, they would prefer some claver-talk, such as "Black-head, painted-face and Mr.Jin (Shanshan) played Huang Tianba in Zhonghe Theatre; The performance was excellent and the stentorian voice would make the ears tingle even if you are listening in the next door." Some

□一品香澡堂局部 Detail of the Yipinxiang Bath House

闲篇儿，什么“黑头、花脸、金爷(少山)在中和戏园子，扮演黄天霸，字正腔圆，味儿那个足，嗓子那个亮堂，就是隔着戏园子的墙根听，那音儿都震耳朵”。还有一些善聊的人，不知从哪里道听途说听来的故事，说得更玄：“侠盗燕子李三，飞檐走壁，专偷有钱人家的钱财，接济缺食少衣的一帮穷哥们儿，大有杀富济贫的义举，这一来二去，闹得京城不少吸食民脂民膏的贪官污吏吓得整天不敢出门，急得像热锅上的蚂蚁似的，生怕身轻如燕的李三登自家的宅门。”侃者的表情是眉飞色舞、绘声绘色，听的主儿更是急着知道下文：“那后来呢?”

斗转星移，光阴荏苒，以上所谈的事儿早已是猴年马月老掉牙的旧皇历了。如今中国步入市场经济的大潮之中，国人的思想更趋多元化。然而不论新一代的追星族怎么赶时髦讲时尚，精明的商家怎么翻新花样，它也永远代替不了澡堂子在老北京人心中挥之不去的那一份美好情感。因为它是原汁原味的京都市井文化的一个组成部分，越是过早失去的，怀旧的人们越是迫切地渴望能重新得到。

conversationalists would talk some incredible stories from hearsay, “the knightly Thief Swallow Li San, who could leap onto roofs and vault over walls, grabbed the rich’s fortune and gave financial help to the poor lack of food and cloth, and gained a reputation to rob the rich and help the poor. So many malfeasants in the capital dared not to go out and were anxious like a hen on a hot girdle for fear that the Swallowlike Li San would enter their houses.” The expression of the talker was enraptured and lively, while the listeners were more anxious to know the following and asked, “what next?”

As time passed, everything has changed so much, and the affairs mentioned above have gone as times gone by. It’s really far away from the point, let’s back to our subject. Now China has entered into the tide of market economy and people are more apt to multi-thought. However, no matter how quickly the new generation of idolater’s fashion changes, no matter how many new games the shrewd bussinessmen raise, nothing could replace the feeling of old bathhouses lingering in the heart of Beijing natives forever, because it’s a part of the pure city culture of Beijing. What we lost too early was just what we wanted to regain eagerly.

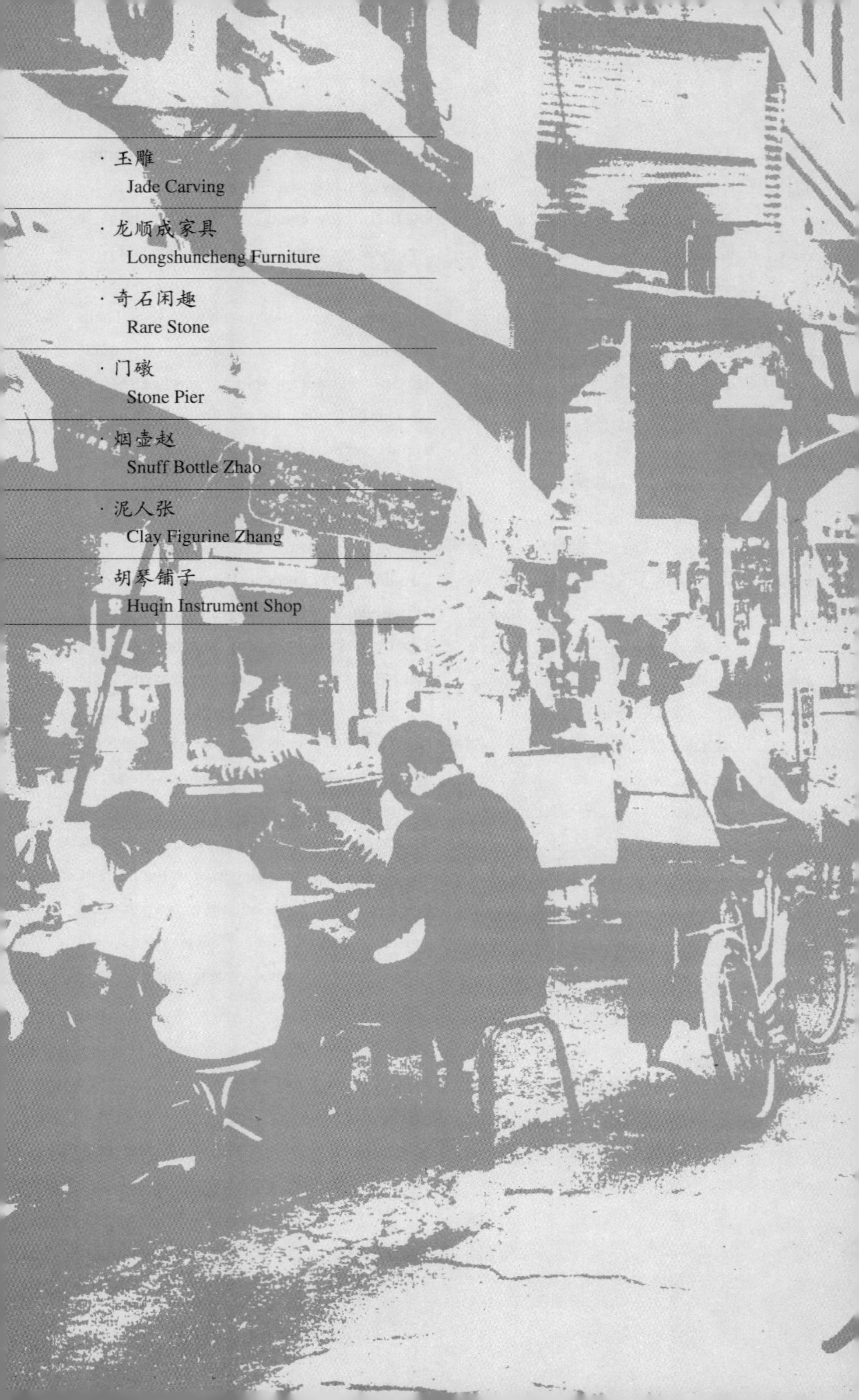

- 玉雕
  Jade Carving
- 龙顺成家具
  Longshuncheng Furniture
- 奇石闲趣
  Rare Stone
- 门礅
  Stone Pier
- 烟壶赵
  Snuff Bottle Zhao
- 泥人张
  Clay Figurine Zhang
- 胡琴铺子
  Huqin Instrument Shop

古玩与匠艺人

Curio and Handicraftman

玉雕
Jade Carving

□ 黄玉双鱼花插 Double-fish Work Made of Yellow Jade

在中国五千年来的悠久文明史中，收藏艺术自始至终占有非常重要的地位。像在文物收藏领域里的赏玉、玩玉、藏玉，更是源远流长经久不衰，现在在北京、上海、广州、天津等大城市仍颇为盛行。玉器最早起源于一万年前，为中国最古老的三大工艺品种之一。它以其绚丽的色彩、奇妙的质地、精湛的制作技艺、典雅的造型和优美的纹饰著称于世。

在中国玉器行当里，流传着“天下美玉出和田”之说。和田位于新疆昆仑山山脉的中部，这里的玉材极为珍贵稀有，自古以来就闻名天下。除新疆的和田盛产高质量的美玉以外，还有辽宁的

Chinese culture has a long history of 5,000 years,in which art collection always plays an very important role. For example, in the field of antique collection, jade appreciation,playing and collection are of long standing, and are still very popular in large cities such as Beijing, Shanghai and Guangzhou. Being one of the most ancient craftworks, Chinese jade is 10,000 years old. It is famous all over the world for its ornate color, wonderful quality, good technique, marvellous appearance and pretty ornamentation. There is a saying in the field of jade making that the jade produced in Hetian is the best jade in the world. Hetian is a place in the middle of the Kunlun mountain, where the jade is very precious and well-known. Besides, people also provide plenty of jade for the development of jade carving in other places, like Xiuyan Town in Liaoning, Qilian Mountain in Gansu and Du Mountain in Henan.

Jade has four characteristics of mildness, smoothness,stiffness and density. Its color is naturally soft, beautiful and pure. This is just like a person’s skin. The jade is so stiff that it can’t be pierced by irons. The jade also has a very dense and even structure. Jade is divided by the craftsmen in this field into two kinds, Nephrite and Jadeite. Nephrite is made of hornblende, in particular tremolite. It is square and very dense,

岫岩、甘肃的祁连山、河南独山的玉石等，这些地方都为玉雕艺术的发展提供了充足的玉材货源。

玉石具有天生的“温、润、坚、密”四大优点，色彩天然柔和、赏心悦目、油润无燥。这一点又恰似人的肌肤。还有坚韧不拔、钢铁难攻、组织紧密、结构均衡的特性。玉器行里的匠人们将玉石细分为软玉和硬玉两大类别。软玉即由角闪石族矿物中的透闪石为主组成的，质密块状，呈纤维状结构，这是软玉细腻和坚韧的主要原因，新疆和田玉就属于这种。清代乾隆年间大量进入我国的翡翠（红色为翡，绿色为翠，以红、绿色最为珍贵闻名）属于硬玉。

清代的玉器行有京作、广作和沪作，三大门派风格也不大一样。特别是乾隆在位期间，玉雕作工更是十分讲究，规矩方圆须一丝不苟，凡是直线的地方必要笔直，凡圆形的部位必如满月，凡窝角必须圆润，尖角则一概要锋利，一件器物任何部位都要注意修整打磨，雕琢要玲珑剔透方为上品。纹饰题材基本上沿袭明代，以吉祥长寿的题材为主，同时亦出现了大量的以山水和古代诗词为创作题材的玉器。由于乾隆皇帝嗜好古玩玉器，曾多次降旨要匠人仿造商周时期的青铜、宋代陶瓷等器型的玉器，并特别喜欢将历代玉器加以改制并刻上“乾隆年制”的款识，使玉雕艺术在乾隆年间达到中国历史上的巅峰水平。乾隆时期高超的代表性杰作有“关山行旅图”、“丹台春晓图”、“大禹治水图”、“会昌九龙图”、“云龙石瓮”等。

此外，以“凤凰”为创作题材的也

and has fibrous structure. These are the main reasons that nephrite is delicate and stiff. The jade produced in Hetian of Xingjiang is just a kind of nephrite. The jade, which was introduced in large quantity in Qing Dynasty, was jadeite, and the jade is called *Fei Cui* in China. *Fei* is the red jade while the green jade is called *Cui*. The red and green jade is the most famous and precious.

The jade trades in Qing Dynasty have three kinds, jade of Beijing, Guangzhou and Shanghai. They are of very different styles. In particular, during the period of Emperor Qianlong in Qing Dynasty, jade carving has very strict requirement. Lines must be very straight, and rotundity should be like the full moon. Angle ought to be very smooth and cusp must be very sharp. Only through carefully making, the jade can be made into a wonderful craft which is exquisitely carved. The theme of the carving, mainly blessing and longevity, is basically descending from Ming Dynasty. Meanwhile, there was also jade about mountain, river and poem. Emperor Qianlong was very fond of curio and jade,and he ordered the craftsmen to make the jade, imitating bronze in Shang and Zhou Dynasties as well as ceramic in Song Dynasty. He also liked to redesign the

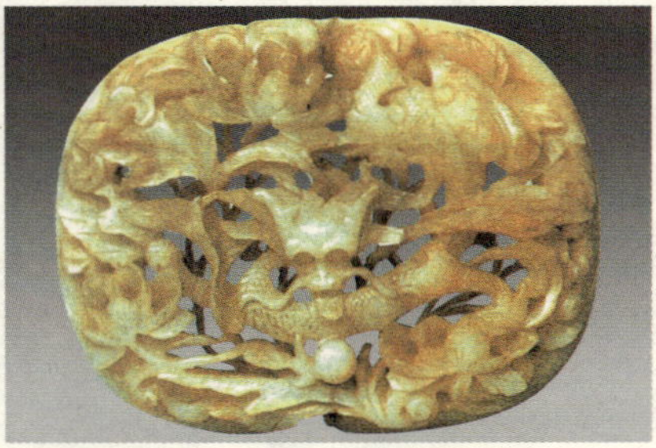

□ 玉石佳作　Exqusite Work of Jade Stone

□ 白玉镂雕竹节花鸟佩
White Jade Baldric Carved with Bamboo,Flower and Birds

为数不少，“凤凰”乃古代神话传说中的神鸟，在“凤凰”身上，寄托着广大劳动人民对光明幸福的无限向往。清代较为常见的玉雕工艺品，便将鹦鹉的嘴、锦鸡的头、鸳鸯的身、仙鹤的足、大鹏的翅膀和孔雀的羽毛组合而成，纹饰多为“龙凤呈祥”、“单凤朝阳”等，其最初的构思均来自“凤凰”。北京的老玉器行，明清至民国时期主要集中在崇文门外的花市、前门打磨厂和琉璃厂一带。玉器行业，虽然历经不少艰难曲折，但到现在仍有着强盛不衰的生命力。

ancient jade and have them carved with inscription “Made in Qianlong Period”. What he did impersonally made the jade carving reach the peak in history. In Qianlong Period, the magnum opus included *Walking in Guanshan*, *A Spring in Dantai*, *Yu the Great Taming the Mighty River*, *Nine Dragons in Huichang* and *Stone Jar in Yunlong*.

Besides, phoenix is also a common subject. Phoenix is a divine bird in Chiese ancient mythology. People anchor their hope for brightness and happiness in pheonix. The popular jade carvings in Qing Dynasty consisted of the parrot, head of golden pheasant, body of mandarin duck, feet of crane, wings of roc and feather of peacock. The ornamentations are mainly “dragon and phoenix appear bliss” and “one phoenix heading towards the sun”. Their ideas originally come from phoenix. From Ming and Qing Dynasties to the Republic of China, the old jade shops of Beijing were mainly in the workshops in flower market of Chongwenmenwai, polishing factory and Glazed Pottery production factory of Qianmen. Although the jade industry has gone through many difficulties, it still has a strong vitality today.

龙顺成家具

Longshuncheng Furniture

□ 龙顺成古式家具 Archized Furniture Made in Longshuncheng

位于京南永定门外的龙顺成中式家具厂，是一家有着百余年历史的专做硬木家具的老铺面，原先位于京城东珠市口三里河的金台书院附近，直到20世纪中后期才迁到永定门，就是现在的厂址。这家老字号从初创起，就亮出老店特有的经营方式，即秉承传统的前店（展卖结合）后作坊（即现在称之的生产车间）模式。以制作寻常百姓居家过日子离不开的桌、椅、柜、箱、橱等日用家具为主，同时也针对客户所需单独定

Standing outside Yongdingmen in the south of Beijing, Longshunsheng Antique Furniture Shop is an old factory specialized in making hardwood furniture. It is over one hundred years old and is originally situated near Jintai Institute, Sanlihe, East Zhushikou, Beijing. It was moved to Yongdingmen in the middle and late of last century and is still there today. From its beginning, this old and famous factory has a unique mode of operation, traditionally selling in the front shop and making furniture at the back workshop. It

制。

翻开中国硬木家具发展的浩瀚史册，就会发现我国明清之际的家具制作水平之高、工艺之繁、造型之美均已达到巅峰。其实上述成就并不是“空中楼阁”，无疑它都是在前人付出大量心血的基础上发展而来。据史料记载，远在宋代便在家具的设计上注意到了人体学的问题，造型以简单朴素为主。到了明清，随着政治、经济的稳定，人民生活水平的提高，客户对硬木家具的需要大大增加。而皇宫大内和不少珠宝店、大铺面对家具的要求，又使“龙顺成”这种老铺面要做出某些特殊的东西，由此为家具制作朝着高质量以适应不同阶层所需提供了良好、严格、有序的客观环境。“龙顺成”老店铺抓住这难得的机遇，有幸成为清朝宫廷造办处指定的皇家家具制作的惟一厂家。从此“龙顺成”得到了一个辉煌的大发展时期，朝着专为皇宫御用服务方面转向，在产品线条、表面花活、雕刻的分寸感、擦腊等系列工艺方面，都逐步适应皇宫近乎苛刻的要求，从而使其承制的宫廷家具也具有了庄重、华美、典雅的宫廷艺术特色。

“龙顺成”这一享誉京城的老字号，其悠久历史可追溯到清朝同治十三年(1874年)。当时一位山东的王姓木匠，凭着高超精湛的木工手艺携家带口独闯皇城，时隔不久便在北京前门外大街鲁班馆开了家并不起眼的桌椅铺。老理讲大凡店铺开张，甭管规模大小经营何种商品，总得起个吉利些的雅号才成体统，于是王掌柜通过朋友，请一位赴京赶考的年轻举子同乡帮忙。好友受托至

mainly provides products for everyday life, such as desks, chairs, cabinets, boxes, and closets. It also makes furniture according to the requirement of the client and processes with imported materials, etc.

When you look forward the development of Chinese hardwood furniture, you will find that as early as Ming and Qing Dynasties, level of furniture making, complexity of technique and charm of appearance were all the highest. But the achievements were gained by no pain, they were the result of hard work of our ancestors. According to the historical resources, as early as Song Dynasty, our ancestors had already paid attention to the somatic anthropology. The furniture at that time turned out to be very simple and plain. In Ming and Qing Dynasties, as the stabilization of the society and the improvement of life, people required a lot of furniture. Meanwhile, Longshuncheng had to make some special furniture to meet the requirements of the imperial, jewelry shops and large shops. This supplied a good, strict and ordered environment for furniture making to meet the needs of different social ranks, and became an industry with high quality. Taking this opportunity, Longshuncheng became the only factory nominated by the royal court to make the royal furniture. From then on, Longshuncheng developed very quickly and provided furniture particularly for the royal court. It gradually met the harsh requirements of the court, no matter products' lines, appearance, carving, wax or other aspects. Thus, its imperial furniture became grand, outstanding and elegant.

This old and famous Beijing factory,

会馆说明来意后，举子没有任何推辞，立即在八仙桌上摊开宣纸，握笔思忖片刻，题名“龙顺成”，寓在天子脚下买卖兴隆吉祥顺利之含义。果然借这一吉名，生意从此“福星高照”，善动脑筋又相当勤奋的王掌柜努力使产品不断翻新，进一步开拓和占领市场。这样经过二十几年的辛勤培育，终于使其制作的硬木家具在皇城根里成为一个知名度颇高的品牌。

到了光绪二十五年（1896年），王家根据市场风云变幻的情况，审时度势地将自家铺面与毗邻的两家木工铺子（吴、傅）合并，仍叫“龙顺成”，此番组合壮大了实力。店铺的硬木家具制作，朝着锦上添花的道路发展，在品种、质量上狠下功夫，最终形成其配套的工

□ 古式家具　Antique Furniture

Longshuncheng, has a history as far as the 12th year of Tongzhi (1874). At that time, there was a carpenter whose first name was Wang. He was from Liangshan, Shandong, a place where the Liangshan heroes came. Skilled in carpentry, Wang along with his whole family came to Beijing. After a short period of time, he opened a small shop selling desks and chairs in the Luban Shop, outer Qianmen street. People always said that no matter how big your shop is and what you sell, you should give it a good name, so shopkeeper Wang told one of his friends to ask a scholar for help. The scholar was his countryman who was taking imperial exams in Beijing. Wang's friend met the scholar and asked him to help Wang, and the scholar agreed. He put the rice paper on the desk at once. Thinking for a moment, he wrote down three characters "Long Shun Cheng", which meant the business would be prosperous in the city where the emperor lived. It lived to its name. From then on, the business became very thriving. Shopkeeper Wang was very clever and studious. He tried hard to improve products and explore and occupy new market. After twenty years of hard working, he finally made his hardwood furniture a famous brand in Beijing.

In the 25th year of the emperor Guangxu, according to the market, Wang family took the opportunity to merge with two nearby carpenter shops(the first name of their shopkeepers were respectively Wu and Fu). Longshuncheng was still the name and the shop thus became more competitive. The hardwood furniture making turned to be better and better. It paid much

□ 宫廷家具 Furniture in the Court

艺化流程。龙顺成的家具制作首先是把好头道关，即认真选材，以达到完美无瑕、过硬精良的高标准，再有便是注重每道工艺，环环相扣，绝不能出纰漏。此外他们在每种产品构思造型上开动脑筋，如既要恪守家具坚固耐用的立足之本，又要体现中国传统硬木家具的文化品味。经王掌柜和另两家股东不断推陈出新，龙顺成生产的家具在几十年间已达到二三十种。随着“龙顺成”字号的箱、桌、椅、柜、条案逐渐深入千家万户，其声名不仅轰动京城还远播华夏，生意一宗接一宗，十分红火，工匠也由最初的十几人增加至二百来号人。由于“龙顺成”的家具特别坚固结实、持久耐用，京城内外流传着“龙顺成”家具百年牢的说法。

围绕这个，还有一个在京城流传甚广的故事呢。话说清朝光绪年间的一个初秋，前门外一家颇有名气的酒家，这天来了一南一北两拨儿食客，席间众人推杯问盏猜拳喝令煞是热闹。待酒足饭饱即将退席之际，两桌客人因久别重逢格外高兴，烧酒喝得有些过量，一会儿双方便因言语不和发生口角，于是借着酒劲儿大打出手，顿时屋内桌椅板凳飞

attention to the variety and quality of the hardwood. At last, it formed a strict work flow. First, select the material very carefully to meet a high standard. Second, pay attention to the details and never make a mistake. Third, they thought about the appearance of the furniture. It not only should be indestructible and durable, but also should have a flavor of Chinese tradition. At least, when people who knew little about furniture saw their products, they would conclude that those are the authentic traditional Chinese furniture. As shopkeeper Wang and stockholders from the other two shops launched more and more new products, some furniture had twenty to thirty kinds in just several decades. As Longshuncheng sold boxes, desks, chairs, cabinet to more and more families, its name became more and more famous both in Beijing and other places in China. Business was booming. The number of the workers grew from under 20 to more than 200. Because the furniture in Longshuncheng is indestructible and durable, there is a saying in Beijing that the furniture in Long Shuncheng can be used for a hundred years.

There is also a well-known story in Beijing about it. One day in the autumn in the years of Emperor Guangxu in Qing Dynasty, people from the south and north both came to a famous restaurant. During the feast, the atmosphere was very soft. But just before finishing eating, the guests from two tables became very excited as they hadn’t seen each other for a long time. They had drunk a lot. After a while, they quarreled and fought with each other. There flied

□清式雕花紫檀木床 Rosewood Bed Made in Qing Dynasty

来飞去。恶战之后自然是狼藉一片，待掌柜和店小二出来收拾店堂残局的时候，发现其中不少桌椅都摔散了架，而惟独刻着“龙顺成”字号的家具除了漆皮儿磕掉几块外，其主体结构则丝毫无损。不久这件不大不小的事就传遍北京城，继而使“龙顺成”家具愈加远近闻名，每天从早到晚买主儿不断。这些人当中既有达官显贵、买卖 人家，也不乏知书达理的文人墨客和平民百姓。总之，在过去的老北京，有身份的人家均以“龙顺成”硬木家具点缀府邸居室客厅，拥有一件或数件龙顺成老字号的花梨、紫檀、红木、鸡翅木品种家具成为一件很光彩的事。

“龙顺成”在它百年的风雨历程中，继承和发展着中华民族传统文化，在不断创新中开拓前进，在家具中包容着未来与历史。面对新世纪，这家老字号正面临着新的发展与挑战，“龙顺成”接待了大批国内外宾客，使百年老字号和它的产品越老越有味、越老越有嚼头。

desks and chairs in the restaurant. People were crying. Everything was in a mess. After the fight, the boss and waiters came out to clear the mess up. They found that many desks and chairs were broken, except the furniture marked with Longshuncheng. Their main structures were still very solid. Soon this spread across Beijing and made Longshuncheng even more famous. Every day, buyers came from morning to evening continuously. These buyers included persons of rank, businessmen, literary men and the common people. In the past in Beijing, families of high rank liked to put some Longshuncheng furniture in their houses. It was very grace for them to have some furniture made of rosewood. For more than 100 years, it is because of its good faith that new and old clients in Beijing trusted it very much. It met a lot of difficulties during the development, but it is still standing. People often praise it as “desks and chairs of Longshuncheng are indestructible” deserves the reputation.

During its 100 years’ development, Longshuncheng inherited and developed traditional Chinese culture. It continues to innovate and progress. It sees the future and history of furniture. It gathers experiences. In the new century, this old and famous brand is facing challenge and continuing to develop. Longshuncheng receives a lot of guests from home and abroad, thus, the older this brand and its products, the more special flavor it will have.

奇石闲趣

Rare Stone

在如今的北京城，上至雪染两鬓的古稀老翁，下到稚气未脱的青少年，或者是一掷千金的款爷，或者是出没于写字楼的高级白领等各阶层的人士，都有玩石的痴迷者。尽管人们玩石、收石、藏石目的各不相同，但是却都能感受到这个行当带给玩石人的眼亮和心跳。

要聊起这个行当里的事，那段子可就长了。他们当中附庸风雅的伪君子有

□故宫绛雪轩前木变石 Woodfossil Stone in front of the Jiangxuexuan in the Forbidden City

Nowadays, there are many people crazy about stones through out Beijing, including old men in grey hair, innocent teenagers, rich men and office workers with high salary, etc. Though people have different goals to play and collect stones, they can got excitement in this field.

There are a lot of stories to tell in this field. There are people pretending to be elegance. There are also lots of innocent people who have just joined it. And there is an indispensable force in which people collect stones only for selling. The real experts who know stones a lot are very rare. In fact, it is a traditional and long history for people in Beijing to collect stones. It started from Tang and Song Dynasties and thrived in Ming and Qing Dynasties. Emperor Kangxi and Qianlong were just experts in this field. They boasted to collect all the peculiar stones in China. Their descendants inherited their hobby. For example, Fu Xuezhai, one of the emperor's relatives in late Qing Dynasty, was famous for collecting gold, peculiar stones, books and paintings in his early life. He was well-known through out Beijing because he always paid a lot to collect rare stones. There were also celebrities in modern times who like the peculiar stones, such as Zhou Enlai, Shen Junru, Chen Shutong, Mei Lanfang, Xu Beihong, Lao She and Ai Qing, etc.

之，初学乍炼的雏儿亦为数不少，为经济利益所驱使的大倒、二倒更是一支不容忽视的力量。而真正意义上的懂石，鉴赏、收藏都在行的门里人则实在是凤毛麟角。其实藏石风气在北京城有着传统与悠久的历史。从老根上说起，它起始于唐宋，兴盛于明清。远的不说，康熙、乾隆祖孙二人就是天下名石收藏的大家，曾有搜尽中华奇石于一身的壮志雄心。他们的这一雅兴荫及子孙后代。譬如世人皆知的清末皇亲国戚，早年以金、石、书、画四绝著称的溥雪斋老先生，就以重金收藏、观赏怪石和稀有之石而名噪皇城。近现代的名人钟情于石的还有周恩来、沈钧儒、陈叔通、梅兰芳、徐悲鸿、老舍、艾青等。

玩石、赏石说白了玩的就是一个眼力。如果不具备慧眼识石的本领，玩到最后完全有可能人财两空，落下一个无穷的笑柄。在这里，可以提到一位奇石收藏家金启旺。此君不但勤于读各类书籍，并且以搜集天下不同地方的名石为

It demands excellent insight to collect and appreciate stones. If you don't have this quality, you won't devote yourself in this field like the others. Otherwise, you will not only lose the money, but also become a joke of your relatives and friends every day. A famous collector of peculiar stone, Jin Qiwang,was introduced in the following. Mr.Jin likes reading books of all sorts. Meanwhile, he devoted his whole life to collecting famous stones of different places. As an expert, he has lived with stones for more than forty years. His study has an elegant name, Qi Shi Zhai, so we can see how crazy he is. He has never be cheated in this field because of his great insight and discretion.

Jin Qiwang's study is a small yard consisting of three bungalows. It is situated in a narrow bystreet in Xuanwu District, Beijing. The whole study is covered with vines. The small yard is covered with green Boston Ivy. The host used one and a half rooms as bedroom and kitchen. In the other rooms, he exhibits eight boxes and

□颐和园乐寿堂院中青芝岫
Qingzhiyou in the Summer Palace

毕生之追求。启旺先生身为门里人又乃行家里手，已与名石相依相伴长达40余年，从其书房的雅号“奇石斋”，可知其对石头的钟情与痴迷。可以毫不夸张地讲，在玩石头上还真没走过眼，没让别人蒙骗过，这恐怕得益于其精到的眼力和一贯的小心谨慎。

金启旺拥有的奇石斋，是一座由三间平房组成的小院，它坐落在北京宣武区一条不起眼的狭小胡同里，整座房子均被密密麻麻的青藤所覆盖。不大的院落置身于浓郁的绿色爬山虎之中，除一间半作为主人的卧室兼厨房以外，其余的房间内分别有序地摆放着8个大小对称的多宝格和茶几等硬木家具。这样的室内布局给客人以既古朴又典雅的感觉。这里有被金启旺称之为“镇宅之宝”的一尊“广西菊花石”。玩石的人都知道，好石、奇石应是来自产地的菊花原石为最佳，它绝不能有丝毫的人工修饰的痕迹，特别是在灯光下观石效果最好，其端庄、平稳、造型等特征，一切均来自大自然这支妙笔。金家的菊花原石约有80厘米高，40厘米宽，分为两色，从中间往上是几朵石状的菊花，错落有致地镶嵌在土红色的石岩上。石菊花表现有聚有散、疏密相间，颇可人意，其中有两朵菊花的花瓣恰好分布在奇石的转折点上，居然呈现立体状，真让人感到大千世界造物主的神奇。石菊花的开放就像我们生活中常见的波斯菊那样，花蕊为凹凸不平的白色结晶体，细长的管状花瓣从中心呈放射状向四周徐徐散开，绽放得生动而亲切，用手一摸，可感到菊花石温润、细腻，宛如一性格温

□ 恭王府花园内名石独乐峰(李明德摄)
Dule Peak in the Mansion of Princess Gong

some famous hardwood furniture like tea table. The eight boxes are of symmetrical size and contain his treasure. This arrangement is of primitive simplicity and elegance. There is a stone named chrysanthemum stone in Guangxi. Jin Qiwang calls it the most precious thing in his study. In this field, people all know that the most rare stones are the original chrysanthemum stone from the producing areas. It should not contain any signs of manual work. It is best to watch stones under light. Nature made the stones elegant, smooth and good appearance. Jin’ s original chrysanthemum stone is about eighty centimeters high, and fourty centimeters wide. It has two colours. There are a few chrysanthemum from

柔、善良的女子，在诉说岁月的沧桑……

清人张尚瑗在《石里杂识》一书中提到："吉水永丰（今江西吉水县）有石，青质而黄章，章为菊花，金花粲然如画。"这是古代较早的对菊花石的记录文字。菊花石质硬且坚，寒冬微温。它盛夏凉彻骨，哈气成雾，转而会聚为珠粒，日丽则泽艳，时阴而色暗。在造型壮美而又妙不可言的菊花石上，一朵朵石菊花昂首怒放，仿佛为"奇石斋"留下阵阵扑鼻的"花香"。

中国有四大名石遐迩闻名。它们依次为杭州太湖石、安徽灵璧石、广东英石、南京雨花石。名石虽不会讲话，但它同样犹如性格鲜活丰满的人物，具有灵动神韵，独具风姿，一石一型，从不雷同，给人以清新悦目、洗炼纯朴之感。奇石之奇，怪石之怪，使醉心于石的藏家产生无限宽广的遐思，总想揭开它那严实而神密的面纱，破解大自然带来的千古之谜。石头也像人一样，它有顽强的生命，有独立的性格，有不向邪恶低头的刚强品质，有崇尚一切真善美的志向。

其实细细一琢磨，在石头身上所体现的一切，不正是我们做人所应该永远追求的吗?一块人性化的好石头蕴含其中的既有柔和婀娜的美，也同样包含着内在与刚劲的美，正因为如此，它让每一位藏石人对其总是一往情深。进而再剖析石头与藏石人之间的关系，不管您承认也好，不信也罢，其实这是有一种缘分涵盖在里面的。比如说有的价值连城的天下奇石，不论世上多少人为之苦苦追求，为此劳作奔波，寻觅许多年，甚至不惜下很高的经济筹码，可最终还是

the middle to the top, spreading in the reddle rock with good order. The stone chrysanthemums are either intimate or sparse. The petals of two chrysanthemums are right on the turning point of the stone. Thus, they appear to be solid! The nature can really do whatever he wants. The bloom of chrysanthemum is just like the way Calliopsis does. The pistil is an uneven and white crystal. The slight petals spread around. It's a vivid scene. When you touch the chrysanthemum stone, you will feel it gentle, smooth and exquisite, just as a mild and virtuous girl who is telling you her story through time.

Zhang Shang'ai in Qing Dynasty wrote in *Talking about Stones*: "In Jishui town Jiangxi, there was a stone which was black and yellow. The yellow part was chrysanthemum. It is like a painting." This is the early record about chrysanthemum stones. Chrysanthemum stone is solid and stiff. It is warm in winter and very cold in summer. When it's sunny, its colour will be bright and when it's cloudy, its colour will be bleak. Once, I saw for myself that on the marvellous chrysanthemum stone, the chrysanthemum was in full bloom. I can even smell a rich bouquet in the study Qi Shi Zhai.

In China, there are four kinds of famous stones: Lake Taihu stone, Lingbi stone in Anhui, Ying stone in Guangdong, Yuhua stone in Nanjing. The stones can not talk, but they have a unique flavor, just like people. Each stone has a model. They are all different. It is pleasing to both the eye and the mind. Stone collectors think a lot about the stones. They always want to unveil it and discover the secrets of nature. The stones,

□ 中山公园青莲朵
Qinglian Flower Stone in Zhongshan Park

与其失之交臂。而一些深藏在大自然中的有情之石，不论其经历多少磨难和坎坷，总是能够来到真正爱它、欣赏它内在美及高雅品味的藏石人手中。您能说这不是因果关系在奇石与藏石人之间有缘的感情体现吗？

like people, have strong life and independent characters. They will never kneel down to evil and they also respect honest, goodness and beauty.

In fact, if you think it carefully, you will find that the quality of stones just like the Character that we should seek. A good humanized stone is not only grace in appearance, but also beautiful inside. Therefore, every collector has a love story with stones. Believing it or not, there is a predestined relationship between collectors and stones. For example, some people can never find the invaluable stones, no matter how hard and how long he tried or how much he paid. However, some collectors, who love stones and appreciate their beauty from heart, can get the peculiar stones covered deep in nature. It surely shows that the relationship between stones and collectors is doomed.

门礅

Stone Pier

“小小子儿，坐门礅，哭着喊着要媳妇。”这首古老的民谣不时勾起人们对老北京四合院门礅的那一缕缕眷恋情愫。然而，伴随着旧城区大规模的市容改造，在推土机的隆隆轰鸣声中，最能代表老北京古建筑风貌的四合院越来越少，坐落在拱型门楼两旁的许多门礅自然也难于幸免。

门礅的种类可谓多种多样，而老北京四合院的门礅，据专家考证大多为

□ 海波寺胡同 24 号的门墩

Stone Pier in NO. 24, Haibosi Hutong

“Little boy sits on the pier, crying for a wife here, what’s for? Chatting in the day and companying at night, combing hair in the early morning.” This balladry descirbes the kids who live in the quadrangle playing at the front door. It shows clearly that the pier has been connected closely to the chlidhood of many people. Such an old balladry often reminds people of the stone piers in front of the old Beijing courtyards. Stone piers are usuallly laid by the sills of the wooden doors of the quadrangles. But whereas with the municipal reconstruction, so many courtyards has been demolished in the roaring of bulldozers, people could see less and less stone piers on both side of arch gate of the courtyards.

Stone piers have all kinds of appearances. According to the introduction of experts, most of Beijing courtyard stone piers are made in Ming and Qing Dynasties, and its formal name is “gate drum stone”. Chinese endowed stone with verve and nimbus, so it had a long history and brilliant culture carved on the stone, wishing for a better life. There are two types of stone piers, and one looks like a drum aside and the other is square one. The drum-shaped piers almost have a longer history while the square ones were carved within one hundred years. The design of piers doesn’t vary a lot which all includes a

明、清两代时制作，它的学名为“门鼓石”。古代先人赋予石头以神韵和灵气，从而将一段段悠久的历史和灿烂的文化镌刻在这石礅上以表示对美好生活的祈盼。

在中国的古代社会，门礅是上至官商富贾，下至黎民百姓的老宅院门楼两旁必不可少的门第装饰。就其雕刻的图案来说，大多为须弥莲花基座，雕刻内容以龙、凤、麒麟、狮、虎、仙鹤、花草等为主。门礅的雕工无疑都是相当考究。此外，鸟兽、花草的造型，纹式的精美等方面，还体现了院中主人地位。譬如位于北京西城区柳荫街的恭王府花园，亭、台、宅、院为主的

□ 雕有石狮子的抱鼓石　Drum Pier with Lion Pattern on

little lion on the top with rich carving pictures on the front and the side face. There is a story of the crouchinglion of the pier. It is said that the dragon has nine sons and each is good at one skill. While, this son is acute and alert that enables him to be a good guard. It is tellable that so many lions were carved differently but each is elegant and exquisite. As for the carving pictures on the pier, they all show originality in a unique style.

In ancient Chinese society, stone pier was a necessity for gate decoration no matter it was high social family or ordinary people’s house. The relief carved on it mostly had a Lotus base, and the main content would be dragon, phoenix, Kylin, lion, tiger, crane, flowers and grass, etc. The craftsmanship of those carving is quite subtle. The type of the carved figure also implies the social status of the owner of the house. Take the Mansion of Princess Gong for example. Located in Willow Shade Street of Xicheng District, all the old style buildings within the garden are put among the water and rockeys. The south faced bright red gate and the delicately carved stone pier has shown the high status of this place. The stone pier has given the whole garden a wonderful feeling. While looking around the whole city, the stone piers of all the courtyards around the city are not so fortunate as that of the Mansion of Princess Gong. Most of them are in bad shape, only a few are exceptions, still capable of telling people of their wonderful history. The drum-shaped stone block in Xiaoxiangfeng Alley of Changqiao, Xicheng district, the box-shaped stone pier of No. 1 Shengfang alley of Jianguo gate, and the Lion-shaped stone block of No. 67 of

古建筑整体掩映在绿荫、假山、碧水、叠砌的太湖石中间。坐北朝南、雕梁画柱的朱红色大门和大门口那对雕刻着华丽纹式图案的一双门墩，无不显示着恭王府花园那独有的雍荣华贵，门墩作为不可或缺的点缀，为这古色古香的王爷府恰到好处地添了一笔。不过纵览京城东、西、南、北许多四合院的门墩，它们就没有恭王府花园的门墩那么幸运了。其中有很多早已斑驳破败，只有为数很少的门墩保持还算完整，偶有极个别的精品仿佛在向世人诉说往日里的无限风光。西城区厂桥小翔凤胡同的“抱鼓型门墩”，建国门盛芳胡同1号的“箱子型雕式门墩”，东四八条67号“狮子型门墩”的造型和雕刻内容各有特色，就其精雕细琢的石刻水平完全可用至善至美来形容，仔细观赏宛若一幅幅底蕴深厚的古画杰作展现在大家面前。

门墩之所以能够世代延续，除了它的装饰作用外，更为重要的是透过它体验无尽的历史沧桑。通过一幅幅极富想像力的图案，让人体会到先人对福寿双全、封侯挂印、岁岁平安的殷切企盼。

□ 图案精美的方门墩 Exquisite Square Stone Pier

Dongsibatiao, all had special character and the contents are quite different. The only thing in common, is their perfect carving craftsmanship. The reliefs are just like some highly valued ancient painting works.

The reason that stone piers could last for so many years, is not only for decoration, but also its reflection of the long history. Through the imaginative figures of the reliefs, we could tell that the ancient people are wishing for good fortune, and a sound and safe life.

烟壶赵

Snuff Bottle Zhao

“内画鼻烟壶”作为一种高雅的艺术品，按其产地可分为京派、冀派、鲁派等若干个派别。具体到鼻烟壶的造型、原料等更是千变万化，其中尤以瓷壶和料器类为多，荸荠扁的造型较为普遍。极为稀有的鼻烟壶则是玛瑙壶和玉壶两个特殊门类。在明清以来的数百年间，古今各路的收藏家、鉴赏家、玩家，公认为万里挑一的上等烟壶的选材非玛瑙、翡翠、玉石类不可，且“内画”这一关键手艺须出自这个行当里顶尖的名家高手。

赵步云是一位收藏圈里的名人。在北京古玩城、红桥、潘家园等几处旧货市场，只要一提到鼻烟壶收藏大家“烟壶赵”，行内没有几个人不知道的。赵君祖上几代人，均是在紫禁城里专为皇上、皇后、妃子把脉看病的宫廷御医。在过去的皇权社会里，能够供奉朝廷当上皇差，不仅其家族风光无限，而且实惠多多，每每药到病除之后，自会有几件古玩珍品、名人字画之类的赏赐。“烟壶赵”就是在这种特殊的家庭氛围下成长起来的。其实要论起他的嗜好那是相当广泛的，对古玩、字画、瓷器、摆件等都挺在行。但是凭心讲，真正让“烟壶赵”情有独衷的却是“内画鼻烟壶”的珍品收藏。行内人几乎都门儿清，鉴定

Snuff bottle with interior painting dated much later is an exquisite artwork, and could be classified into several styles according to its source, such as Jing School, Ji School, Lu School. The painting is finished from inside-out with iron oxydal mixed with water. To make an inside painting in a bottle, a painter must work on the rubbed inside surface through the mouth of the bottle. This created a milky white surface suitable, which were applied subsequently. Snuff bottles of this genre include landscapes, flower pieces and other works. These were created in a day or less of painstakingly intricate brushwork and are truly works of art. As to the shape and materials, most are made of ceramics and special material, and the shapes are mostly flat. Agate and jade material snuff bottle are quite special. In several hundred yeas, all the collectors, and connoisseurs agreed the best snuff bottle must be made of agate, emerald or jade, and should have the best painter in this field to do the inside painting.

Zhao Buyun is a famous collector, whose name is well-known in several big relics markets in Beijing. Zhao’ s ancestors were used to be doctors for imperial families. In the old society, if someone were serving the imperial family, not only could he have a high social status, but also he could get some gifts, such as old Chinese

一件鼻烟壶的市场价值，首先得看它出自哪家的窑口和画篇，上等佳品非古月轩马家老铺面莫属。聊起早年马绍轩的拿手绝品“鼻烟壶”，赵先生手上还真有一件，那就是其太祖做宫廷御医时，一年春天为隆裕皇后（注：清末光绪皇帝的皇后）治好病后隆裕特别恩赐的一件皇室收藏的珍品玉壶，此壶是以纯正的新疆和田玉的玉皮子为底料，经过多道工序打磨加工制作出来的。“鼻烟壶”艺术品中尤以玉壶质地最佳，其中一块玉石又以处在表层的玉皮子的料质才可堪称为上佳，它具有晶莹剔透、柔美滑润、纹路清晰等优点。而且该烟壶中的画篇内容更是相当精彩，为“柳宗元独钓寒江雪”，它将古韵悠悠与诗情画意涵盖在作品中，一边是风度翩翩的古代大诗人柳宗元，一边是其流传千古的著名诗

paintings and other precious items, especially after curing the imperial families' illness. Snuff bottle Zhao was brought up in such an environment and he has known much about curio, calligraphy and painting, ceramics, etc, but he was especially interested in collecting inside painted snuff bottle. It's known to connoisseur that the market price of a snuff bottle should be determined by its source and the content of the painting, and the best works must come from the Ancient Moon Shop managed by Ma Family. Zhao Buyun has one of the genuine works of old Ma Shaoxuan. It was a gift that the Queen of Longyu, Emperor Guangxu's wife, gave his great grandfather after he cured her illness. This jade snuff bottle was grinded and polished with many processes, from a piece of the best Hetian Jade of Xinjiang Province. Jade snuff bottle texture is the best, and

□ 鼻烟壶　Snuff Bottle

句，二者相得益彰。所以无论从内画风格的细腻、人物之传神、选料之在行等诸多方面，都可堪称马绍轩鼻烟壶中的精品。

鼻烟壶行当里有许多奇闻趣事。烟壶赵的屋子中北墙的多宝格里有一个鼻烟壶，造型精巧别致的烟壶上，雄鹰立在地上昂首抬头，望着一轮明亮的皓月，形象逼真栩栩如生。另外一件和刚才那件图案十分近似的烟壶，不细看根本没什么不同，但内行知道，这是一件可以以假乱真的十足的假货。为什么这么讲呢?假壶是松枝上落着苍鹰，真壶则恰恰相反，真是不入哪行儿，不知道哪行的门道精深呀!

烟壶赵室内多宝格上有各种颜色、各种款式，不同年代的鼻烟壶。其中有著名的红楼梦中的“金陵十二钗”、“高亮赶水”、“王婆子骂鸡”等内画鼻烟壶的绝品，真是令人终生难忘。古玩行当乐子多多，只有您置身其中，才能体会到其中的妙不可言。

the upper layer of the jade is even better. It has the character of being soft and clean. Inside Zhao Buyun's snuff bottle, the painting Liu Zongyuan fishing on snowy river which describes the famous poet Liu Zongyuan in Tang Dynasty and his famous poetry and mixes the ancient charm with poetry, is particularly expressing. From the painting to the material, it could be considered one of the best artwork of Ma Shaoxuan.

Snuff bottle collection field has many interesting stories. On the shelf of north wall of snuff bottle Zhao' s house, there is a special shape snuff bottle. It was painted with an eagle standing on the ground, looking at the bright full moon. There is another snuff bottle with almost the same painting, and outsiders would never tell the difference. It is a fake one, because the eagle was standing on a pine branch.On his shelf, there are many snuff bottlees with all kinds of color, shape and history. Some of them have the wonderful paintings on them, you will never forget them when the pictures get into your eyesight. Curio field has much happiness, and you can only feel it when you really get into it.

泥人张

Clay Figurine Zhang

在我国民间艺术的百花园中，有被平民百姓赞誉为奇葩的"彩塑艺术"。而一提"彩塑艺术"，人们马上会联想到名扬海内外的已故民间艺术大师"泥人张"。泥人张吸取前辈艺人的精华，并巧妙融入自己的聪明才智，用双手塑造出一个个艺术精品，在技艺方面达到一种大艺术境界。

□ 泥人张作品 The Work of Clay Figurine Zhang

In Chinese folk arts, there was a peculiar one called colored sculpture art. As long as it is mentioned, people would immediately think about the folk art master Clay Figurine Zhang, who has already passed away. Clay Figurine Zhang took the experience of old artists, and used his own talent, to create one after another great artworks.

Clay Figurine Zhang, with the real name Zhang Changlin (1826 - 1906), lived in Tianjin City, Qing Dynasty. Old Tianjin was a business port, and a lot of poor folk artists with their special skills were making a living there. Within all of them, Clay Figurine Zhang was the most successful. He would like to take a place in pier or downtown to do his business. The good thing was he could easily get in touch with ordinary people, and finish the statue in leisure chatting. His work has the appearance and spirit of the person right in front of him. With time passing by, his real name was forgotten, and the name of Clay Figurine Zhang was getting more and more famous.

Clay Figurine Zhang' s colored sculpture art came from his long term practicing. Besides, he would particularly absorb nutrients from the famous literary works. All the characters within old literary works, such as the *Story of Three Kingdoms*, *the Story by the Water*, *The Dreams in*

"泥人张"大名张长林(1826~1906年),字明山,生活在清朝中叶的天津卫。作为当时通商口岸的老天津卫,聚集着许多穷困潦倒,但却身怀绝技的民间艺人。而在这许许多多的艺人当中,又以精于捏塑艺术的张长林最为成功。他一般喜欢在码头或闹市随便摆上个地摊儿。这样做的好处是,可以非常方便直接地与平民百姓接触,闲谈中变戏法似的就将眼前的人物捏好,而且人在眼前可以对照,作品形神兼备,深受当时民众的喜爱。日久天长,张长林的名字被人们忘了,而"泥人张"却声名远播。

"泥人张"的泥塑艺术,来自他长期的实践。此外,张长林还特别注意从文学名著中吸取艺术营养,用于丰富自身的人物创作。其中我国古典文学名著《三国演义》、《水浒传》、《红楼梦》、《西厢记》、《花木兰从军》、《西游记》等一系列的故事人物,经他之手转瞬间便捏合成活灵活现的故事人物,其中既有亭亭玉立的古代少女、端庄贤慧的少妇,又有渔人、樵夫、掌柜、铁匠、举子、秀才、鬼神、狐仙、钟馗、狐狸精、哪吒等,三教九流五行八作,无所不包。

"泥人张"的彩塑不仅在天津被称为"天下第一绝活",还影响到北京的清朝皇室。据史书记载,在道光、咸丰、同治年间都曾请"泥人张"本人到北京供过皇差,现在我们还能从颐和园、故宫等皇室园林中看到"泥人张"的一组组令人赞叹不已的泥人杰作。尤为值得一提的是,早在1915年的巴拿马万国博览会上,"泥人张"的众多艺术作品,就代表中国登上国际艺术的殿堂,并一举荣

the Red Chamber, *Hua Mulan in March*, and *Journey to the West*, would soon came out alive from his hands. He had made slim ancient girl, elegant young wife, fisherman, shop owner, blacksmith, literator, ghost and spirit, gods, any character you would think of.

His colored sculpture not only got famous in Tianjin, but also spred into the Forbidden City. According to history records, Clay Figurine Zhang was called into Beijing to do certain works for the imperial family, which allows us to see his works in the Summer Palace and Forbidden City. In 1915, many of his works got exhibited in the Panama International Exhibition, and claimed

□ 挖耳僧 Ear-picking Monk

获20多枚奖牌，为中国赢得了极高的荣誉。在“泥人张”后，张玉亭对“泥人张”的彩塑艺术的继承和发扬起了重要作用。张玉亭(1863～1954年)，字兆荣，是“泥人张”第二代传人。在长达70余载的创作生涯中，张玉亭的作品多达两万多件。他很好地继承父辈彩塑艺术的精髓，涉及的领域则更加广泛，在彩塑捏制技艺方面也更精湛。在艺术方面其将写实与夸张巧妙地结合在一起，泥人形象美不胜收。张玉亭有一件堪称泥塑珍品的“挖耳僧”，作品栩栩如生、活灵活现，本来挖耳这个动作是很不雅的，但观赏者却可从“挖耳僧”的情感神态中，看到真实生活一幕的再现。“泥人张”艺术历经100多年的坎坷，子承父业，代代相传的“泥人张”后代们，正在向人们奉献着越来越多的好作品。

over 20 medals. After Clay Figurine Zhang, another man who had an important role in inheriting and developing this art, was Zhang Yuting (1863-1954). He is the second generation of Clay Figurine Zhang. In his life of over 70 years, he had made out more than 20000 pieces of works. He inherited his predecessor’s best part, and experienced more social life, which allowed him to get over the previous Clay Figurine Zhang. He could manipulate his work with reality and exaggeration, and from the outline of the monk of his masterpiece, *the Ear-picking Monk*, we could see a real life scene. Philosophers say : “Art comes from life, and is higher than life.” Clay Figurine Zhang’s colored sculpture making was exactly so. Clay Figurine Zhang has lasted for over 100 years, the descendants of Clay Figurine Zhang would provide more and more fine works to the ordinary people.

胡琴铺子

Huqin Instrument Shop

在北京南城琉璃厂路东有个十分不起眼儿的四合院，黑色底漆、金黄字体的牌匾悬挂在小小门楼儿的上方。这就是名噪京城、为菊坛及海内外票友们熟知的京胡制作世家——史善朋竹琴社。

史善朋老先生祖藉京东通州西集，生于清末宣统元年（1909年）。史善朋小时因家境所迫，年方9岁便经亲戚介绍来到北京琉璃厂"马良正老胡琴铺子"当学徒，这一学就是整整10年。在老北京，大凡从旧社会走过来的人都知道，手艺圈儿里广为流传着这么一种说法，即"教会徒弟、饿死师傅"，由此可见那个年代的人要想掌握一门谋生的手艺是多么艰难。而史老先生自幼聪颖过人、心灵手巧，他处处留心，明着师傅不全教，暗地里自己长心眼偷着学艺。时间一久，凭着多年如一日学艺人的手勤、腿勤、嘴儿甜等品行，史善朋逐渐博得师傅、师兄的好感，在他们高兴之余口若悬河之时也偶尔传播了他一点京胡制作的门道儿。有道是"快马不用鞭催，响鼓不用重锤"，这一来二去，随着学徒生活时光的延伸，遇事喜欢多动脑筋、善于琢磨的史善朋终于将京胡制作的关键选料工艺和制作绝活熟记于心。

到了20世纪20年代初，历经世间沧桑磨砺的史善朋老先生，总算盼星星

There is a very common courtyard with a black-background and golden-charactered tablet hanged over the gate at the east of Liulichang Road, southern part of Beijing, and here was the famous Shi Shanpeng Jinghu Instrument Shop.

Shi Shanpeng, born in 1909, came from Xiji Tongzhou District, in the east part of Beijing. Due to the poor condition of the family, he was introduced by a relative to be the apprentice of Ma Liangzheng Huqin Instrument Shop of Liulichang, when he was just 9 years old. He stayed there for 10 years. People who experienced the old society all know, there used to be a saying among craftsman, "teach the apprentice all, the master die in starvation". Learning all the skill of one profession is very difficult. Shi Shanpeng was quite smart, and his master did not teach him everything, but he tried every chance to learn. After some time, he got along well with all the apprentices and his master. They might tell him a bit of the methods of making Jinghu now and then. He finally managed all the technique and special skills of making Jinghu.

Early in 1920s, Shi Shanpeng finally finished his apprentice period after experienced all the hardship. He formally set up his Shi Shanpeng Jinghu Instrument Shop at No. 81 of Litieguai street of Liulichang, which lasted for over 80

盼月亮似地熬到学徒期满。一向年轻气盛、踌躇满志的他，很快便在琉璃厂李铁拐斜街81号正式顶门立户，从事起靠手艺活维持生计的营生，创立了至今约80多年历史的老胡琴铺子史善朋竹琴社。史老身居皇城脚下文人雅士常来光顾的宣武区琉璃厂，这里浓郁厚重的文化氛围对他影响很大，同时亦培养和造就了史老尊礼重义的性格。胡琴铺子开张前后，已在这块地面上儿扎下根的史老广交新朋更不忘旧友，因此人缘儿特好，大家纷纷前来史家铺面捧场儿。其中“史善朋竹琴社”的第一代牌匾，就出自清朝末年中国最后一位翰林张伯英老先生之手，可见史老为人交友涉及面之广。

据史老的长子史致贤先生介绍：史老生前有一最大嗜好，即从青年时代起就喜欢骑自行车，如那个年代时髦的“白金人”、“三枪”、“菲利浦”等名牌，老先生均骑过而且经常绕京城兜风。颇为有趣的是“史善朋竹琴社”铺面儿的家底就是史老在故交亲朋的规劝下，把两辆自行车推到当铺，卖了32块现大洋后开创的京胡小作坊，此后才有了若干年后“史家京胡”风光八面名噪华夏的好日子。

史老先生制作的京胡，在梨园、戏迷、票友中久负盛名。这当中除了京胡制作的特殊技巧外，还在于史老能在原有基础上继承和发扬光大京胡的某些制作特色。最具典型和有代表意义的是他能根据京剧不同的流派，制造出与其特点融合为一体、音色又十分和谐的京胡。这在很大程度上为京戏曲调的优美

years till now. The place of Liulichang was often visited by well educated people, and old Shi was deeply influenced. After his shop's opening up, he kept a good relationship with people of this place, which greatly helped his business. The first tablet of his shop was written by the last imperial literator, Zhang Boying.

According to the introduction of Shi Zhixian, his eldest son, Shi Shanpeng was very interested in riding bicycle. He used to ride with the famous brand bicycles of that time, and go around the city. His friends and relatives persuaded him to send his two bicycle to a pawnshop, and set up his little shop with the 32 big coins gained. This was the origin of his little shop which later on got famous in Beijing.

The Jinghu he made was quite famous among Beijing Opera field. The reason is that he not only managed the special skills of making Jinghu, but also he developed some of the character' s of

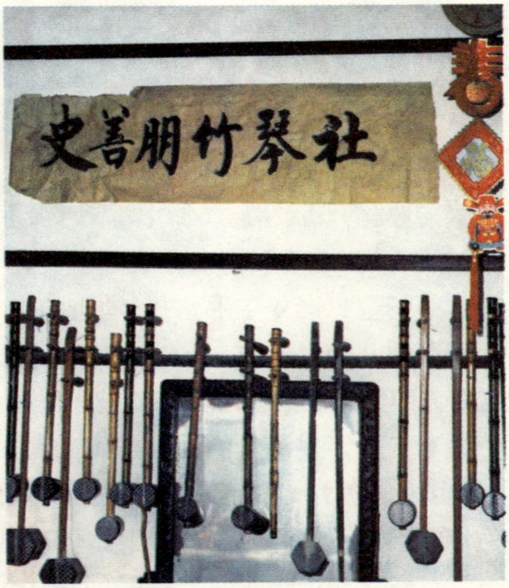

□ 史善朋竹琴社制作的胡琴
Huqin in the Shop of Shi Shanpeng

动听作出了极其宝贵的贡献，使之真正融入正宗高雅的京剧艺术中。史老先生毕生钻研京胡制作这门手艺，不少名角儿和琴师与他交往多多。如著名京剧表演艺术大师梅兰芳先生的三位琴师徐兰沅、王少卿、姜凤山都是他熟悉的朋友，他们不时抽空在一起切磋京胡演奏及制作方面的问题，这也使得史老制作的京胡曾为梅先生的京剧“梅派表演艺术”增添重彩。与梅大师同时代的已故著名京剧四大须生之一杨宝森先生，解放前足迹就遍及国内各大城市，为他担任京胡伴奏的琴师便是其长兄杨宝忠先生，杨宝忠先生一生操史善朋老先生制作的几把京胡走天下。当年杨宝森先生的多出精典剧目风靡京沪，与杨宝忠先生精湛高超、美妙绝伦的京胡演奏以及京胡醇厚的音色不无关系。过去，北京各大戏园子里戏单子上除印上名角名段打头牌的醒目内容外，紧随其后还要依次印上诸如“杨宝忠操琴、鼓师杭子和击鼓”等相应字眼。老戏迷一见上边这几个腕儿级人物登台献艺，便乐此不疲地连夜排队买票。有时一出戏尚未拉开帷幕，正宗主角儿杨宝森杨老板(旧时对唱戏名家的尊称)还没有登场，深谙梨园门道的戏迷们，总要以雨点儿般的掌声先为琴师杨宝忠老先生那悠扬、动听的京胡演奏叫几个好儿，来个碰头彩儿。而这令人美不胜收的艺术效果就是通过史善朋老先生亲手制作的俗称“黑老虎”(琴担为黑色)，“黄老虎”(琴担为黄色)的著名京胡演奏出来的，许多资深的老戏迷对此记忆犹新。现在这两把堪称国宝级的京胡就保存在京南虎坊桥湖

Jinghu making. The most important skill is he could make some particular Jinghu, which could have a special harmony with the style of certain Beijing Opera performer. In this way, his Jinghu greatly increased the charm of Beijing Opera. Shi Shanpeng researched the Jinghu making skills for all his life, and some famous Beijing Opera masters and Jinghu players were his friends. The Jinghu players, Xu Lanyuan, Wang Shaoqing and Jiang Fengshan, who used to work with famous Beijing Opera master Mei Lanfang, are among them. They would get together and talk about the problems about Jinghu making. These friendship helped him to promote his skill even better, and made Mei Lanfang' s performance having a more graceful effect. Another Beijing Opera master Yang Baosen used to act all over the big cities of China right before the liberation. His elder brother was his Huqin player, and the several Huqins he took with him was also made by Shi Shanpeng. Yang Baosen' s performance was highly praised in Beijing and Shanghai at that time, and such a success of course had a direct connection with the perfect playing of Yang Baozhong' s Jinghu playing. In the old times, the big Beijing Opera theatres not only would put out the most important player' s name, but often would put out the name of the Jinghu player's name as well. Experienced fans would wait outside the ticket house all night, as long as these names were on the advertisement. Before the performance formally started, the fans would give enthusastic applause to the Jinghu playing of Yang Baozhong, and the wonderful sounds were from the “Black Tiger” and the

广会馆内京戏博物馆的展室里，供喜爱中国传统文化的各方人士前来参观。

回味往事展望明天，真是感慨万分，一代名琴伴随一代名角儿、名师的风光与辉煌走过它那如烟的岁月。史老毕生制作胡琴儿，多把流芳于世的好琴、名琴均出自他的双手。几十年的作琴生涯，为史善朋老先生赢得了京胡制作史上“一代宗师”的盛名和美誉。史老先生于1961年早逝，实在令人惋惜。每当戏迷、票友聊起过去京城梨园群星荟萃时，就会自然而然回忆起王少卿为梅兰芳先生演出的“贵妃醉酒”之京胡伴奏，而杨宝森先生演唱他的拿手儿好戏“文昭关”、“击鼓骂曹”时，又让一些曾深临其境的戏迷们仿佛又一次沉浸在杨宝忠先生迷人的京胡演奏艺术的魅力之中。以上这些艺术效果，无不凝聚着史善朋老先生的聪明智慧和耗费大量心血制作的一把把名琴的功劳。

经历无数风雨的“史善朋竹琴社”这家京城老胡琴铺子，犹如老树再发新枝，其祖传的京胡制作80多年中从未断档，一直后继有人。正如年过六旬的史老先生的长子史致贤先生所言：“我们家为什么三代人一直开着这个老胡琴铺子呢？为的就是让这门传统手艺活儿别失传，不能对不起老祖宗，更不能对不起大老远慕名来的戏迷朋友……”

“Yellow Tiger” which was hand-made by Shi Shanpeng. Now these two Jinghu was kept in the Beijing Opera Museum of Huguang Assembly in Hufangqiao, southern Beijing.

In those old days, a famous Jinghu would accompany some famous Beijing Opera master or a famous Jinghu player for a long and great period of time. Shi shanpeng made Jinghu for his whole life, and left quite many high quality products. Several decades of work has made his fame in the history of Jinghu making. Shi Shanpeng died in 1961 when he was just over 50 years old. When Beijing Opera fans chat about the best times of the old days, they would naturally remember Wang shaoqing’s amazing Jinghu playing in Mei Lanfang’s Imperial Garden, Yang Baosen’s best performed *Wenzhao Pass* and *Curse Cao by Druming*, and would remind of Yang Baozhong’s Jinghu playing. All these wonderful effect were coming from the great Jinghu made by Shi Shanpeng.

Now Shi Shanpeng Jinghu Shop has lasted for so many years, but their old craftsmanship has never been forgotten. 60 years old Shi Zhixian, the eldest son of Shi Shanpeng once said: “The reason our family keep this old Jinghu shop, is not to have the traditional craftsmanship lost. We can’t disappoint the ancestors and the fans coming to see this place.”

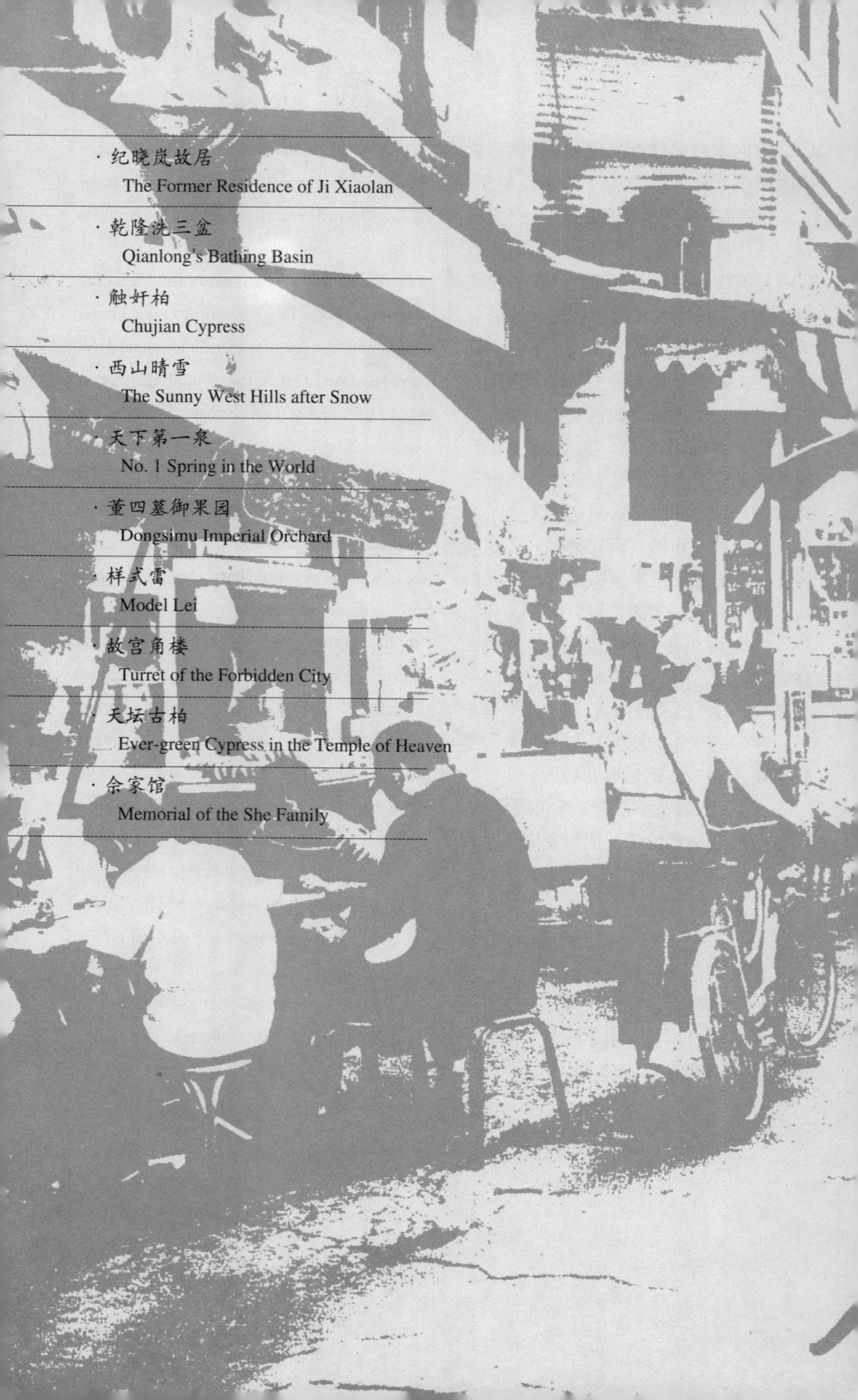

古迹与典故

Relic and Legend

纪晓岚故居

The Former Residence of Ji Xiaolan

位于北京城城南珠市口西大街241号的纪晓岚故居，整座建筑古色古香，玲珑别致，是昔日老北京的许许多多四合院之一。在清朝中叶乾隆年间，这里住的是翰林院侍读大学士、礼部尚书纪晓岚。到今天，这所老宅子已有近300年的历史。

纪晓岚(1724～1805年)，名昀，号春帆，祖籍直隶河间府献县崔尔庄人，以总纂《四库全书》而名满天下，不仅是一位博览群书的大学问家，还是一位机智而富有幽默感的大名士。纪大学士生活的年代，就是世人皆知的“康乾盛世”，天子乾隆在这龙座上一坐就是60年，使封建统治达到了中国历史上最后一个巅峰，但是大清国从此由盛到衰，在乾隆执政的中叶便开始下滑。在乾隆盛世时期，乾隆将开馆修《四库全书》的重任委于一代才子纪晓岚。按现在的话来说，纪晓岚绝对是“上知天文，下知地理”的一位全才。据史书记载：纪文达公诗词歌赋无所不通，出口成章，妙语联珠，其在历史、文学、天文、地理诸方面都有很深的造诣，乾隆在高兴之时，也会甩出这么一段话：“朕三日不见纪昀，就像缺了些什么。”不过在皇权社会里，在喜怒无常的皇上身边供奉皇差，可不是一件容易的事，平常有哪点

Ji Xiaolan's former residence is located in No. 241 of Zhushikou west street, Southern Beijing, and it is one of the many old graceful courtyards built in old times. During the mid of Emperor Qianlong's period, the owner of this place was a high rank official and famous Confucian Ji Xiaolan. Till today, this old courtyard has been there for almost 300 years.

Ji Xiaolan was born in 1724, and died in 1805. He was from Cui'er village in Xian County, Hebei Province, and was famed in compiling the *Siku Encyclopedia*, also known as *the Imperial Collection of Four*. He was not only a great scholar, but also a humorous personage. Ji Xiaolan lived in the famous and great time of Kang-Qian when Emperor Qianlong held his power for 60 years. This was the highest point of Chinese history, but from the mid of Qianlong's time, Qing Dynasty started to decline. Emperor

□ 纪晓岚故居 The Former Residence of Ji Xiaolan

侍候不周，一旦触怒了龙颜，随时都有脑袋搬家的可能。民间有句非常贴切的话说“伴君如伴虎”。纪学士依靠自己的足智多谋，在大兴文字狱的年代里，几次逢凶化吉，因而仕途还算顺畅，没有经历太多坎坷。从纪公中了进士到去翰林院供职，一路官运亨通，最后荣任翰林院总纂官。一生当中，纪晓岚参与了许多重要典籍的修订和编稿，为继承 和保存中华民族悠久灿烂的文化作出了可贵的贡献。

几百年来，人们一直怀念这位与刘罗锅子齐名的诙谐和幽默大师纪昀。民间传说，他连皇帝老子的玩笑都敢开，而且开得既巧妙又恰到好处，因此不仅从来没有受到过任何处罚，反倒每每令龙颜大悦。纪公嘲弄同僚，特别对一些没有真才实学，只会阿谀奉承、溜须拍马的势利小人，以特有的幽默无情地给予鞭挞。对无恶不作的太监和横行霸道的贪官污吏，纪公更是给以大胆辛辣的嘲讽，为无权无势的黎民百姓和有正义感的清官鸣冤叫不平。他无论去什么地

□ 纪晓岚故居的古藤
Old Wisteria in the Former Residence of Ji Xiaolan

Qianlong entrusted Ji Xiaolan as the director of compiling the *Siku Encyclopedia*. In modern terms, he is someone who knows everything. In history records, he was a great scholar and every word he said would be wonderful and charming. He had great accomplishments in History, Literature, Astronomy and Geography. Qianlong once said: “I would be feeling uncomfortable if I haven’t seen him for 3 days.” While in feudal society, serving the emperor was something very dangerous, and if someone irritated the emperor for a minor issue, he might be beheaded. There used to have a famous saying among people that staying with the emperor is just like staying with a tiger. Ji Xiaolan was smart enough to make himself safe, though several times he had been dangerous enough, and finally was raised to the position of compiling director of imperial scholar institute. In his life, Ji Xiaolan compiled lots of important books, and made invaluable contribution to Chinese culture.

In several hundred years, Ji Xiaolan and another famous personage, Liu Yong, was never forgotten by people. In folk stories, Ji Xiaolan was brave enough to make fun of the emperor. His jokes were funny and appropriate, so he could escape being punished but often made the emperor happy. He liked to tease his collegues, especially those incompetent greasiness. He was sarcastic to the eunuch and corrupted officials. No matter where he went, his witness and humors would be left there. It is said once Ji Xiaolan and He Shen accompanied the emperor going on the Great Jing-Hang Canal. The great canal was winding with many anabranches and there were

方，总是能够将长期养成的机智、幽默、出口成章的本领发挥得淋漓尽致。据说乾隆皇帝有一次乘船沿着京杭大运河下江南游览，纪晓岚、和珅二位朝廷命官奉旨随行侍驾。皇上的大龙船一路顺流南下，不知不觉就到了直隶境内的沧州地界，也就是离纪晓岚家乡不远的地方。当初大运河河道蜿蜒曲折，且支流众多，分别从不同的位置汇入古运河的主流。在其中有一条宽敞的入河口处，两岸垂柳成行，水草十分丰美，沿河土地松软肥沃，冲积成连绵起伏的一个个小小沙丘。在风儿不断拍打下，河边的河水形成一个个圆圆的小浪窝儿，当地老百姓俗称其“王八窝”。乾隆在船上看到此情此景，觉得很有意思。遂转过头问身边的纪晓岚：“纪爱卿，这两岸的许多坑穴，到底是怎么一回事儿呀!”纪晓岚闻听乾隆所言，正琢磨着如何回答才能令龙颜喜悦，可没成想老奸巨滑的和珅在一旁诡秘地一笑，凑上前去说：“皇上，您还不知道吧，这可是纪大学士的老家呀!”和珅有意戏弄纪晓岚，将大自然形成的景观说成是纪晓岚的老家，那纪晓岚不就成了“王八”！然而，兴趣正高的乾隆并不知道和珅要弄纪晓岚的真实用意。可纪晓岚对和珅的用意自然是心知肚明，他一边捋着胡子，一边眯着眼睛缓缓道来：“禀告万岁，这河中穴窝又多又密，皆是因河深所在。”“河深所在？纪爱卿快快细细道来。”乾隆忙问。“皇上，您细瞧这一段河水泛绿，浪多拍岸，形成大小不等的一个个浪窝，老百姓都晓得凡是河深的地方，才出现这么多祸国殃民的王八窝。”“河深”与

□ 阅薇草堂　Yuewei Grass Study(Early in 1900s)

many willows on the banks. In one of the major branches in Cangzhou, not far from Ji Xiaolan's homeplace, the river water made many sand dunes and caving, well called Tortoise Cave by local people.

When the ship reached the river, Emperor Qianlong saw the caves and felt interesting. He turned around and asked Ji Xiaolan: “How comes those caves?” Ji Xiaolan was thinking how to answer this question, and He Shen replied to the emperor with a secretive smile: “Your Highness, maybe you do not know, here is the homeland of Ji Xiaolan.” He Shen was intentionally teasing Ji Xiaolan, implying that Ji Xiaolan was a tortoise. Qianlong didn't get the real meaning of what he said, but Ji Xiaolan understood his purpose. He responded: “Your Majesty, such many cave is caused by the deep water(He Shen).” Qianlong was curious, “tell

"和珅"二字为谐音，和珅自然明白纪学士是在乾隆皇帝面前反唇相讥，心中暗自叫苦不迭，黑麻子脸因为生气憋得像一块红猪肝。短短一则小故事就向人们展示了一代名儒机智聪慧、蔑视权贵的高风亮节。

如今漫步在这座恬静、古朴的灰砖小院里，凝视着院中天井里据说是北京城里最古老的紫藤萝，仿佛纪公亲手植古藤的情景就发生在昨天一样。如今，植藤人早已乘鹤西去，但老藤仍然枝叶繁茂，绿荫缭绕，香气袭人。不难想像，当时幽雅清静的环境也许曾为纪学士撰写《阅微草堂笔记》一书中的一些精彩篇章赋予过神奇的灵感，故而才使之成为了一部不朽的传世佳作吧。

me why it is caused by deep water." Ji Xiaolan said: "the water looks green here, and making all kinds of twists, people all know, whenever water is deep, it would come with lots of Tortoise caves." Deep water had the same pronunciation with He Shen's name in Chinese. He Shen understood Ji Xiaolan was teasing back, and got quite upset about what he said. From this little story, we could see the personality of Ji Xiaolan.

Walking around this quiet and ancient style little courtyard, looking at the wisteria, it seems it was planted by Ji Xiaolan yesterday. Now Ji Xiaolan had passed away for a long time, but the wisteria was still high and green. Within such a nice and elegant environment, Ji Xiaolan wrote down some of his best works.

乾隆洗三盆

Qianlong's Bathing Basin

雍和宫位于北京东城国子监街一带，是北京城内最大的喇嘛教寺院，亦是著名的藏传佛教艺术馆和全国重点文物保护单位。这所寺院几百年来一直以其恢宏的建筑、精美的佛像、丰富的文物驰名海内外，曾两次作为“潜龙宅”的特殊经历更使它闻名遐迩。

这里最初是清圣祖康熙皇帝第四子胤祯居住的府宅，1708年胤祯晋升为“和硕雍亲王”，此处宅院遂被称为“雍亲王府”。1722年老皇帝康熙驾崩，和硕雍亲王继承帝位，年号雍正。胤祯承继大统后，按老规矩则很快迁到紫禁城皇宫里主持朝政。1725年，雍正颁布圣旨把其以往一直居住的府邸改作行宫，并御笔赐名“雍和宫”。雍正在位只有短短的13年，于1735年突然间一命归天，其子弘历继承皇位，年号“乾隆”。而乾隆皇帝又恰恰出生在“雍亲王府”，这便是两次“潜龙宅”的由来。

在雍和宫法轮殿的后部、五百罗汉山前，有一个玻璃罩，罩内放着一个硬木雕刻的须弥座，座上摆放一尊用老紫檀木制作而成的盆托，托内嵌着一只木盆，这就是雍和宫内著名的文物珍品之一“洗三盆”，又称“鱼龙变化盆”。盆外围的雕刻技艺十分精湛，内容亦是极富想像力。只见海水卷起层层浪花，蛟

□ 雍和宫万佛阁

Thousand-of-Buddha Hall in Yonghe Lama Temple

Yonghe Lama Temple, located in Guozijian Road, eastern part of Beijing city, is the biggest Lama temple in Beijing. It is the artistic garllary of Lama Buddhism and the national first grade relics protection site. Its fabulous building, beautiful Buddha statue, various relics have made its fame around the world, and its history of twice being the residence of would-be emperor would make it even more well-known.

Originally it was the residence of Emperor Kangxi's forth son, Yinzhen. In 1708, Emperor Kangxi raised Yinzhen as Infante, therefore his residence was named after his title. In 1722, Emperor Kangxi passed away, and Yinzhen became Emperor Yongzheng. After his inauguration, Emperor Yongzheng moved into the Forbidden City. In 1725, Emperor Yongzheng gave an order to change his former residence into

龙翻江倒海昂首向上的雄姿跃然于盆壁，而在中心位置一个胖娃娃则双手扣住盆沿，神情极其诙谐，孩子、蛟龙、浪花的造型自然合一，妙趣横生。据史料记载，清代乾隆皇帝生下三天之际曾用它洗过澡，所以又称“乾隆洗三盆”。

单就中国民间“洗三”习俗来说，从古到今不论帝王将相还是平头百姓，谁家生了小孩都要遵守“洗三”的老民俗。清代崇彝所著《道咸以来朝野杂记》讲道：“三日洗儿，谓之洗三。”大概这样做可以洗去所谓婴儿自“前世”带来的污垢，并可保佑其一生平安、吉祥顺利。

康熙五十年（1711年）八月十三日，弘历诞生于雍王府内东书院的如意室。其生母钮祜禄氏，生于清康熙三十一年（1692年），先祖为大清国显赫的开国元勋额亦都。钮祜禄氏在十三岁时就被当

□ 雍和宫万佛阁弥勒佛像
Mile Buddha in the Thousand-of-Buddha Hall

his Xanadu, and gave it a new name Yonghe Palace with his personal autography. Emperor Yongzheng has been in power for only 13 years, and died in 1735. His son Hongli, Emperor Qianlong, inherited his power. So the Yonghe Palace was also known as the residence of would-be emperor.

At the backside of Falun Hall in Yonghe Palace, right in front of the Five-hundred-Arhat Hill, there is a wooden basin with a rosewood support, which is covered with a glass dome and based on a Buddha Holy Seat carved of hardwood. This is one of the most famous relics of Yonghe Lama Temple, called Xisan Basin, also known as Fish Dragon Transformation Basin. The relief on the outside of this basin was carved quite lively, and the content is very imaginative. On the sea waves, a dragon is flying from the sea into the air, and at the center of the relief, there is a lovely baby with both hands holding the edge of the basin. The baby, the dragon and the sea water come together into a quite beautiful picture. According to history records, Emperor Qianlong was bathed with this basin on the third day after his birth. That's why it got the name of Qianlong Xisan Basin. In term of the *Xisan* in Chinese, no matter ordinary people or royal families, new born baby has to be bathed on the third day of his birth. In the book *Social Miscellaneous Since Emperor Daoguang and Xianfeng*, authored by Chongyi of Qing Dynasty, bathing on the third day of the new born baby is called Xisan which means to wash away the filth from the baby's previous life, and bless it with a safe and sound new life.

On August 13th of 1711, Hongli, the later

时身为贝勒爷的胤祯选为侧室，二十岁时生下一子，取名弘历，也就是后来的乾隆皇帝。据说当年钮祜禄氏在侍奉胤祯近八个年头时才身怀六甲，可以想见当时她的心情是相当复杂的，因为自己虽入主四贝勒爷府邸却始终无缘扶正。如果这回命中注定生下个千金将不会给自己的命运带来任何转机，说不定在这人多嘴杂的雍王府还可能招致更多的闲言碎语。可万一苍天有眼能让其生出个小王爷，凭着母以子贵这条皇室祖辈延续的老规矩，不仅能扶正，而且可以得到雍亲王的更多宠幸。钮祜禄氏就是在这种复杂的心情中等到了临产。伴随着一声婴儿嘹亮的啼哭，一个白胖胖的小

□雍和宫内的乾隆洗三盆

Qianlong´s Bathing Basin in Yonghe Lama Temple

Emperor Qianlong was born in the east study in the Yonghe Palace. His mother, Niugulu, was born in 1692, a descendant of E'yidu family, which had made great contribution to the establishment of Qing Dynasty. When Niugulu was only 13 years old, she married as a concubine with Yinzhen who was just an ordinary son of Emperor Kangxi. When she was 20 years old, she gave birth to a boy, and named him Hongli. It is said when she got pregnant after her marriage with Yinzhen for 8 years, she had many thoughts. Since she married Yinzheng, she never got raised as the lawful wife. If she gave birth to a girl, she would not change her fate for a bit and would even bring more fussy talks within this palace. But if she gave birth to a boy, considering the old rule of royal family that the mother got her place from her son, she might have a chance becoming the lawful wife of Yinzhen, and get more love from her husband. She awaited her labor in these thoughts. A lovely prince came to this world with a loud and clear cry, and her wishes came true. The baby was her first child and she hoped quite considerate, desperately that her son could have a great and prosperous life. She told her maid: "Today is the day for my son to have the bath, I don't want to use the old basin. I have seen a wooden basin behind the Buddha niche of the east building before, and it looked nice and great, let's use that." The maid fetched the basin as told. This basin was in a color of dark brown, carved with dragon flying over the sea water. It seemed to indicate something.

Later on, the Lamas got known about this event, and put this basin right in the Falun Hall.

王爷降临人间，天随人意的钮祜禄氏喜极而泣。很快孩子已降生三天，必须要洗澡，即民俗“洗三”。钮祜禄氏虽初为人母却想得十分细致，特别想为儿子弘历图个一生吉利，大福大贵。于是她唤来奶妈吩咐道：“王姥姥，今儿个是弘历‘洗三’的日子，可别用原来的盆洗。我头些日子看见在东暖阁佛龛后面有个木盆，又干净又气派，就用它洗吧。”丫环按吩咐不一会儿就将木盆取来，这盆为紫褐色，盆壁上一朵朵浪花高高托起蛟龙，一幅龙镇四海之气势，预示着什么……

后来雍和宫的喇嘛们知道这件事后，特地把这只檀木木盆供奉在法轮殿内。因此盆是乾隆皇帝沐浴用过的盆，皇帝乃真龙天子，所以盆内一年四季必须供上供品，祈求真龙天子为天下子民带来太平盛世。钮祜禄氏自然母以子贵，先后被晋封为熹妃、熹贵妃。乾隆龙袍加身后，又被尊为崇庆皇太后。喜好游山玩水的乾隆也常携母同游。据史料记载，在乾隆期间，她和儿子乾隆到过边陲塞外、清东陵遵化、江南的苏杭、东北祖籍盛京、五岳之首泰山、佛教重地五台山等古迹名胜。从乾隆五年(1740年)崇庆皇太后五十岁以来，乾隆还几次为她举办万寿庆典。乾隆四十二年(1777年)正月，崇庆皇太后病逝，享年八十六岁。

清圣祖康熙皇帝八岁登基，在位六十多年，政绩显赫、国势强大，同时也为以后的“乾隆盛世”打下了坚实的政治与经济基础，其功之高、在位时间之长是为清朝其他皇帝所不及的。此外康

Since this basin was used to bath Emperor Qianlong, sacrifices should be put in the basin all year, wishing the emperor giving people a peaceful and prosperous time. Hongli's mother, after her son's birth, got her title raised again and again. When Hongli became the Emperor, she naturally became the Empress of Chongqing. Emperor Qianlong loved traveling, and often took his mother with him. On history records, she had been to places like northern border, Zunhua's Eastern Mausoleum of Qing Dynasty, Suzhou and Hangzhou of Southern China, Shenyang at northeast, Taishan Mountain, and the great Buddhism site of Wutai Mountain etc. Since her 50th birthday in 1740, Emperor Qianlong has hold several big celebrations for her. In 1777, she passed away at her 86.

Emperor Kangxi got into power at 8 years old, and ran this country for over 60 years. His political feats was greater, and the time holding power was longer than any other emperors of Qing Dynasty, which greatly benefited the country and created the condition for the Great Time of Kangxi and Qianlong. Besides, Kangxi also held

□ 雍和宫法轮殿　Falun Hall in Yonghe Lama Temple

熙子孙数量之多也为清朝历代君主之最，据史料记载：康熙一生共育有三十五个儿子、二十五个女儿，孙子、孙女达一百多个，有些孙子辈的他连见都没见过。作为当朝天子，康熙能有众多的龙子龙孙无疑是个好兆头，自然预示着大清江山稳坐、绵延万年。但如果从另一个角度看，就会发现因康熙在位时间长、皇子多，而导致各种人际关系过于错综复杂。太子的两次废立，皇储位缺引起的纷争，直到临终时也处理不好。而民间纷传的雍正靠改旨篡位，以及继位后杀兄弑弟等事至今仍难辨真假。由用“鱼龙变化盆”为弘历“洗三”一事所引出，民间还流传着这样一种说法：雍正能当上皇帝那全是沾了儿子弘历的光。据说某年夏初，身体尚健的康熙在圆明园举行皇宫诗会，集中对年龄稍大些的皇子、皇孙进行一检验，看看他们各自的文采如何。这天一大早，只见皇子、皇孙们个个踌躇满志、精神焕发，准备在皇阿玛、皇爷爷面前一展才华。偏巧，那天胤禛和十岁的儿子弘历因事稍迟了些。可一到殿前，就见小弘历径直朝康熙皇帝面前跑来，带着童音脆生生地道：“皇爷爷，孙儿弘历给您请安。”康熙见弘历聪明可爱，便问：“弘历啊，你今年几岁啦？你阿玛教你作诗了么？”弘历仰着头，明亮清澈的眼睛看着康熙，小嘴甜巴巴地一一作答，而且答得特别精彩，让老康熙乐得嘴都合不上了，兴奋的他已将雍亲王和众皇子皇孙们都忘在了一边。对皇孙小弘历疼爱有加的康熙皇帝，决定把孙儿带在身边加以培养，不久又破格封

the record of descendents. According to history, Kangxi had 35 sons, 25 daughters, over 100 grandson and granddaughters, some of his grandsons never even met him. Everything got two sides. It’s a good sign for Kangxi as the emperor with so many descendants that indicated the stability and long lives of Qing Dynasty. But on the other side, the fact that he held power for so many years and had so many descendants, would lead to very complicated personal relationships. Crown prince was deposed twice, his sons fought for principality, and all these disputes were not settled when he died. Rumors about Yongzheng changed his father’s order to get into power, and killed his siblings when he became the emperor, was still undetermined till now. And because of the story of Hongli’s bath with the Fish Dragon Transformation Basin, it’s said that Yongzheng was crowned emperor with his son’s benefit. It was said in an early summer, Kangxi was holding a poetry party in Yuanmingyuan Garden, checking his sons and some of his grandsons’ literature level. In that morning, all his sons and grandsons were well prepared, hoping to show their talent in front of Kangxi. Yinzhen and 10 years old Hongli was delayed by something else, but when they arrived, Hongli ran directly to Emperor Kangxi and said: “Grandpa, I am here.” Kangxi found the smart and lovely boy, and asked: “Hongli, how old are you? Has your father told you writing poem?” Hongli looked at him and provided brilliant answers, which made Kangxi very happy, even forgot about Yinzhen and other descendents. Kangxi liked Hongli very much and decided to

弘历为“和硕宝亲王”。随后又在圆明园内另建一处宅院供弘历居住，这就有了日后康熙在琴棋书画、治国安邦等诸多方面对弘历的栽培。这期间不时有人臆测，康熙可能有意把帝位传与皇孙弘历。可那样做又的确不合乎清代祖制，所以，这才有了胤祯继位，年号雍正。雍正驾崩后，弘历顺利继承帝位，开创了清朝的又一盛世——“乾隆盛世”。

take him himself, and soon gave him title as an infante. Later on, he ordered to build a place for Hongli to live in, and taught him the methods of ruling the country. During that period, people imagined that Kangxi had the intension of passing his crown to Hongli. But such an action was not in line with rules of Qing Dynasty. That’s why Yinzhen became the coming emperor and passed his power to Hongli after his death, then came the Great Time of Qianlong.

触奸柏

Chujian Cypress

□孔庙 Beijing Confucian Temple

坐落在京城的国子监街上的北京孔庙，是元、明、清三代皇帝祭祀孔子、举行国家祭典的重要场所。它始建于元代大德六年（1302年），占地22000平方米。院内由雄伟壮观的古建筑群落组成，亦有反映了中国数百年来科举制度的珍贵文物题名碑，以及集儒家经典著作为一处的“十三经碑林”等多个重要的历史文化遗产。北京国子监孔庙院内植有在册的参天古树约106棵，其中树龄最高同时也最富传奇色彩的当属大成殿门前

Beijing Confucian Temple, located in Guozijian Road, is the site for emperors of Yuan, Ming, Qing Dynasties worshipping Confucius and holding national ceremonies. It covers an area of 22000 square meters first built in 1302, and there are magnificent buildings, precious stele reflecting hundreds of years of imperial examinations, and steles of 13 holy scriptures of Confucian sutra, etc. There are also 106 registered old trees, within which the oldest and the most legendary one is the Chujian(Feel

台阶下的“触奸柏”。据说该树已有700余年的树龄，但至今仍茁壮挺拔、古意浓浓，硕大的树冠宛如一把翠绿的大伞，给游人带来无比的清凉。多少年来围绕这株历经七个世纪的古柏，一直流传着一个妇孺皆知的故事。

明世宗朱厚熜(即嘉靖皇帝）在位期间，是明朝历史上政治最为黑暗、吏治极端腐败的一个阶段。他本人昏庸无能、很少过问国家政事，给了奸相严嵩可乘之机。严嵩（1480~1567年）字惟中，又字介溪，江西分宜人。早年在家乡时，父亲是个权倾一方的官吏。严嵩年龄稍大，中了个进士，自此开始步入仕途。嘉靖二十一年（1542年）严嵩入阁，负责协助当朝天子处理政事。博得明世宗的宠信后，严嵩揽权擅政达20余年。嘉靖皇帝甚至在一次御前朝会上说:“世上没有杀严嵩的刀、斩他的剑。”大权在握的严嵩在朝廷内外心狠手辣。

话说这年朝廷科举考试来临，深受嘉靖皇帝信任的严嵩，奉命前来国子监孔庙代天子行祭孔的礼仪。此次祭孔活动中，主角严嵩所乘的由八个人抬的大轿子居于队伍中心位置，街道两旁站满了店家和百姓。一个时辰后，严嵩等一大批祭孔官员就来到了孔庙。经过一套整衣正冠的必备程序后祭孔大典开始，瞬间大成殿门前鼓乐齐鸣，典礼官高声诵读经文。作为肩负代天子行祭孔使命的严嵩在文武百官簇拥中，迈着四方步向孔庙殿门缓缓走来，结果刚要迈上殿前台阶，风和日丽的天空中突然刮来一阵强风，万没有想到风吹古柏树枝竟然挑掉了严嵩头上的官帽。严嵩脸上顿时

Treacherous) Cypress in front of the Great Achievement Hall. It's said that the tree has been there for over 700 years.It is still flourous and exuberant and its great canopy looks like a huge umbrella, shading the hot sunshine. In the history, there is a well known story about this 700 years old cypress.

During the period of Zhu Houcong's government, people saw a darkest and most corrupted history in Ming Dynasty. The emperor was not only incompetent, but also not willing to manage the states affairs. Such a political condition gave a chance to a treacherous man, Yan Song. Yan was from Fenyi, Jiangxi Province and his father was a local official with great power. When Yan grew up, he passed the imperial examination and started to serve in government. In 1542, he got into the central government, assisting the emperor to manage the political issues. He got the trust of the emperor and held the power to himself for over 20 years. The emperor once said in a high command meeting: “There is no sword could touch Yan Song.” With the emperor's support, Yan got very cruel to his competitors inside and outside the government.

It's said that one year an imperial examination was to begin soon, and the emperor ordered Yan Song to come to the Confucian Temple to hold a ceremony on behalf of the emperor himself. On the day of the ceremony, Yan Song came to the Confucian Temple in a 8-person-carried dooly, with businessman and ordinary people standing on both sides of the street. After certain necessary procedures, the ceremony got started, and the ceremony marshal loudly read out ceremo-

□孔庙院内触奸柏
Chujian Cypress in Beijing Confucian Temple

大惊失色，心想刚才还万里无云，哪来的一阵邪风呢！莫非有什么不祥之兆等着我呢？作贼心虚的他转而想到自己身为当朝首辅大臣，以往干了那么多伤天害理的缺德事儿，树了那么多的敌，此时似乎被杀的一个个不散的冤魂正张牙舞爪从阴曹地府里向他扑来……随行的官员看到这一幕一下子也怔住了，当下人把乌纱帽捡起递送给严嵩。严嵩恼羞成怒、沮丧至极，继续祭孔的念头儿荡然无存，只见面容铁青的严嵩重新戴上官帽，而后使劲一甩手，随即带着手下的官员一溜烟儿似地离开了孔庙。由于其平日一向作恶多端，所以人们世代相传认为是老古柏显灵能辨忠奸，故称“触奸柏”或“辨奸柏”。

nial article, while musical instruments were sounding. Yan Song went in front of all high officials up the steps leading to the Great Achievement Hall. Just at that time, a strong wind came from nowhere and the old branches of the cypress accidentally picked out Yan Song's official hat. Yan Song was appalled, thinking where this strong wind came in such a good weather, and whether it would be some kind of bad implication. Then he remembered that he had done so many bad things after he became the first minister. It seemed that the ghosts of all those people he had killed was coming to grab him for revenge. The officials behind him was stunned by this scene when a servant picked up his hat and gave it back to Yan Song. Yan Song was so upset that he totally had no interest in holding ceremony any more. He put on his hat and led officials out of the Confucian Temple. From then on, people thought this old cypress had the capability to tell who was righteous and who was treacherous, and so named it Chujian Cypress or Bianjian Cypress. In Chinese, *Chu* or *Bian* means to recognize, and *Jian* here refers to Jianchen, which means a treacherous court official.

西山晴雪

The Sunny West Hills after Snow

提起乾隆，那可是清代一位福份不浅的皇帝，光在这龙座上一坐就是六十余年。在早儿上有爷爷康熙、父亲雍正为其打下坚实的政治基础，在位期间国内无大的战争，而且天公也十分作美，风调雨顺，国泰民安。这些为生性喜欢游山玩水的他，提供了一个旅游享乐的绝佳机遇，一生六下江南不说，每每游览名胜古迹、欣赏良辰美景之时，好大喜功的乾隆时不时就会为各地的一些景点起名，众大臣又投其所好一通儿阿谀奉承，当仁不让的他御笔一挥，新名即“应运而生”。这种事例不少史料均有记载，太远的不讲，北京西郊就有“西山晴雪”。在清朝以前，这里原名“西山积雪”，是远近闻名的燕京八景之一，位于香山静宜园内。

香山在北京城西北部40余里的地方，这是一座林木葱郁、幽静秀丽的天然植物王国，早在明清时期便闻名遐迩。无数文人墨客为它的壮美飘逸、杏花飞香、黄栌遍布山坡、玉泉山山泉清澈甘甜而陶醉不已，留下了许多留芳千古的传世华章。一个寒冬，外面雪花在尽情地飞舞，漫山遍野裹上了一层层银装，此时刚上完早朝的乾隆凭窗远眺，瑞雪兆丰年的惬意之感涌上心头，脑海里情不自禁地浮现出“西山积雪”那银

□燕京八景之一“西山雪晴”
The Sunny West Hills after Snow

Qianlong was an emperor with great fortune, and he had been in power for over 60 years. Before him, his grandfather Kangxi and father Yongzheng had paved a smooth way, and there was no big war under his rule and rarely natural disasters. All these provided him a perfect condition for travelling. He had been to Southern China for 6 times and had the habit to give names to the sceneries. His high officials knew he loved to be flattered, thus a lot of new names had come into being. Such examples could easily be found in history records, and the Sunny West Hills after

妆素裹的美丽景色，遂决定暂时放下案头的公务，吩咐手下文武百官，备上车马踏着皑皑白雪，浩浩荡荡前往香山，欲一睹冰雪世界中“西山积雪”的俏丽容颜。

雪中的香山，景色果然格外迷人，春秋时节翠绿的山峰如今被厚厚的白雪轻柔地覆盖着，高高的鬼见愁山顶更是冰清玉洁。乾隆一边登山游玩，一边尽情欣赏这冬日里香山特有的雪景。回想以前若干次御驾香山，都是以春、夏、秋三季居多，那时的香山满目碧绿，沿山而下的涓涓溪水，曲曲弯弯足有数里之长，一个个美景尽收眼底。乾隆在一块巨石上，远远望去，此时天空的雪花还在纷纷扬扬地飘洒着，乾隆兴致特高地观赏着雪景，只见一株株迎风傲雪的松柏、白杨、黄栌、山桃映入视野，几只野兔在雪地中互相追逐，身为皇帝的乾隆也抑制不住心中对大自然由衷的赞美之情：“西山雪景，真是名不虚传，妙哉！妙哉！”沉思片刻，若有所悟的乾隆接着说道：“前人为什么起名称之‘西山积雪’呢?此番雪中美景竟然用如此的名字，不免令人感觉有难脱俗套之意，你看如何呢，刘爱卿？”乾隆冷不丁这么一问，让跟随乾隆几十年，此次奉命侍驾的宠臣刘墉有点措手不及。不过脑袋瓜儿稍微一转悠，刘墉便明白了自诩文韬武略都无人可比的天子的想法，忙躬身答道：“回皇上，微臣才疏学浅，不敢贸然进言。”乾隆素知刘罗锅儿平常弯弯肠子就特多，如今竟然在自己面前也卖起关子来，不过好在乾隆今天正在兴头儿上，并没怪罪于刘墉，反而

Snow is just one of them. Before Qing Dynasty, the Sunny West Hills after Snow was called the West Hill Snow Cap, and it was one of the 8 most beautiful scenes in Beijing.

In the west of Beijing, there is a lovely natural paradise for plants, the Fragrant Hill, about 20 kilometers faraway from Beijing. Its quietness and beauty had been well-known to people early in Ming Dynasty. Countless liberators had been amazed by its beauty, and wrote so many great articles about it. In a cold winter day when it was snowing, the whole landscape was soon covered with white snow. Qianlong was just back from the court and the snow flakes reminded him of the beautiful scenes of the West Hill Snow Cap. The emperor decided to drop his work temporarily, and asked his officials to enjoy the wonderful snow-white landscape in the Fragrant Hill.

The Fragrant Hill was quite beautiful within the snow, and all green hills became white. Qianlong enjoyed the scenery while climbing the hill. He had been here many times, but mostly in other seasons with little creeks winding around and all kinds of color filling into his eyes. Now he got on a huge rock, and all kinds of trees quietly stood there with several hares running on the snow-covered mountain. He was amazed and said, “The west hill snow is really great and wonderful! Why liberators call it West Hill Snow Cap? Such a nice scenery should not have such an ordinary name. What do you think about, Liu Yong?” Liu Yong had not prepared to answer his question, but he had been with Emperor Qianlong for several decades, and knew his real intension right away, so he said: “Your Majesty, I am not

笑容满面地说："以朕之见，定名为西山春雪为佳；或者称为西山云雪亦不为过……"总之，乾隆接连说出了几个名字，又都被自己一一否定，众人见状均不敢多言。此时乾隆见天色已晚，一声令下，暂且回去。翌日起了个大早儿，乾隆又和刘墉等人再次来到香山脚下。雪后的香山景色更为壮观，只见几只花喜鹊在林中粗大的柳树梢儿上叽叽喳喳叫个不停。老话说"喜鹊一叫，喜事自然来"，乾隆也深信这一民间传说，精神为之一爽，一行人迈着轻快的步伐，又一次来到昨天起名的那块位于半山腰的山石旁边。乾隆顿时龙颜大悦，一挥手唤来刘墉，金口吐出玉言："刘爱卿，以朕之意，就取名为西山晴雪，更为贴切。""太绝了!太妙了!皇上，真不愧为当今大清国文武双全的圣主。"刘墉一整套的溢美之词犹如事先背好了一样脱口而出。从此，燕京八景之一的"西山积雪"便被乾隆皇帝改为"西山晴雪"了，这就是流传几百年的乾隆的众多故事中的一个。

a liberator, I don't have any comment on this." Qianlong also knew Liu Yong very well, and was not satisfied with such an answer. Fortunately he was in a good mood and told Liu Yong with smile:"I assume it could be named as West Hill Spring Snow, or West Hill Cloud Snow." He raised several names and rejected them immediately. On the second morning, Emperor Qianlong took Liu Yong and several officials back to the foot of Fragrant Hill. The scenery got even more magnificent and a couple of pied magpie was singing on the willow tips. There was an old Chinese saying, "Pied magpie sings, good things comes." All of them climbed the hill in a fast pace, and soon reached the huge rock they had came the day before. Emperor Qianlong was very happy that he called Liu Yong to come close, and told him, "Liu Yong, I had a good name now, Sunny West Hills after Snow, how do you think?" Liu Yong had already prepared a whole set of flattering words for him. From then on, West Hill Snow Cap was replaced by Sunny West Hills after Snow.

天下第一泉

No. 1 Spring in the World

□京西名山玉泉山 Jade Spring Hill

北京的西山如诗似画，它既有太行山挺拔壮美的气魄，又含几许黄山青翠秀丽的风韵。其中位于西山东麓的支脉玉泉山，更是以它独特的自然风光、文物景观而驰名。尤为值得一提的是，玉泉山有一处四季流淌的泉水，这就是曾被清代天子乾隆敕封的“天下第一泉”的玉泉。古籍《习成集》一书中有这样的记载：“玉泉山在京城西三十里西山之麓，有石洞，泉自山中而出。洞门刻有玉泉二字，泉味儿干洌。上有石岩，名吕公洞。其上有芙蓉阁，金章宗避暑处。其在山之阴者，泉自下涌。”描述了当初这里迷人的景色，而由此演变而来的燕京古都八景之一“玉泉垂虹”，更使这处景点声名远播。

居住在此的先民相传，西山群峰有很多的泉眼，“西山遍地泉，大小一百

The West Mountain in Beijing is idyllic and there is not only the upright and magnificent verve of Taihang Moutain, but also the verdant and elegant charm of Huangshan Moutain. Among others, Yuquan Hill, a branch range, located at the east foot of the West Mountain, is well-known for its unique natural scene and cultural relic spot. What is worth mentioning is Yuquan, a spring running in all seasons in Yuquan Hill, which have been conferred the title of No. 1 Spring in the World by Emperor Qianlong. It's recorded in the book *Xi Cheng Collection,* “Yuquan Hill lies in the foot of the West Mountain, 15 kilometers away from the west of Beijing. There is a cave in Yuquan Hill and spring flows out from the Hill. The cave door is engraved with two characters *Yuquan* and the spring tastes sweet and cool. Upon the cave is a rock which says Mr. Lv's Cave. On the rock is Lotus Pavilion where Emperor Zhangcong in Jin Dynasty ever passed summer holidays. Lotus Pavilion is located in the north of the Hill and spring gushes down it.” This book describes the enchanting scenery of Yuquan Hill at that time. “Yu Quan Chui Hong”, one of Yanjing (Ancient Capital) Eight Scenes evolved from this makes the sight spot even more famous.

The peasants lived there said that the West

□玉泉山裂帛湖 Liebo Lake in Jade Spring Hill

眼，香山三百寺，无寺没泉眼”。西山泉水虽多，但要说哪一口山泉水质最佳，则首推有“天下第一泉”之称的玉泉。据当地年事已高的老辈人讲，我国古典文学巨匠曹雪芹在创作《红楼梦》时，曾在西山正白旗村一带生活多年直至去世。穷困的曹雪芹居住在西山一个十分简陋的院落里，它就位于林深草密的一条山谷中并与这眼泉水相邻。有天一大清早，好友鄂比来到曹家小院做客，信口问道：“西山诸峰有这么多的泉眼，不知曹兄为何偏偏喜欢这眼泉的水呢？”曹雪芹轻轻一笑答道：“西山大大小小约三百个山泉，为兄我几乎都尝过了，可以讲句不算夸张的话，哪儿的泉水也不能与这眼山泉相提并论。它不仅水质甘甜、清冽，而且用此泉烧开的水沏茶，茶叶便会徐徐舒展、茶水清澈、香气四溢，尤为不同寻常的是，品尝过后，唇齿留芳，疲劳顿消，兄弟您品尝一下如何？”鄂比将信将疑，说道：“依小弟看来这西山其他的山泉水质也并不一定就

Mountain has lots of spring mouths. They said that spring of various sizes all over the West Mountain were more than one hundred. There are three hundred temples in Fragrant Hills and each temple has its spring mouths. Though there is plenty of spring in the West Mountain, Yuquan Spring with the No. 1 Spring in the World has superior quality over others. According to the aged people, Cao Xueqin, the great master classical literature, ever lived in Zheng Eight Banner of the West Mountain Village for many years until death when he was writing *Dream of the Red Chamber*. The villagers said, in former days, Cao Xueqin lived in a simple and crude courtyard which was located at a valley among dense forest bordering upon the spring mouth. One morning, his friend E Bi came to visit Cao's courtyard and asked him thoughtlessly: “There are so many spring mouths in the West Mountain, why do you prefer the spring water from this one?” Cao Xueqin answered with smile: “The West Mountain has nearly 300 spring mouths, big and small, and I have tasted them all. Without exaggeration, no other spring can be regarded as the same with this one. The spring is sweet and cool. In addition, if you boil this spring water and make tea, the tea leaf will unfold slowly, and the tea is limpid and the fragrance overflows everwhere. What is unusual is that after you drink the tea, your lips and teeth will retain the fragrance and you are free from fatigue. Would you like to have a taste?” Half believing and half doubting, E Bi said: “As far as my knowledge is concerned, other spring water in the West Mountain is not so inferior to this one! Did you too exaggerate about

差到哪儿去呀！曹兄所言是否有些言过其实呢？”曹雪芹解释道：“这西山远近三百泉固然水质也堪称上乘，不过要看和谁比了。如果拿它们与我家大门前的这眼泉水相互比较而论，从本质上讲真乃天地之别也。”鄂比觉得曹雪芹说得有些神乎其神了，可又不能马上找出令人信服的论据来反驳，只好暂时作罢。

过后时间不长，便到了春花怒放的阳春时节。因事外出多日的鄂比刚从城里回来，便踱着四方步来到曹家小院，本意想约曹雪芹共同踏春，去享受一下无限春光，可偏巧这天曹雪芹不能相陪，在向鄂比略表歉意的同时，拜托他回来时顺便捎一壶曹家门前的山泉水，供沏茶用。离开曹家后，鄂比像以往一样，在西山的东南隅尽情畅游后，忽然想起了雪芹所托之事，赶紧走到曹家门前的山泉边，用瓢把泉水舀起装在随身所带的小壶里，然后来到曹雪芹家中。雪芹此时写作正暂告一个段落，见鄂比从外边游玩归来，便招呼他进门，一边说古论今一边烧水沏茶，不一会儿水就烧开了。曹雪芹起身沏了一瓷壶茶闷上片刻，再倒进两个小盖碗，并将其中一碗递给鄂比。有些口渴的他率先饮了起来。哪知雪芹刚呷了两小口儿，立刻感觉味儿不对，马上向鄂比问道：“兄弟带回的这水不是我家门前那口泉眼的吧？”鄂比顿时一惊，故作镇静地应道：“这水确是您家门口不远的那眼泉的水。”雪芹说：“这水我敢断定不是我家大门前那口泉的水，而是两眼山泉水掺合在一起的。”

鄂比见曹雪芹口气如此坚定，心想

it? ”Cao Xueqin explained: “There is no doubt that the three hundred spring mouths in the West Mountain, near and far, is superior in quality. But that's just depends on which one to compare with. If comparing them with the spring water at my doorway, it is really the distinction between the heaven and the earth.” E Bi thought what Cao Xueqin said was miraculous, but he couldn't find convincing argument to talk back right away, so he had to let it be.

Quickly it came to be the spring. E Bi who went out on business came back and walked slowly to Cao Xueqin's courtyard. E Bi has intended to invite Cao Xueqin to go out for a walk to enjoy the beautiful spring scenery, but unfortunately Cao Xueqin couldn't accompany him. So Cao Xueqin expressed his apology, at the same time, he requested E Bi to bring a bottle of spring water with him at Cao Xueqin's doorway to make tea when he came back. Leaving Cao Xueqin's courtyard, E Bi enjoyed his travelling and suddenly called to remember the affair entrusted by Cao Xueqin. He bailed out the spring with ladle and poured it into the small bottle he brought along with him and then he came to Cao Xueqin's family. When Cao saw E Bi come back from outside, he asked him to enter his courtyard. They talked about the ancient times and the contemporary era, at the same time Cao Xueqin boiled water and made tea. After a while, the water was boiled. Cao Xueqin stood up to make tea in a porcelain pot. He poured the tea water into two bowls with lids and passed one bowl to E Bi. As Cao Xueqin was very thirsty, he took the lead in drinking tea. After just sipping a

□ 玉泉山第一泉　No.1 Spring in the World

他刚才是不是没在家中写书，而是尾随自己出去了呢，于是反问道：“曹兄何以判断这水不是您家门口那眼泉的呢？”雪芹笑着说：“这碗茶水，我刚喝上两口，就知道这是两眼泉的泉水掺合在一起的，上面的水水轻，是我家门口那眼泉的水，下面的水水重，是别处的山泉，两口泉的泉水明显味道不同。”鄂比一看自己要的小把戏被曹雪芹说穿了，只好笑眯眯地如实道来。其实自打二人为泉水质地优劣发生小小的分歧后，鄂比就一直想试一试曹雪芹对泉水的研究真如他本人所言的那样吗，所以鄂比借这次单独踏青之际，先去香山玉皇顶上将那里的泉水灌上半壶，然后再来到曹家门口那眼泉里加上半壶，最终将整壶水提到曹家烧开沏茶，以检验一下曹雪芹能否辨别出来，结果没成想曹雪芹只喝上一两口就一语道破，这下可让喜欢开玩笑的鄂比佩服得五体投地。他敬佩地说：“曹兄，您不愧为与茶圣陆羽齐名，一世为墨客，终生作茶仙呀！”

随着时光的推移，有关这眼泉是“仙泉”的故事越传越远、越传越神，吸引得附近的山民都来这取水。后来更有传言：“常饮这眼山泉水，能祛邪治病、

little, he immediately felt the flavour was different, and said at once, “The spring you brought must not be the one at my doorway.” E Bi was taken aback by this, but he pretended to be calm and answered: “The spring is the one not far from your doorway indeed.” Cao Xueqin said: “I can conclude the spring is not the one at my doorway and it is a spring mixture from two spring mouths.”

Because Cao Xueqin was so sure about the difference between the two kind of spring, E Bi thought to himself that Cao Xueqin must have followed him. So he asked Cao Xueqin: “How can you judge the spring is not the one at your doorway?” Cao Xueqin answered with laugh, “When I just drink a little, I know this spring is a mixture of two spring mouths, because the upper spring is the one at my doorway that is light, and the lower one is from elsewhere that is heavy. The tastes of the two kinds of spring is markedly different.” Since the little trick was disclosed by Cao Xueqin, E Bi had to tell him the truth with laugh. He said with admiration: “Hi, Mr. Cao, you are as famous as Lu Yu, and you are not only a famous writer, but also a tea immortal.”

As time went by, the story about the Immortal Tea went farther and farther away and became increasingly miraculous. More and more neighboring villagers came to draw spring water there. Later on, the rumor went like this: “Drinking the spring water frequently will remove evil, cure illness and prolong life.” This was just a joke spreading among ordinary people, but it was heard by eunuches and they reported to Emperor Qianlong, who conferred the name No. 1 Spring in the World to the spring. From then on, this

延年益寿。”这本是民间戏言，却被听到的太监们奏报给了天子，于是乾隆皇帝御笔一挥赐名“天下第一泉”，征为皇室御用，由朝廷专门刻碑并派官兵把守。随之在以后几百年间，西山附近的百姓只能眼巴巴瞧着宫廷里的拉水车来来去去，谁也甭想再喝这泉的水了。

spring was used by the royalty exclusively, and the court engraved a stele for the spring. So for several hundred years since that time, the common people near the West Mountain could only hopelessly witness the wagon carrying water in and out of the court, and no one could drink the spring water again.

董四墓御果园

Dongsimu Imperial Orchard

□董四墓御果园遗址 Relic of Dongsimu Imperial Orchard

在连绵起伏的北京西山群峰中，有一座景色别致、幽静壮观的碧绿青山——金山，它东起红石山口，西至香山主脉。其中位于金山脚下，有一个依山傍水的美丽山村，它的名字叫“董四墓村”。这里地肥水美山青树翠，得天独厚的自然环境，使这里早在明末清初就成为名噪京城的“皇家御果园”。据《养吉斋录》一书中记载：“董四墓村在玉泉山北，产桃最美，仁宗（即清嘉庆皇帝）尝以赐朱文正公”。由此可见几百年前的“董四墓御果园”，就以大桃味道鲜美深受当朝天子的垂青。昔日从山下到半山腰，映入眼帘的俨然是一幅果树的绿色画卷。过去北京老百姓吃到的梨、杏、苹果等，这里出产的占相当的一部分。据讲小小的董四墓村，几乎囊括当年北方所有常见的时令水果。虽然瓜、果、梨、桃之类的水果，全国不少省份同样

Jin Hill, stretching from Hongshi Mountain Pass in the east to the main Fragrant Hills range in the west, is a sequester, grand and dark green hill with unique scenery in continuous and undulant West Mountain. At the foot of Jin Hill, there stands a beautiful village called Dongsimu Village. With advantaged natural environment, Dongsimu Village has become famous Imperial Orchard in the end of Ming Dynasty and the beginning of Qing Dynasty. It's recorded in the book of *Yangji Zhai Record* that Dongsimu Village yielded the best peaches and that Emperor Jiaqing of Qing Dynasty ever tasted the peach and conferred it to Mr. Zhu Wenzheng. It's told that in the past when you walked up from the mountain foot to the mountainside, what you saw just liked a green picture of fruit trees. In former days, a considerable percentage of the pear, apricot and apple that old Beijing civilians ate were from here. It is said that the small Dongsimu Village nearly produces all the common seasonal fruits in north China and that the fruits here have been designated as tribute for more than 200 years, so the fruits in Dongsimu Village must have its unique characteristics.

The topography of West Mountain is high in the west and low in the east. The encircling high mountains and dense forest ward off the sand

□ 董四墓御果园遗址 Dongsimu Imperial Orchard

出产，而这里的水果能在200余年来被指定为朝廷贡品，自是有其独特之处。

西山一带地势西高东低。这里群山环抱、山高林密，挡住了隆冬时节来自塞外的风沙，从而能使果园长年气候湿润，在冬无严寒、夏无酷暑的环境中生长。每当大地复苏春暖花开的时候，一股股清澈甘甜的泉水由山岩石缝中淙淙流下，滋润养育着园里的一株株果树。在纵横交错的山谷中有难以计数的山泉，如冷泉、黑龙潭等，这些泉水又被巧妙地连在一起，顺着山谷河套流入董四墓村，浇灌了御果园中的果树。"董四墓御果园"中的桃树栽培最早可追溯至明代中叶，经不断的品种改良，到清代才逐渐将栽培面扩大。在清廷内务府把"董四墓御果园"产的水果指定为御用贡品时，还重金招募了一些果树栽培高手加盟。这使得果园的水果始终保持着在形、色、香、味上的高品质，也使这里所出产的水果更加远近闻名。而在种类如此多的果品中，又以果园产的大桃儿名气叫得最响。

传说清代乾隆年间的一个秋日，多

blown by wind from north of the Great Wall during winter time, so it is moist in all time of the year with no chilliness in winter and no hotness in summer. Whenever spring comes and flowers blossom, limpid, sweet and cool spring water will flow down the slot of rocks, moistening every fruit tree in the orchard. In the interlaced valley, there is countless spring such as Cold Spring and Black Dragon Spring and so on, which link each other by spring skillfully, flowing into Dongsimu Village along the valley river, irrigating the fruit trees in the imperial orchard. The peach planting history of Dongsimu Imperial Orchard could trace back to the middle period of Ming Dynasty. With continuing breed improving, the planting area expanded gradually in Qing Dynasty. When the Inner Affair Office of Qing Court designated the fruits of Dongsimu Imperial Orchard as tribute to emperor, the court recruited a group of master-hands with high salary to plant fruit trees, which kept the fruits high quality in shape, color, flavor and taste, and also made the fruits even more famous far and near. Among the various fruits, the big peach produced in the orchard enjoyed superior reputation.

The story goes that in an autumn day during Qianlong' s Reign of Qing Dynasty. Emperor Qianlong who had been busy with government affairs wanted to go out, so he ordered Ji Xiaolan, Minister of Li Department and the writer of *Imperial Collection of Four*, and other ministers with him travelling in West Mountain. Emperor Qianlong planned to visit the sightseeing spot to relax himself and look in his mother in Fragrant

日忙于朝政的乾隆皇帝这天想出去散散心，便命礼部尚书、编纂《四库全书》的纪晓岚和其他大臣侍驾，到西山游玩。此行乾隆打算游览一下西山的名胜放松放松，也顺便到香山看望太后。圣旨一下，随行人员赶紧收拾行装陪乾隆上路，只小半天光景，君臣一班人便到了离香山行宫不远的金山脚下，这次御驾出游正值金秋好时节，那微带凉意的秋风吹拂着乾隆，他四处眺望，被果园中红艳艳的桃子吸引了。乾隆的举止被正在旁边的纪昀看个正着，他瞅着乾隆紧盯桃园那若有所思的神态，心中对圣上所想的事情便猜到了八九分，当下略一沉思，便笑么滋儿的走上前去叩头禀奏道："皇上，您看眼前这果园里的鲜桃儿有多漂亮啊！听说是用玉泉山的泉水浇灌的桃树，故而桃子肉儿厚、汁儿多。如今老太后身子骨欠安，圣上何不趁前去探望之机，带上两篮鲜桃子让太后尝尝，太后一高兴，身子骨肯定会好起来的。"纪昀所言，正中乾隆下怀。乾隆高兴地说："纪爱卿，知朕者，世上只有纪大学士你呀！"

在君臣轻松的谈笑中，侍从已摘好了两篮又大又新鲜的桃子，于是一行人马继续前行，来到了香山行宫……几天后乾隆听说老太后自打吃了自己带去的鲜桃后，身子骨儿大为好转，没出三天就凤体康复了。乾隆自是欣喜万分，御笔将董四墓村果园赐名为"董四墓御果园"，并指定这里的水果为御用贡品，还给果园招募了一些栽培的果树能手。从那以后，"董四墓御果园"历经了长达近200年的风光，直到清帝退位。

Hills by the way. The retinue quickly tidied up luggage, and soon the monarch and ministers arrived at the foot of Jin Hill not far from Fragrant Hills Xanadu. The emperor's journey happened in golden autumn and the slightly cool autumn breeze fanned Emperor Qianlong. He looked around and was attracted by the red peaches. Ji Xiaolan noticed the behavior of Emperor Qianlong, and knew what the emperor was thinking about. He walked to the emperor with smile and said: "Your Majesty, how beautiful the fresh peaches in the orchard are! I hear that the peach trees are irrigated by the spring water of Yuquan Hill, so the peaches have thick flesh and rich juice. Right now the queen mother is unwell, why not take this opportunity of visiting to bring two basketful of fresh peaches for queen mother to taste. She will recover her health with rejoicing." Ji Xiaolan just hit Qianlong's heart and Qianlong said happily: "It is only Mr. Ji Xiaolan who knows me in the world."

With light-hearted talk and laugh, the chamberlaine had picked up two basketful of big and fresh peaches. Then the travellers went ahead to Fragrant Hills Xanadu. Several days later, Qianlong heard that his mother had recovered completely since she ate the fresh peaches. With gratulation, Qianlong named Dongsimu Village Orchard as Dongsimu Imperial Orchard, and designated the fruits there as tribute for imperial usage. In addition, the court also recruited a goup of master-hands for planting peach trees in the orchard. From then on, Dongsimu Imperial Orchard witnessed glory for nearly 200 years till Qing Emperor laid down the sceptre.

样式雷

Model Lei

□泰陵神道碑亭 Tablet Pavilion in front of Tailing Mausoleum

在历史悠久，有着八百多年建都史的世界文化名城北京，集中了许多举世闻名的名胜古迹。在漫长历史长河之中，我们的祖先用智慧和勤劳，建造了一座座规划整齐、巧夺天工的建筑。像故宫、颐和园、天坛、中南海等一大批古建筑，就是工匠们将技术与艺术巧妙结合的一组组经典之作。

明末清初，有一个非常有声望的宫廷建筑师雷发达，其家族又名“样式雷”。据相关史料记载，清朝的“样式雷”一族共有八代人供奉朝廷，从“样式雷”北京支系的雷发达入京，至光绪年间仍在崇陵工作的雷现采为止。雷家原为江西人，籍隶南康府建昌县。明朝末年木匠雷玉成为避流寇之乱，与子振声、振宙举家迁移金陵石城。清兵入关后，为重修李自成农民军所烧毁的宫殿，雷振

As a famous historical cultural city in the world, Beijing was established as the capital more than eight hundred years ago, so there were numerous world-famous places in Beijing. In the long history, our ancestors created a lot of wonderful architectures of perfect layout with their wisdom and hardwork. A great many ancient architectures such as the Forbidden City, the Summer Palace, the Temple of Heaven and Zhongnanhai, were just the classic masterpieces created by the craftsmen, which combined the technique and art perfectly.

In the late Ming and early Qing Dynasties, there was a reputable imperial architect named Lei Fada, whose family was called Model Lei. According to the historical data, from Lei Fada, who traveled to Beijing and opened a business in Beijing, to Lei Xiancai, who worked for the construction of Royal Tomb Chongling until the reign of Guangxu, there were totally eight generations of the family working for the Qing Court.

It's said that the family of Lei came from Jiangxi, originally living in Jianchang County in Nankang Area. According to the relative documents, the lineage of the family of Lei had lasted for a hundred years in Yuan Dynasty. It's recorded that the ancestor of Family Lei, Lei Yucheng, who was a carpenter at that time,

声的儿子雷发达与堂兄发宣，一同应募北上入京，这就是“样式雷”的发祥。

据雷金玉碑记载：“清康熙年间修建海淀延平工程，曾祖考雷金玉领楠木作工程，引正殿上梁，得蒙皇恩召见奏对，蒙亲赐内务府总理钦工处掌案，赏七品官，食七品奉。又因曾祖考七旬正寿，得蒙皇恩亲赐，命皇太子乾隆书‘古稀’二字匾额，供奉原籍大堂，七十一岁寿终。由内务府传，仰蒙皇恩赏盘费一百余金，奉旨驰驿归葬，圆寂江苏江宁府江宁县安德门西善桥。”这里所说的“海淀延平工程”上梁事就是指畅春园正殿九经三事殿上梁之时（为康熙二十七年至二十九年间，具体无从考）。因正殿上梁是建造中非常重要的仪式，康熙皇帝也亲临施工现场观礼。当年上梁是大木作最后一个关键环节，雷金玉时年恰好三十岁，其身手敏捷，猱升而上，只见他手握利斧三五下便手落榫合，相当出色地完成了任务。天子康熙见此顿时龙颜大悦，高度赞赏雷金玉的高超技艺，特颁旨召见他前来问话。康熙发现雷谈吐不凡，见多识广，当面就赏雷金玉为正七品官，让其总管皇家钦

□ 清东陵景陵　Jing Mausoleum in the Eastern Royal Tombs of Qing Dynasty

moved to Stone City of Nanjing with his two sons Zhensheng and Zhenyu, to avoid the bandits in the late Ming Dynasty. When the army of the Qing came in through the Shanhai Pass, Lei Fada, Lei zhensheng's son, and his cousin Faxuan traveled to Beijing at the request of Imperial Household Agency, which was planning to reconstruct the palace burnt down by the peasant army of Li Zicheng. So this is the beginning of the story of Model Lei.

The records in Lei Jinyu's stele read that in the years of Emperor Kangxi in Qing Dynasty, the family's ancestor Lei Jinyu participated in the Yanping construction of Haidian District, and finished the work of placing the beam of the building. For his achievement, the emperor called him in and honored him with the title chief imperial designer of Imperial Household Agency, enjoyed the treatment of the grade-7 officer. In his 70th birthday celebration, the emperor obliged him a stele inscribed in Prince Qianlong's handwriting: “*Guxi*(seventy years of age)”, which was presented in his ancestral home. When He died at the age of seventy-one, the emperor awarded him one hundred *liangs* silver and assigned Imperial Household Agency to give it to his family for the expense taking his body back home through post-house.

What was worth referring was something happened in the construction of the main hall in Garden of Everlasting Spring (It's between the 27th and 29th year of Kangxi, but the exact time wasn't affirmed) . Placing the beam in the construction of main hall was an important ritual, so Emperor Kangxi presented the construction

□ 承德避暑山庄烟雨楼 Cloud-and-Rain Building in the Imperial Mountain Summer Resort

工处的工作。而在此以前，雷金玉只是管装修的楠木作的一个普通工匠而已。此后，雷金玉先后参加了多项皇家建筑的设计和施工工作。当其因病死后，雍正皇帝又下圣旨通过驿站把雷金玉的遗体送回原籍安葬，这在当时是非常高的一种礼遇。在清朝统治中国的二百多年来，雷发达、雷金玉的子孙后代一直继承祖业为朝廷服务，因此深受历代皇帝的赏识，创造了宫廷建筑设计中令人叹为观止、独具一格的样式，所以被当时广大匠人尊称为“样式雷”。清代几乎所有的皇家建筑工程，大多都由“样式雷”家族直接主持设计和施工，譬如圆明园、颐和园、玉泉山、北海、清东陵、清西陵、承德避暑山庄等。

“样式雷”家族的古建筑风格与布局可谓千变万化，以依山傍水、清雅别致为主要风格，着力突出自然与人文景观的组合，根据不同条件，恰到好处地将一组组风格迥异的房舍，建成错落有致的古典式院落。格局设计严谨是其特点之一，步入院中给人以古朴华丽、曲

site for himself. At that time placing the beam was the last crucial step in the construction, and thirty-year-old Lei Jinyu was agility and talented, who ascended quickly and wielded his axe skillfully, completing the job perfectly. Emperor Kangxi was very delighted and appreciated his skill very much, so the emperor asked him to come up and talked with him. Kangxi found that Lei had a wide knowledge and had his own opinion, so Kangxi granted him regular grade-7 officer and the director of Imperial Construction Board on the sot, while Lei Jinyu was only a common craftsman in a workshop in charge of fitment before that. After that, Lei Jinyu joined in designing and constructing many imperial constructions. When he died of illness, Emperor Yongzheng issued an edict to carry his body back to his hometown through post-house, which was regarded an unusual courteous reception.

During more than two hundred years of Qing Dynasty rule, the offsprings of Lei Fada and Lei Jinyu inherited their ancestors’ position in the court and were appreciated very much by emperors of all dynasties. Due to the incredibly originative model building of the imperial construction they created, they were addressed respectfully by the craftsmen at that time as Model Lei. Almost majority of the imperial constructions in Qing Dynasty, such as the Yuanmingyuan (Garden of Eternal Spring), the Summer Palace, Jade Spring Hill, Beihai Park, Eastern Royal Tombs of Qing Dynasty, Western Royal Tombs of Qing Dynasty and the Imperial Mountain Summer Resort, were designed and constructed directly by Family of Model Lei.

径通幽的美好感觉是其二。而最能体现“样式雷”绝佳才华的是，能够在弹丸之地中因地制宜，将以小见大、以秀取胜的建筑风格体现得淋漓尽致。如在数组小巧玲珑的配套建筑物里，辅以中国古典名著中人物画的图案点缀在内檐的硬木上，如此妙笔更为雍荣华贵的皇家园林起到画龙点睛的作用。我国古代有八仙过海的神话传说，而传说中的蓬莱、瀛洲、方丈三座仙山又是诸神居住的仙境所在地。现在北京城中的中南海瀛台，就是昔日“样式雷”后代雷廷昌禀承皇帝旨意，巧借修筑瀛台，用来迎合其想改变枯燥无味的宫廷生活的想法而建造的。瀛台这一组古建筑的构图之美妙，营造水平之精湛，堪称中国建筑史上的经典杰作，它因而也最大程度地体现了“样式雷”建筑风格和思想。瀛台为中南海的一个组成部分，是一座四周环水的人工小岛，它位于碧波荡漾的中南海中间，因而又有南台之称。这里曾是清朝皇室从事政务、避暑、游览等主要活动的场所。在“戊戌变法”失败后，这里是慈禧幽禁光绪皇帝的地方。清初，“样式雷”的后代雷廷昌在领授皇命

□颐和园苏州街北侧 Suzhou Street in the Summer Palace

Ancient constructions created by family of Model Lei were incredibly variable in style and design, while the main style was elegant and unique, surrounded by mountain and close to water.They were stressing on the combination of natural and human scenery and taking the advantages of the landscape to arrange different style into an orderly classical compound. One of their features was the preciseness in layout design.The most outstanding characteristic of Model Lei was taking advantage of the landscape in a tiny area and interpreting the style to see the great vision within the small. As for the inside ornament of groups of delicate complex, they would paint some designs of characters in Chinese classical literary works on the hardwood, adding the finishing touch to the magnificent imperial garden with wonderful techniques. In China there are legendaries about Eight Immortals Crossing the Sea, and three Immortals' Mountains Penglai, Yingzhou and Fangzhang, which were the fairy land where the immortals lived. Yingtai in Zhongnanhai of Beijing, was constructed by the former Model Lei's offspring, Lei Tingchang. As a component of Zhongnanhai, Yingtai was an artificial island surrounded by water. It is located in the midst of Zhongnanhai, so it's also called Nantai, and it's the main place for Qing Emperors to handle state affairs, summer and excurse. After theWuxu Reform Movement failed, Empress Dowager Cixi immured Emperor Guangxu here. In the early days of Qing Dynasty, Lei Tingchang took the order of Emperor and had a good understanding of Emperor's intention, so he planned out a blueprint of a fairyland of

□圆明园大水法遗址 Grand Waterorks works in Yuanmingyuan

以后，自然对皇帝内心的真正想法心知肚明，因而就有了将瀛台建造成一个人间仙境的蓝图。像亭、台、楼、阁，均以古代典藉中的相关描写和出处为佐证，注意周围环境与整体景观的和谐，使两者之间起到交相辉映的最佳效果。远看粗壮的古木参天照眼，近观奇花异草散发沁人心脾的芳香，还有造型独特的一座座太湖山石镶嵌其中，各个景点间通过小小石桥连接在一起，美丽的小岛被碧水清波环抱在中间。“样式雷”家族创造的古代建筑艺术之精髓，一直被应用至今。“样式雷”家族为全人类留下了一幅幅不朽的艺术画卷。

human. He wanted to make Yingtai a visional and fascinating place away from tedious court life, so as to satisfy the need of the emperor to enter the fairy. The composition of building complex in Yingtai was so wonderful, and it's constructed so skillfully that it could be surely called a classical masterpiece in Chinese architectural history. The pavilions, terraces and towers were totally designed according to the descriptions in ancient books and records, and the style was in the pursuit of harmony between the surrounding environment and the whole sight, achieving the best effect of mutually supporting and reflecting. From a distance visitors can see the high old trees erecting to the sky, while standing closely, they can see rare flowers and grasses setting out refreshing fragrant, with unique Taihu Stones dotting everywhere. Spots are connected by little stone bridges and beautiful islands are surrounded by clear water. The traditional construction art which was created by the family of Model Lei is used until now. Model Lei left a great many enduring art scenes to human.

故宫角楼

Turret of the Forbidden City

□ 紫禁城外看故宫角楼　Turret of the Forbidden City

北京故宫曾是明清两代帝王行使最高权力的地方，也是中国古典宫廷建筑的集大成作品。除了内部巧夺天工的建筑外，环绕故宫城墙的四隅，还有被京城老百姓俗称为“九梁、十八柱、七十二条脊”的精美角楼作为点缀，为故宫的富丽堂皇锦上添花。

故宫角楼的建造有一个民间流传甚广的故事。明朝初年，朱棣皇袍加身做了永乐皇帝后，却时时不忘自己当王爷时的北京，执意要将南京城废弃，北上迁都于北京。迁都圣旨一下，满朝文武哗然，反对者居多。朱棣大怒，下旨规

The Palace Museum(the Forbidden City) was the imperial palace of Ming and Qing Dynasties, and is an outstanding model of Chinese classical imperial architecture. In addition to the ingeniously constructed buildings inside, there was a beautiful turret building in each corner of the palace. The unique structure was described vividly by Beijing natives as 9 beams, 18 columns and 72 ridges, adding to the beauty and magnificence of the Palace Museum.

The story about the turret of the Palace Museum was told from mouth to mouth in the folk. In the early days of Ming Dynasty, after Zhu Di was acclaimed Emperor Yongle, he always wanted to come back to Beijing where he settled as a prince, and insisted to abandon the city of Nanjing and move the capital northward to Beijing. When he issued the decree, all the civil and military officials were very astonished and the majority dissented from him. Zhu Di was furious about this, and ordered that everyone who disagrees on moving the capital be killed without exception. Thus no one dared to offend him.

It' s said that Zhu Di ordered his favorite minister to take charge of the project and asked him to add a unique and ingenious turret in each corner of the Palace Museum so as to make the

□故宫角楼近景 Turret of the Forbidden City

定凡反对迁都者"一律格杀无论"，至此再无人敢有任何犯上之举。

话说朱棣派往北京负责建造皇宫的亲信大臣被要求在外城墙的墙头，也就是在紫禁城城墙的四个犄角上，再加盖四座样式别具一格、造型精巧华丽的九梁十八柱七十二脊角楼，目的是为了衬托庄重华丽的主体建筑。亲信大臣哪里敢有丝毫的怠慢，赶紧回到家中简单地收拾行装，昼夜兼程赶往北京，到了京城就直接下榻在京南一座专门侍奉皇差的会馆里，并立即吩咐手下人将当时京城几十家大包木厂里有头有脸的工头、匠人都召至会馆，传达皇帝的圣旨，并责令他们一定要在五个月之内按圣旨建成四座角楼来。

亲信大臣吩咐之后，匠人们一时半会儿也拿不出更好的主意来，只好相约去分头想办法，大家伙心里都特别明白，这可是人命关天的大事!五个月不知不觉已过了一半儿，可是匠人仍然没有理出更好的头绪和拿出切实可行的方案

magnificent palace standout. The minister didn't hesitate and left for Beijing at double speed day and night. Hardly had he settled in an assembly hall especial for imperial envoy in the south of Beijing when he told his following to summon all the prestigious taskmasters and craftsmen of several dozen main workshops in Beijing, and conveyed the message to them from the emperor. He ordered them to build four turrets according to Emperor Zhu Di's demand in five months.

Receiving the assignment, the craftsmen just hadn't any good idea, so they determined to think about it separately. They all knew quite well it's a task relevant to their lives! Half the five months had passed quickly, but no one could think up a satisfying and efficient design. During the period, some craftsmen successively worked out several turret models, but all of them were thrown over due to some dissatisfaction in the style and configuration.

One day, a young craftsman named Fulai had nothing to do, so he walked out of yard of the workshop, strolled to Wenyu River and cooled himself under the shade of willows on the bank. Suddenly, he heard somebody hollering in the distance, "Sir! Sir! Guoguo (katydid)! Sell! Not expensive!" Fulai looked up and saw a healthy and energetic old man who carried two strands of katydid cages made of wheat stick on the end of the shoulder pole. Fulai suddenly got an idea. He observed the katydid cages connected by thin hemp rope carefully and found both design and figure of them was very ingenious just like the elaborate Chinese architectures of the fairyland

来。这期间，有的匠人分别烫制出几种角楼模型，但都因样式及结构与圣旨不符而遭否定。

这一天，一个年轻的工匠叫福来的在包木厂里闲来无事，便走出门遛遛达达地来到城北温榆河岸边的柳树下歇凉。忽然，从老远的地方传来一阵阵吆喝声："客官！客官！买蝈蝈喽!好听还不贵呀！"福来循声望去，只见一位鹤发童颜、声如洪钟的老翁用扁担挑着两大串串在一起的秫秸杆蝈蝈笼子。福来顿觉眼前一亮，继而仔细揣摩这些用细麻绳连在一起的蝈蝈笼子，发现它们无论构思的灵巧还是造型的别致，都犹如古人描述的蓬莱仙境中的亭、台、楼、阁。更巧的是，其形制和皇上要求的角楼完全一致。福来和许多匠人一样，正因为角楼的事情一直没有着落而心中烦闷。如今一看到这些大自然中鸣叫的绿蝈蝈和精巧别致的小蝈蝈笼子，灵感随即而来，顿时有几许轻松之感。福来立刻买了一笼蝈蝈。

当福来提着蝈蝈笼子进屋的时候，一连数日愁眉不展的匠人们都劈头盖脸地埋怨他不着边际。面对伙伴们的责备，福来慢慢地说："大家都过来仔细瞧瞧，这个蝈蝈笼子构思设计有多巧妙啊，你们看里面的梁啊，柱呀，脊呀什么的都有，我特地在回来的路上数过了，正好是'九梁、十八柱、七十二条脊'。"大家闻听此言，都争着抢着挤到蝈蝈笼子跟前来数。太绝了，蝈蝈笼子真好似一座小巧玲珑、栩栩如生的"九梁、十八柱、七十二条脊"角楼。

一阵喧闹过后，大家情绪渐渐平静

□ 仰视故宫角楼　Turret of the Forbidden City

(the place where the immortals lived) described in the ancient books. Just as other craftsmen, Fulai was worried about the design of turret all the time. The sight of the green katydid from the little nature and elaborate katydid cages gave him inspiration. Immediately Fulai felt relaxed, and he bought a cage of katydid at once.

When Fulai came back with the katydid cage, other craftsmen who had been anxious for several days all blamed him for the fiddle-faddle. In response to people' s blame, Fulai said slowly: "Please come and have a look at it. How ingenious was the cage! You see, there are beams, columns and ridges inside. I have counted carefully on the way; it' s just 9 beams, 18 columns and 72 ridges." Hearing that, everyone crowded to look and counted the inside components of the cage. It' s wonderful that the cage was very like a exquisite and visual small turret with 9 beams, 18 columns and 72 ridges.

As the tumult passed, they gradually calmed down. Taskmasters and craftsmen sat around the katydid cage and researched it earnestly and carefully. Before long, they worked out the blue-

下来，工头和匠人们围坐在蝈蝈笼子旁边，进行了一番认真研究与仔细推敲，并按图很快烫出纸样，做出了精巧的实物模型。有道是天助人也，匠人们终于在皇帝规定的期限内建造出巍然屹立于紫禁城城墙四个角上的美丽角楼。

这个富有传奇色彩的故事祖祖辈辈儿讲了足有好几百年，人们都风趣地说:“当年卖蝈蝈笼子的老翁，十有八九是鲁班爷下凡为人间排忧解难来的。”多少年来，来到紫禁城脚下，看见这四座凝聚先人智慧的角楼，人们就会情不自禁地想起蝈蝈笼子的美妙传说。

print accordingly and made a delicate physical model. As people always said, Heaven helps us all. Craftsmen finally built four beautiful turrets on corners of the Forbidden City before the deadline. This legendary story was told by generations for thousands of years. It' s said tastily the old man selling katydid cages was probably Lu Ban, who descended to the earth to help craftsmen solve the problem. For so many years, people would always remember the beautiful story about katydid cage whenever they come to the foot of the Forbidden City and sightsee the four turrets which embodied wisdom of the ancient people.

天坛古柏

Ever-green Cypress in the Temple of Heaven

□天坛古柏林 Ever-green Cypress in the Temple of Heaven

天坛是中国历史上建造年代最早、规模最大、保存最为完好的一组供帝王祭祀用的古建筑群落。除祭天的主体建筑祈年殿外，还有皇穹宇、回音壁、圜丘等一组组辅助性建筑，它们同样都是天下驰名的。这里只对皇家园林天坛另外一种景象"古柏"作一较为详尽的介绍。

天坛位于北京城南的崇文区，占地约4000亩，整个园内共植有六万余株各类树木。其中历经人世沧桑的古树达3500余株，而树龄在300多年以上的一级古柏约1150余株，数量之多居北京各大公园的首位。古柏有"珍贵的活文物"的美誉。远在明朝永乐四年(1406年)天坛始建的初期，在各主要建筑周围便将有帝王树之美称的桧柏、侧柏植于景点周围。至清乾隆盛世时代，社会稳定，又

The Temple of Heaven is the earliest, the best preserved, also the largest building complex for worshipping heaven in the history of China. Besides the main construction, the Hall of Prayer for Good Harvest, there is a group of supportive building, such as the Imperial Vault of Heaven, the Echo Wall and the Circular Mound Altar, which are also world-famous sightseeing spots. This article would only give a detailed introduction of another scene, the old cypresses in the Temple of Heaven.

The Temple of Heaven is located in Chongwen District, south of Beijing with an area of almost four thousand *mus*. It's a classical garden mainly for worshipping heaven, and there are over six thousand various kinds of trees in the garden, of which more than 3500 trees had a long history, and the number of first-grade old cypresses over 300 year-old is nearly 1500, more than any other famous parks in Beijing. The cypress has a reputation of rare living cultural relic. Back to the 4th year of Emperor Yongle, Ming Dynasty, when the Temple of Heaven was first built, there had been many cypresses and arborvitaes called Monarch Tree surrounding the main constructions. When it came to the Glorious Reign of Emperor Qianlong in Qing Dynasty, the society was stable and Emperor Qianlong

对天坛进行了一番大规模的改建。乾隆还多次颁旨在天坛的内坛、外坛补种大量的柏树，形成了如今成片古柏、古槐与建筑交相辉映，令人生发思古幽情的独特景观。

围绕坛庙植不同种类的树木自古就有先例。《论语》中就有这样的记载：“夏后氏以松，殷人以柏，周人以栗。”今天当游人漫步天坛之际，徘徊在古柏树林中，会惊叹一组组的宏伟建筑和古树景观，犹如人类的神来之笔，来自自然的一种清新，陶醉着四面八方的游客。纵观整个公园，苍翠照人的古柏棵棵雄浑壮美，枝繁叶茂。据专业人士介绍，在成片的柏树林中，能看见的古建筑其实只占总体的1／20，其余皆为绿云般的不同柏树所覆盖。古柏组成的片片林海

□天坛古柏林全景 Cypress Wood in the Temple of Heaven

changed and enriched the Temple of Heaven in a large scale, so as to present his godliness to the heaven. During the period, he issued edicts more than once to plant a great many cypresses around both the Inner Altar and the Outer Altar. Therefore today there are forests of cypress and pagoda trees surrounding the architectures, creating an unique scene which may bring people into a remote thinking.

It' s an ancient custom to plant various kinds of trees around altars and temples. In the Analects, there were records such as “The Xia sovereign planted the pine tree about them; the men of the Yin planted the cypress; and the men of the Shang planted the chestnut tree”. Today when tourists walk in the Temple of Heaven and wander in the forset of old cypresses, they would marvel at the scenery of groups of magnificent architectures and old trees. It' s such a wonderful artificial atmosphere with freshness of the nature that tourists from all over the world would immerge into it. All over the park, old verdant cypresses look beautiful and full of vitality. Experts introduce that with the coverage of cypresses, actually merely one twentieth of the architecture in the garden are visible. The sea of cypress forests, magnificent constructions center such as the Hall of Prayer for Good Harvest and groups of ingenious architectures complement with each other and creat a solemn and peaceful atmosphere in the Temple of Heaven together.

It' s important to realize that the effect of famous trees decorated in the scenery is just as good as the historic site itself. Take the famous

□掩映在天坛古树群中的建筑
The Buildings Surrounded by the Cypress Wood

与雄伟壮观的中心建筑祈年殿等以及一组组精巧辅助建筑相辅相成，共同营造了古天坛肃穆宁静的氛围。

古柏中特别值得一提的是，有不少名木植于各景点间，其影响足可以与所在的名胜古迹相媲美，如名扬五湖四海的“九龙柏”。它位于皇穹宇的西北角，这棵树的主干纵向褶皱，将古树分为九股皱折，似九条巨龙缠绕向上腾空般的神奇，因而得名“九龙柏”。“问天柏”，植于祈年殿附近，兀立挺拔的树木中有一枝杈单独伸出，造型宛若古人峨冠长袖，昂首挺胸，手臂直指天际。1986年，一位游人发现此树的状况酷似我国古代的爱国主义诗人屈原，因而突发奇想，冠以“屈原问天”的名字。此外，还有与长廊毗邻的“柏抱槐”、“迎客柏”等名木，各自有其独特的风采。

古柏在天坛扎根数百年，迎风傲雪仍然枝干粗壮，高挺着它那一年四季永披绿装的硕大树冠，与这里良好的自然条件密不可分。同时，为保护这片珍贵的存世不多的古柏树林，园中的广大园林工人和科技人员通力合作，加大科研

Nine-Dragon Cypress for example. It is located on the northwest corner of the the Imperial Vault of Heaven. The tree trunk has crimples in the longitude, and looks like comprised of nine dragons coiling and flying; hence it' s named Nine-Dragon Cypress. Located about the Hall of Praying for Good Harvest, the erected Asking-Heaven cypress has a single branch reaching out, just like a person who wears a high hat and long sleeve cloth points his finger directly to the heaven. In 1986, a tourist found that there were sameness between the figure of the tree and Chinese ancient patriotic poet Qu Yuan, so an ingenious mind came to him and he called the tree Qu Yuan Asking-the-Heaven. Besides, there are famous trees such as the Cypress Holding-Pagoda tree and the Guest-Meeting Cypress adjacent to the Long Corridor, and each has a special taste.

Growing in the Temple of Heaven for hundreds of years, old cypress undertook all the challenge and test, always erecting with its large crown ever-green all the year around. It's due to the favorable natural condition; meanwhile, in order to protect the rare cypresses existing in the world, the workers in the garden coordinated with technical staff, strengthened scientific research, and maintained the old cypress with scientific method and technique, playing an important role in keeping the old cypress growing healthily. Moreover, considering the needs of real situation in the process of old cypress' s growing, they took measures accordingly, including digging deep well, laying bricks for breathing and setting support for feeble trees and so on. These efficient and practical measures all

□ 浓密柏树林中的祈年殿神厨及长廊 Sacred Kitchen and Long Corridor in the Thriving Crypass Wood

力度，以科学的方法和手段养护古柏，为古柏的茁壮成长洒下许多辛勤的汗水。他们还考虑到古柏在生长中的一些实际需要，相应采取开挖深水井、铺设通气砖、支撑弱树等一系列有效务实的措施，都收到了良好的效果。

二十多年以前，时任美国国务卿的亨利·基辛格访问北京期间曾来天坛游览。基辛格对中华民族传统文化无限赞叹，对随行人员发出这样耐人寻味的感慨："建筑物和房子容易建造和保存下来，而这么多粗壮的大树能保留几百年乃至更长的年代，是一件非常了不起的大事情，在这一点上，只有在东方古国中国才能做到……"

had good results.

It's said that seeing once is better than hearing a hundred times. More than 20 years ago, when the former United States Secretary of State Henry Kissinger visited Chinese capital Beijing, he came to the Temple of Heaven and highly praised Chinese traditional culture. He sighed with emotion to the entourage: "It's easy to build and preserve architectures and houses, but it's really something to preserve so many sturdy trees for hundreds years, even longer. Only the ancient oriental country China could achieve that……" No matter the people living under the walls of the Palace or the foreign friends coming for the first time such as Kissinger, Beijing's Temple of Heaven and cypress always have more or less some fascination which is difficult to describe.

No matter in spring or in summer, in autumn or in winter, when you want to avoid the uproar and find a good place full of nature pleasure in Beijing, the Temple of the Heaven is the first choice. The scenery here would give you a happy mood, and the natural carpet consisted by green pastures which exist with cypress harmoniously and form a mutually dependent atmosphere. In the days that advocating care for life and health, picturesque scenery and clear environment have uncountable important relation with every one and every family.

佘家馆

Memorial of the She Family

□明袁大将军墓　Tomb of Gen.Yuan

在北京东南部，广渠门内东花市斜街52号(现在的北京五十九中旁边)，有一座苍松翠柏环绕、名震海内外的墓祠，它就是著名的袁崇焕墓。那么袁崇焕到底为何许人呢?人们为什么要世代纪念他呢？其与北京城是什么关系呢?

袁崇焕(1584～1630年)，字元素，祖藉广东东莞石碣镇水南乡守义坊，是明末著名的军事家、政治家。万历进士，官至兵部尚书，督师辽蓟。明朝末年，国势衰弱，民不聊生，吏治腐败，摇摇欲坠的大明江山处在内忧外患的双重夹击

The memorial of the She Family, located in 52nd Oblique Street, Inner Guangqu Gate and surrounded by a forest of pine and cypress, was the world-famous Memorial of Gen. Yuan Chonghuan. Then who was Yuan Chonghuan on earth? Why did people commemorate him for generations? And what's the relationship between him and Beijing City?

Yuan Chonghuan (1584-1630), whose style name was Yuansu, born in Shouyifang Shuinan Village, Guangdong Province. He was a famous militarist and politician of Ming Dynasty and was once entitled the Secretary in the Board of War, and was appointed the Governor of Liaodong with full authority to handle all forces outside the Passes. Towards the end of the Ming Dynasty, the Emperor's rule was waning, and life for the masses was hard with rife corruption in officials. So the tumbledown Ming Dynasty was confronted both rebellion inside and aggression abroad from increasingly powerful Manchu. In the 2nd year of Chongzhen (1629), Huangtaiji defeated all the armies in the path and led up to Beijing with his Eight Banners in less than eight months, threatening Beijing, the capital of Ming Dynasty. Taking the emperor's order, Gen. Yuan led more than ten thousand soldiers from Ningyuan to Beijing and settled along the

□清明之际袁氏宗属前来祭祀

The Family of Yuan Sarficing before the Tomb

之中。而此时生活在山海关外的后金势力却日益强大，不断骚扰内地。明崇祯二年(1629年)，皇太极率八旗兵直逼北京城下，北京危在旦夕。袁崇焕临危授命，率万余名明军火速从宁远增援北京，屯兵在今广渠门、龙潭湖一线。

在这场著名的保卫北京城的生死大战中，袁崇焕率领明军浴血奋战，左右冲杀，身上多处受伤，但他依然毫不畏惧奋勇杀敌。据史料记载，仅广渠门一战就从巳时(上午10点左右)一直战斗到酉时(下午6时左右)，一举重创远道而来、不可一世的皇太极。这场有关北京城生死存亡的决战，前前后后持续长达一个多月，袁崇焕及所率明军在北京人民的大力支持下，连战连胜，最终取得北京保卫战的胜利。

皇太极的八旗军在京城广渠门外与明军的决战中惨败而归，但其对大明政权取而代之的野心则愈来愈强烈。见单靠军事进攻难以奏效，经过一番苦思冥想，便出台了一个反间计，陷害袁崇焕与后金有密约。昏庸的崇祯皇帝果然不辨真伪，听信传言。遂将立下赫赫战功的袁大将军囚禁入狱。崇祯三年（1630

Guangqu Gate and Dragon Pond Lake.

In the famous battle defending the capital, Yuan Chonghuan led the Ming army to fight bravely. Even though he was wounded, he still fought against the Manchurians army bravely without hesitation. It's noted that only the battle in Guangqu Gate had lasted from ten A.M to about six P.M. This time Yuan had a good beat on the extremely arrogant invader Huangtaiji. Under the support of the masses, Yuan Chonghuan's army got successive victories.

Huangtaiji's Eight Banners Soldier was defeated by Ming army in the battle outside the Guangqu Gate and retreated, but their ambition was more and more strong. Realizing that it's unfeasible to achieve their goal by force, they had a new idea, and made up a story that Gen. Yuan had collaborated with the Manchu and would betray the Ming court. The fatuous Emperor Chongzhen were actually tricked by the enemies and ordered to arrest the illustrious Commander Yuan. In the 3rd year of Chongzhen (1630), the imperator of the Ming condemned illustrious Commander Yuan to death in Caishikou wrongly and forbade no one to bury his body. A righteous person from Shunde, Guangdong whose surname was She, didn't want to see such an upright and outspoken commander who would abandon his life to protect the safe of Ming to suffer that, and risked his own life to carry the body secretly at night the next day. Then he buried Yuan in Righteousness Garden of Guangdong inside Guangqu Gate. From then on, he changed his name and determined to guard the tomb of Commander Yuan all his life. He en-

年)，袁崇焕被冤杀在菜市口，暴尸于荒野，眼见刚直不阿为大明江山宁可肝脑涂地的袁大将军就这样不明不白的含冤而死，与袁崇焕同是来自广东顺德的一位佘姓义士，趁着翌日夜深人静，冒着株连九族的危险盗回尸骨，运至广渠门内旧广东义园埋葬。此后他隐姓埋名，立志终身为袁大将军守墓。并嘱托后人也要世世代代为督师守陵，永不做官，不要回祖籍广东，待自己死后，也要把自己葬于此地。佘家后代牢记祖训，一直为袁崇焕守墓至今长达370余年，如今到年过六旬的佘幼芝女士为第17代，这就是广渠门内有名的“佘家馆”。现在散居在世界各国的袁氏宗亲会的许多人每年都要前来这里祭祀先祖。

据材料显示，在明末清初，广渠门周围方圆几十里，通称“广东义园”，原意是为来自广东籍在京为官的人提供一块去世后的公用墓地。自袁大将军遇害在此地安葬后，依照先祖的遗训，历代佘家人就在这里以出租土地和刮绒活为生，日子虽然过得有些拮据，但丝毫不悔。自佘义士以后，佘家世世代代再没有人为官，但一直以读好书、念好书为本。佘家先祖与袁大将军多年来一同为朝廷效力，所以深知袁大将军的为人，他一向廉洁自律，爱民如父，无论是大将军本人和佘家先祖都把忠义二字看得很重。佘家祖祖辈辈300多年来为袁大将军守坟无怨无悔，就是佘家从心眼儿里觉得为这位民族英雄守得值，而且从来痴心不改。

据说袁大将军的妹妹出嫁时，身为兵部尚书的他只陪送给一把小小的泥

trusted his offspring to guard it from one generation to the next and never took government station. Before the death he requested that his body be buried at the same spot instead of carrying back to Guangdong. The offspring of She kept his word in mind and guarded Yuan Chonghuan's tomb for more than 370 years. Today the 17th generation Ms. She Youzhi is in her sixties. This was the famous Memorial of the She's inside the Guangqu Gate. Until now the offspring of Yuan scattering all over the world still come here to commemorate their ancestor every year.

According to Ms. She Youzhi, during the late Ming and the early Qing Dynasties, the area within several dozen *lis* was generally called Righteousness Garden of Guangdong, which meant to be a common graveyard for people from Guangdong Province who took government position in Beijing. According to ancestor's word, generations of She family made a living here by hiring land and doing some handwork after Commander Yuan was buried here. Although the life was hard, they felt no regret. After the righteous person whose surname was She, nobody in the family ever took position in the government, but they always stressed on learning. The ancestor of She worked together with Commander Yuan in the court for many years, so he knew Yuan's personality quite well. Yuan was honest and upright and always put the masses on first. Both Yuan and She took loyalty and righteousnesss as their principle. For three hundred years, this is the reason why generations of She guarded Yuan Chonghuan's tomb without complaint.

□第十七代守墓人佘幼芝女士（左）
Ms.She Youzhi,the 17th Generation of She Family

壶，崇祯冤杀袁大将军之后，抄家者竟然两手空空，一无所得。这几百年间，近现代不少仁人志士，如人民的总理周恩来，社会名流康有为、张伯驹、蔡廷锴、叶恭绰、梁启超等人先后拜谒过袁大将军墓祠。特别值得一提的是，在解放初期北京市政府搞市政规划时，曾计划将原广东义园佘家馆附近的坟墓全部迁移，佘家第15代传人佘恩兆为保袁大将军之墓祠而四处奔走相告，此事还得到柳亚子、章士钊、蔡廷锴、叶恭绰等人的支持，他们联名上书给主席。毛主席很快在1952年作出批示："请彭真同志处理，我意如无大碍，袁崇焕祠墓应予保存，毛泽东，5月16日"。

我们不管领袖还是平民对民族英雄，永远怀有特殊感情，如果袁大将军在天有灵，他会含笑于九泉的。袁大将军生前有两句至理名言："心术不正得罪于天地，言行要留好样与儿孙"。佘女士表示，现在她本人60多岁了，但佘家十几代人历经370多年为袁大将

It's said that when Yuan's sister got married, he only gave her a small pot, although he was Secretary in the Board of War. After Gen. Yuan was killed unjustly, someone sent to confiscate his property found nothing at all. During the last several hundred years, many people of far sight such as Premier Zhou Enlai and the personages Kang Youwei, Zhang Boju, Cai Tingkai, Ye Gongchao and Liang Qichao all visited the Memorial of Yuan Chonghuan. What especially worthy of mention was in the first stage of liberation, when Government of Beijing planed to redesign the layout of the city, the tombs around Memorial of She inside the former Righteousness Garden of Guangdong should be totally moved away. In order to preserve Yuan's Memorial, the 15th generation of the family, She Enzhao appealed to all the people concerned. He got support from Liu Yazi, Zhao Shizhao, Cai Tingkai and Ye Gongchao, and they wrote a letter to Chairman Mao. Mao quickly issued a document in 1952:"Comrade Peng Zhen should deal with this. As for my own opinion, we should preserve Yuan Chonghuan's tomb as possible as we can. Mao Zedong. May 16th."

From leaders to the masses, everyone has a special feeling for Yuan Chonghuan. He would be gratified if he knew that at the other world. Yuan Chonghuan left us two wisdoms, "Bad intention would be hard to exist in the world; Good words and deeds should be passed to offspring." Ms. She indicated that herself had been in sixties, and more than ten generations of her family had guarded Yuan Chonghuan's tomb for 370 years, but they never thought about

军守墓，真是一点都不是为别的，友情、忠义一直是佘家为人处事的座右铭。不论经历多少艰难曲折，始终坚持要上不能愧对列祖列宗，下不能对不起子孙后代。这些平凡的人民都是中华民族的脊梁。

something for return, because loyalty to friendship and righteousness was always their motto. No matter how hard it's, they would live up to the expectation of ancestor and set a good example to their offspring. These ordinary people were really the back of Chinese nation.

大师与国粹

Master and National Legacy

梅兰芳与丹青

Mei Lanfang and Chinese Painting

京剧四大名旦之首、梨园表演艺术宗师梅兰芳先生的高超京剧艺术已经为世人熟知，但梅先生绘画艺术才华则知者廖廖。

京剧乃国之瑰宝，戏曲界名角善丹青者大有人在。如已故武生泰斗“同光十三绝”之一的杨小楼，著名须生、“铁嗓子”余叔岩，名旦荀慧生、张君秋等人都有数量不等的绘画作品存世。但梅兰芳大师不仅仅将习画作为个人嗜好，而是真正将其融入舞台表演，使丹青为戏曲艺术锦上添花。

梅兰芳先生一生为人正派坦诚，十分讲情重谊，结交了不少名人雅士，并不时邀友于家中品茗小聚。一些名扬四海的画坛巨匠成为了梅府的坐上宾，如在晚清民初已享誉中外的国画宗师吴昌硕、齐白石，以擅画仕女、梅花，名扬美术界的汪蔼士，还有著名画家陈半丁，清道光皇帝的四世孙溥心畬等人。这几位堪称国宝级的画家在“缀玉轩”（梅兰芳为书斋所起的雅名）留下了一段段鲜为人知的佳话。

擅画梅花、仕女的汪蔼士老先生，与梅大师通过丹青结交的师生之谊颇具代表性。汪老不仅在画坛久负盛名，还是一位痴情梅派艺术的老戏迷和票友，只要时间允许，凡京城有戏园子上演梅兰

It' s well-known that Mei Lanfang, the most famous Beijing Opera female character performer, had a very high artistic standard, but few people know about his talent in Chinese painting.

Beijing Opera is a costful heritage of Chinese art, and lots of famous opera actors are also good Chinese painters. Such as the old Beijing Opera martial master Yang Xiaolou, Yu Shuyan, Xun Huisheng, and Zhang Junqiu, all had some Chinese painting works left behind. Whereas Master Mei Lanfang not only took Chinese painting as a hobby, but also put this art into his stage performance and enhanced his Beijing Opera.

Mei Lanfang was an honest and quite hospitable person, and had many educated friends in all kinds of art field. He loved to invite friends home, and among these guests there were some famous Chinese painting artists, like Chinese painting master Wu Changshuo, Qi Baishi, and Wang Aishi who is good at painting female figure and plum blossom. There also are famous painter Chen Banding and Pu Xinshe. All these artists with national reputation have left a wonderful story in Zhuiyuxuan, Mei Lanfang's personal study.

Among these anecdotes there is a story that Master Wang Aishi became the teacher of Mei Lanfang in Painting. Wang not only had a great

芳先生打头牌的戏，基本上不落空。在欣赏梅派名戏名段之际，还经常携带纸笔，将梅先生在舞台上塑造的不同角色凝聚于纸上，以供大师比较对照。汪老成为梅先生的至交，经常被请至府邸小叙，是光顾"缀玉轩"的常客之一。1951年，正值百花吐蕊、蜂飞蝶舞的仲春时节，因事离京月余的汪霭士老先生惦念着多日不见的梅兰芳先生，特地选择在五月初一个风和日丽的日子，带着从杭州西湖岸边茶农那里买来的新龙井，前往位于西城区护国寺街的的梅家看望。梅先生见到有些日子没来的老朋友，心中甭提有多高兴了，马上将汪蔼士迎到上房落坐。宾主二人边喝茶边聊天，话题从古延伸至今。这时汪蔼士关切地问："畹华，您的艺名既然叫梅兰芳，这名儿起得冰清玉洁、高雅庄重，如果再研习些丹青，专攻梅兰，那您可真是艺术成双啦。"梅兰芳闻听此言，正合自己由来已久的学画想法，立马答道："汪先生说得好，那恕小弟我不客气了，从今儿个起拜您为师，专习梅、兰、竹、菊如何……"汪蔼士没有推辞微笑着答应了。

□梅兰芳舞台真实布景 Mei Lanfang's Stage Setting Art

□梅兰芳大剧院 Mei Lanfang Grand Theater

interest in painting, but also was deeply amazed by Beijing Opera. As long as he had spare time, he would come to see Mei Lanfang's performance in Beijing without delay. During his enjoyment of Mei Lanfang's show, he would put Mei's figures in stage on paintings for Mei's reference. He had become one of Mei Lanfang's best friend, and was often invited to Mei Lanfang's study. In the mid of Spring 1951 when Wang Aishi just came back to Beijing, he took some new tea bought from tea farmers around West Lake, Hangzhou, and came Huguosi Street, Xicheng District to see his friend Mei Lanfang. Because they hadn't seen each other for a period of time, Mei Lanfang was quite happy of his dropping by, and took Wang Aishi to his study. While they chatted, and enjoyed the tea, Wang Aishi mentioned, "Wanhua, your art name is Mei Lanfang, such a name is quite elegant, but if you could learn some Chinese painting, especially plum blossom and orchid painting, would it be more perfect?" In fact, the same thought have been in Mei Lanfang's mind for a long time, so he answered right away: "That's a great idea.Would you take in me as you student? Could you start to teach me the painting of plum, orchid, bamboo and

从此，梅兰芳先生演戏之余就开始挥笔泼墨，研习丹青。而汪蔼士则尽其所能，将多年来在绘画技巧上的心得体会尽情倾吐：“画画与演戏虽行业不同，但它们有许多共性，如唱戏讲悟性，丹青亦如此，用心血作画持之以恒，日后定能大器晚成……”梅兰芳受益匪浅。经过一段时间的练习，天赋极佳的梅兰芳笔下的一枝枝梅花已经具有了卓尔不群的姿态，似生长在大自然中的梅园那样，迎风霜傲雨雪，争相怒放、香飘四野。所画兰花则犹如盛开在空旷山谷中，幽雅高贵。在作画当中，梅先生努力探求深含其中的动与静、虚与实、神与态等技法，力求达到心灵与大自然的完美融合。

随着绘画艺术的日臻成熟，勇于在传统京戏上推陈出新的梅兰芳先生，及时将两者有机结合在一起，为国粹的进一步繁荣、发展、革新作出了有益的尝试。如先生在其表演过的梅派名剧《西施》、《洛神》、《天女散花》、《黛玉葬花》、《贵妃醉酒》中，就极为巧妙地配合相关剧情，在舞台上一挥而就，把一幅幅佳作奉献给广大观众。据载，梅大师晚年曾欣然挑起排演由河南豫剧移植过来的《穆桂英挂帅》这出大轴戏的头牌，地点在大栅栏的中和戏院，当时演出可谓盛况空前，戏报刚贴出来三天票即告售罄，不少痴情戏迷还是不死心地徘徊在戏园子门前等退票。演出开始前，著名画家陈半丁老先生特地来到后台，把自己精心所画的一幅《铁干红梅》赠与梅兰芳，画面题辞为“老梅越老越精神”，由此表达社会各界人士对这位德艺双馨的老艺术家的由衷祝贺。

chrysanthemum?” Wang Aishi said nothing but accepted. From then on, Mei Lanfang started to learn Chinese painting when there were no performings. Wang Aishi taught him all he knew. He said: “Painting is different from Beijing Opera, but they have quite many similarity. Your art need savvy, the same is painting. Paint with all your heart, and keep on painting, and you will succeed.” Mei Lanfang accepted all his teaching, after some time practicing, the plum he draw has got better and better. The orchid on his painting looked just like in the wild valley. When painting, Mei Lanfang tried to balance all the comparisons including runing and stillness, vanity and reality, in order to reach a perfect harmony with nature.

His painting skill got better, then Mei Lanfang mixed painting with Beijing Opera. His test had some contribution to the prosperous development and evolution of Beijing Opera. In some of his performances, such as *Xi shi, Luo shen, Daiyu Bury Flower, Yang Guifei Got Drunk* and some other works, and he would do some painting on the stage as the story went, and gave those paintings to audiences. According to record, aged Mei Lanfang agreed to perform in a drama called *Mu Guiying Takes Command*, coming from Henan Opera, and he performed in Zhonghe theatre of Dashanlan. When the poster came out, tickets were sold out in 3 days, and many fans still waited at the gate, hoping someone would gave out some tickets. Before the performance, Chinese painting artist Chen Banding brought one of his work *Ironed-Branch Red-Plum* to the backstage, and presented to Mei Lanfang. This was the congratulation of people from all fields to the aged artist.

侯宝林与相声艺术

Hou Baolin and Comic Dialogue Art

□ 侯宝林故居，北京宣武门外香炉5条8号
The Former Residence of Hou Baolin

在北京宣武门外海柏寺街一带，有个叫香炉营五条的狭窄胡同，其中的8号院是已故著名相声表演艺术大师侯宝林先生生活和居住过的院落（1954～1959年）。这是一处由若干间并列的排子房组成的房舍，现已被每家住户垒起的院墙界定为十几个独立的院子，院内有三间普通的北房和东西两侧的厢房，一棵粗大的香椿树扎根于小院的东耳房旁。

At the Haibaisi Street outside Xuanwu Gate, there is a narrow alley called Xiangluyingwutiao. Hou Baolin, the comic dialogue master, used to live in the No. 8 courtyard during 1954 to 1959. There used to be several rows of houses, and now they has been separated into many small courtyards with brick walls. Within the courtyard there are 3 common houses with east and west wing-rooms with big trees in. Beside the east wing-room, there plants a strong Tree of Heaven.

Hou Baolin (1917~1993), born in Beijing, is a great comic dialogue master. He was from a poor family and was passed to old Mr. Hou as a foster son when he was only 3 years old, for poor living conditions. His foster father had been married but hadn't given birth to any children. The family was not rich, and the foster father worked as a chef in a local school to earn their only income.They used to live in Shishahai area of Xicheng District. Because of their financial condition, Hou Baolin only went to private school for several years, but he got matured spiritually in early age. In order to help the family, young Hou Baolin came to southern city with the recommendation of relatives, and easily got into the show ground of Tianqiao, which was the recreational place for ordinary people, and started his life of roadside performance.

侯宝林（1917～1993年），北京人，满族，杰出的相声表演艺术大师。自幼家境贫寒，三岁左右时因生活所迫由家人作主将其过继给婚后无嗣的侯老先生（随养父为侯姓）。养父家当年住在西城区什刹海附近，属城市贫民阶层，生活并不宽裕，全家基本靠养父为附近一所学校当个毫无经济保障的厨师勉强维持生计。侯宝林只断断续续念过几年私塾，但他懂事很早，正如人们常说的“穷人的孩子早当家”，为给家中减轻负担，小小年纪的侯宝林经演艺圈内亲戚朋友的引荐来到城南，顺利地融入到当时专供平民阶层消闲找乐子的天桥演艺场，开始走上了一条民间艺人“撂地”的生活道路（注：行话称“平地抠饼”，指艺人在地摊上表演节目混口饭吃的意思）。

初涉天桥的几年，侯宝林边向师傅学习，边在场子里与师傅共同表演“双簧”，即“现学现卖”（老话儿叫“撂地献艺”）。昔日老天桥从艺人员成份复杂，但也有可以肯定的地方，即人人“身怀绝技”。即便如此，能维持正常生计的也只是极少数人，大多数人过的都是半饥半饱的穷困日子。尽管小侯宝林其貌不扬，人长得精瘦，个头又不高，但艺术天赋与生俱来，浑身上下透着一股子一点就通的机灵劲儿。虽说初涉民间艺人圈，侯宝林却有着一股子初生牛犊不怕虎的精神，丝毫不怯场，而且越是看的人越多发挥越棒。就拿“双簧戏”来说，师傅仅口头连说带比划地示范三两回，表演起来侯宝林竟然能与师傅配合得天衣无缝，一来二去引来不少捧场的人，因此颇得师傅喜欢。随着每天没时没晌的

In the beginning, Hou Baolin learned from his master and at the same time performed in the show place. During that time, the performers at Tianqiao had all kinds of background, but it’s certain that everyone had their own talents. Even so, few of them could make a living and most of the performers led a poor life. Hou Baolin’s appearance was not attractive, but he had some endowment in art, capable of easily learning things with a little teaching. Though he was a freshman in this profession, he never had pusillanimity in the stage, and the more audience there were, the more excited he got. Take a double-reed show as an example, his master only taught him couple of times, and he could cooperate with the master harmoniously, thus his master liked him very much. They offered shows everyday with no time limits, so Hou Baolin’s performing skill got improved quickly. With time passing by, he had attracted many old audiences. This made his master quite happy, and started to regard him with special respect about his apprentice. When a double-reed show was at its climax, little Hou Baolin would come to the audience and said, “Ladies and gentlemen, thank you for enjoying our performance, please forgive us if there is anything unsatisfactory, and do what you can to help us with our performance.” The audience was still waiting for the following show, and would pay him some money happily.

Hou Baolin grew up in such a performance life, and started to think more. He got aware that lots of skilled performers had little audience for their simple way of performing, and decided to manage several special skills to deal with a hard

连轴转，侯宝林的表演技艺愈加娴熟，久而久之已有不少愿看他演出的较为固定的回头客。这让吃了多半辈子开口饭的师傅不由得喜上眉梢，自然高看这位虽入道不长却颇有艺缘的徒弟三分。每当一场双簧高潮迭起、观众胃口被吊足时，小侯宝林总是恰到好处地来到场子边的人群前，双手抱拳客气地说："诸位大爷、大妈、叔叔、婶子，老少爷们，今儿个晚辈当着大家伙的面儿献丑了，有什么照顾不周的地方还请大伙儿多担待，有劳您有钱帮个钱场儿，没钱帮个人场儿……"来此找乐儿的众人正沉浸在兴头上，因此纷纷慷慨解囊。

随着年龄的增长，加上天桥游艺场从艺生活的磨练，勤于思考的侯宝林视野更为开阔。特别是目睹旧社会不少老艺人虽日日拼命演出，可由于艺术表现手法单一还是观众稀少得可怜，侯宝林暗下决心，一定要掌握几种绝活来应付艰难的生活。有心的侯宝林抽空奔波于说评书的、说相声的、拉洋片的、唱京戏的众多艺人的场子旁，认真观摩，边看边在心里头揣摩，偷着学艺以不断丰富自己。在20世纪30年代就已名扬天桥游艺场乃至老北京四九城的，如说评书的吴辅庭、哈辅源、单长德，以说学逗唱的全活儿吸引四方来客的天桥相声老艺人"百鸟张"、"蛤蟆头"、"粉字颜"，凭吹拉弹唱遐迩闻名的"随缘乐"、"哨子马"、"胡胡李"、"口子红"等多个行当艺人的场子边，都留下了侯宝林暗自学艺的身影。这种博采众长的学艺经历所积累的丰富经验，为几十年后侯宝林成为一代相声表演艺术大师打下了扎实全面的艺术功底。

□ 侯宝林与大弟子贾振良
Hou Baolin and His Prentice Jia Zhenliang

life. So he went around in his spare time to watch many other performers' show, and secretly learned their skills. At 1930s, he had made his name in Tianqiao area and the whole Beijing city. He had learnt from story-telling people like Wu Futing, Ha Fuyuan, Shan Changde, and old Comic Dialogue Performers like Suiyuanle, Shaozima, Huhuli, Kouzihong, etc. All these experiences has established the basis for him to become a great Cross Talk master.

In several decades, anyone who saw Hou Baolin's performances gave very high comments about his knowledge in history and culture. His performance gave people an elegant enjoyment, and no matter how many times you see or hear his works, you will never get bored. All these come from his linguistic ability and artistic performance. His works are about various topics, giving several generations of Chinese people endless happiness and laugh. But if we look back, his success has a strong connection with the source of Beijing folk art, with Tianqiao area, and with all the folk artists living in this place. Without this special place, we would not have seen Hou Baolin, a great cross talk master.

数十年来观众欣赏侯宝林的每一段脍炙人口的相声，无不惊叹其浓郁的历史、民俗和文化内涵。侯宝林的相声立意清新、格调高雅，说、学、逗、唱雅而不俗，幽默诙谐，令人百听不厌、百看不烦，充分展现了侯宝林先生杰出的语言天赋和卓越的表演艺术。他的相声段子题材涉猎相当广泛，雅俗共赏，给中国几代人带来过无尽的欢乐和笑声。回首侯老先生成功的背后，离不开老北京平民艺术的发祥地天桥，离不开曾给过侯宝林艺术哺育的众多天桥民间艺人，可以说，没有天桥这片特殊的民间艺术土壤，就不会有日后一代相声表演艺术大师侯宝林。

北洋军阀统治时期，人民生活苦不堪言，迫于生计，侯宝林往往是双簧戏与相声评书轮换演出。但无论是演双簧还是说相声，只要侯宝林往场子中央一站，立即会引来里三层外三层的观众。此时，刚刚20岁左右的侯宝林开始了与另一位相声表演艺术家郭启儒老先生几十年的合作，直到郭老先生在“文革”中因病去世。侯宝林演出的场地不仅是天桥一处，鼓楼、什刹海、东四牌楼、西四牌楼一带的茶馆、书场，西单商场等繁华热闹场所以及广播电台等地，经常是两位相声艺人早年为观众登场送乐、献艺录音的地方。

已有一定名望的侯宝林并没有因观众的认同而陶醉其中。为了在相声艺术方面再上一个台阶儿，侯宝林经曲艺界朋友从中搭桥儿，正式拜20世纪20年代在北京相声界赫赫有名的老前辈朱阔泉（艺名：大面包）先生为师。经几年

During the warlord’s period, people had a really hard time. In order to make a living, Hou Baolin often had to give performance like Cross Talk in turn. No matter what he was performing, all he needed to do was to stand at the middle of the stage, and soon audiences would gather around. At that moment, Hou Baolin started his cooperation with another cross talk master, Guo Qiru. They worked together until Master Guo passed away in the cultural revolution. Hou Baolin gave performance not only in Tianqiao area, but also in tea houses and story-telling theatres in Gulou, Shichahai, Dongsipailou, Xisipailou, even in Radio Station.

Hou Baolin got famous, but he would pursue more. In order to reach a higher standard, with the help of friends in artistic fields, he formally became the apprentice of an old cross talk master, Zhu Kuoquan, who was really famous in 1920s. After several years of learning from Master Zhu, Hou Baolin finally became the best student within all his apprentices. Hou Baolin and Guo Qiru’s brilliant works got broadcasted all over China, and most of Chinese people got to know their names. Except for making performance in Beijing, they would take 3 months to half a year to put on shows in city like Tianjin, Baoding, Shenyang. All the boss of theatres, tea houses and story-telling theatres of those places became Hou Baolin’s friends. Ordinary people in Tianjin and northeast China could easily enjoy their famous works then.

Like many artists who experienced the hardship before the liberation, Hou Baolin welcomed the setup of new China. His artistic life has come

努力学艺得到朱老真传，侯宝林最终成为其众多弟子中最能抓住观众口味、艺术成就最高的一位。拜师后的侯宝林与郭启儒二人合说的一个个精彩相声段子，通过“话匣子”传遍了大江南北，很快声名鹊起，轰动大半个中国。除了在北京演出之外，侯宝林每年还要定时抽出三个月乃至半年时光分别到天津、保定、沈阳等外埠出演。所以上述地方一些剧场、书场、茶馆的老板、掌柜的均与侯宝林成了多年来相识的老朋友，东北、天津等地的观众可十分方便地领略侯、郭二位先生亲口说《三棒鼓》、《珍珠翡翠白玉汤》、《戏剧杂谈》等名段。

和许许多多饱经旧社会痛苦创伤的艺术家一样，侯宝林以喜悦欢畅的心情迎来了新中国的成立，迎来了真正属于自已的艺术上的春天。党和国家十分关心重视这些从旧社会走过来的没有社会地位、吃尽辛酸苦楚的老艺人。这一期间，侯宝林、郭启儒这对老搭档像辛勤的蜜蜂一样深入到工厂、农村、油田、部队，他们边深入生活，边将采集到的素材加工、整理、提炼，很快就转化为风趣幽默、紧扣时代脉博的好相声。侯宝林先生到了哪里，就为哪里的人民带来轻松愉快的笑声。

作为享有极高声誉的一代相声表演艺术大师，侯宝林在新中国成立后的十几年间，与郭启儒多次作为客人，被毛泽东主席、周恩来总理、朱德委员长邀请到中南海等地，将精彩的相声段子献给共和国的缔造者们。侯宝林将自编的《关公战秦琼》、《戏剧与方言》、《三棒鼓》《夜行记》等语言风趣、富有新意

to a blossom. The government cared much about these artists who came from a very low social class and experienced all the hardship. During that period, Hou Baolin and Guo Qiru went into factories, villages, oil fields, military barracks, and collected all kinds of materials and put them into their wonderful new programs, which brought happiness to people.

Being a highly-praised Cross Talk master, Hou Baolin with his partner have been invited as guests to offer performances to Chairman Mao, Premier Zhou En’lai, and Chief of Staff Zhu De. He performed several works authored by him, and the interesting and humorous act gave lots of laugh to these central government leaders.

After the economic revolution, aged Hou Baolin and his partner have performed many cross talk works with economic revolution and ordinary peoples life. In the spring festival party, he performed with Guo Qiru, besides, he have shown a special skill he learned when he was young, called sand calligraphy.

Hou Baolin is not only a great cross talk master, but also the one who loved to find talented person and train them. He came from the old society, but he did not have the bad habits of old artists. In order to develop the cross talk art, he took the problem of training new cross talk performers as a priority. Based on Hou Baolin’s contribution to Chinese Cross Talk art, he was invited to be the linguistic professor of Chinese department of Beijing University. Many famous Cross Talk artists we know, like Jia Zhenliang, Ma Ji and Shi shengjie are all his students.

Hou Baolin’s contributions to the art of Cross

的多个相声段子奉献了出来。两位大师入木三分、滑稽诙谐的精彩表演，常令在座的中央领导人笑容满面。

改革开放后，年事渐高的侯宝林先生与他的另一位搭档、共同演出多年的相声名家郭全宝，表演了很多以开放改革为题材的相声。在春节联欢晚会上，他不仅与郭全宝老先生表演了令人捧腹大笑的相声段子，还将其早年在天桥儿学艺时的绝活“白沙撒字”（学名称“沙书”）这一近乎失传的手艺亮了出来，让全国电视机前的观众大饱眼福。

侯宝林先生不仅是一位卓越的相声表演艺术大师，而且还是一位善于发现人才、培养人才的伯乐和园丁，他艺德高尚、甘当人梯的精神在曲艺界尽人皆知。侯老虽从旧社会走过来，却没有沾染旧艺人的不良习气，而是为了发展相声艺术，将培养接班人当作刻不容缓的关键问题来看待，体现出一位老艺术家的坦荡胸怀。根据侯宝林先生对中国相声表演艺术所作的杰出贡献，大师生前被北京大学聘为中文系语言学教授。侯宝林先生生前交友甚广、为人正直、待人热情，一生真可谓“桃李满天下”。其中倾注大师满腔心血的一些弟子如贾振良、马季、师胜杰等人是家喻户晓的相声表演艺术家。

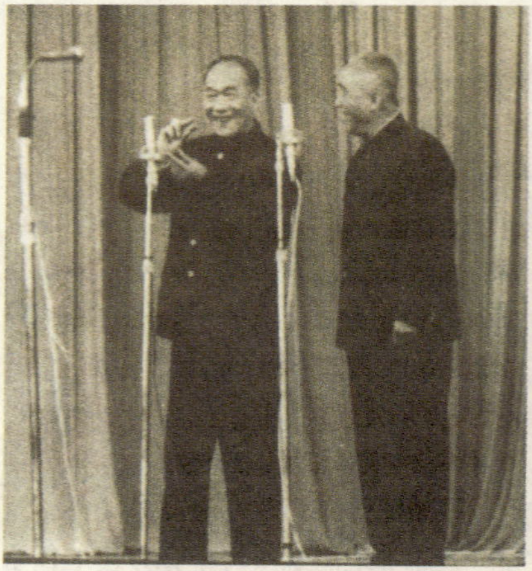

□ 侯宝林和郭全宝　Hou Baolin and Guo quanbao

Talk were numerous. First, he took the lead in purifying the language by getting rid of vulgarities. He re-edited a lot of traditional scripts and performed them on the stage. Second, he stressed the oretical research into Cross Talk while creating and performing. He made friends with scholars, and co-authored on the origin of Cross Talk, A *Collection of Articles on the Art of Cross Talk* and other works. Third, he wrote more than 30 scripts, of which the most representative are *Marriage and Superstition*, *A Miraculous Skill Brings Destruction*, *Lord Guan Fights Qin Qiong*, *Opera and Dialect*, *The Drunkard and The Opera Fan*.

琴书泰斗关学曾

The Master of Peking Qinshu,Guan Xuezeng

□琴书泰斗关学曾
The Master of Peking Qinshu,Guan Xuezeng

"我从小在北京土生土长，没招过谁，从没惹过谁，总想要点强。省吃俭用好不容易，我买了一个电脑，爱如珍宝，小心翼翼，在书包里装。回归路上有人打架，我去把热闹看……"

看过张艺谋导演的影片《有话好好说》的人，一定不会忘记这段音韵悠扬、直白有趣的北京琴书唱腔。但了解北京琴书、了解琴书泰斗关学曾先生的，恐怕还是为数不多。

北京琴书是北京地区鼓曲艺术中最有代表性的曲种，其前身是清道光年间

I was born in Peking

I have never got a rise out of anyone

I only wants to be more outstanding

I led a hard life and saved some money

I have bought a portable book-computer and cherish it

I pack it in a schoolbag carefully

Someone was fighting on my way home

I went to have a look and wanted to know what they are fighting about……"

Anyone who have seen the film *Keep Cool*, which was directed by Zhang Yimou, will never forget the melodious and popular aria from Peking Qinshu among the film. But if they were asked who sang the aria and what is Peking Qiushu, perhaps few people can give an answer.

Peking Qiushu,based on the Five-tone Drum Art which came into being in the period of Emperor Daoguang in Qing Dynasty and was popular in the peasant in the southeast suburb of Beijing and Anci County of Hebei Province (Langfang City,Hebei Province now) during wedding and funeral, is an outstanding Drum-music art in Beijing. There was no special actor who performed Five-tone Drum Art first in towns until 1920s, and in 1930s there came a famous artist, Zhai Qingshan,who was famous for the

兴起于北京东南部郊区和通县一带农村及河北省安次县农村(今廊坊市)的五音大鼓(以三弦、扬琴、四胡、鼓板伴奏，再加上演员的唱腔，合为五音)。五音大鼓起初只是乡下办喜事或逢年过节时庄稼人聚到一块儿自娱自乐的民间艺术形式，到20世纪20年代出现了在市、镇演唱的专业艺人，30年代中期，当时的名角翟青山先生的长篇大书《黄凤配》大受欢迎。有一回翟先生上电台，弹三弦的和拉四胡的没去，只好用一架扬琴伴奏，没想到广播出去以后，听众反映特别好，于是他只留下扬琴，改名为单琴大鼓、扬琴大鼓，亦称单琴调、琴书。

关学曾，满族人，1922年生于北京，幼时家境贫寒，从小便开始分担家庭生活重担，夏天顶酷暑卖青菜豆腐，冬天冒严寒卖山里红、糖葫芦，年关临近挨家挨户送“财神爷”。关老爷子从小便迷上了曲艺，14岁那年，有幸拜在当时琴书行当中声望极高的常德山、石金荣门下学习单琴大鼓，从此开始了长达七十余年的琴书生涯。天资聪颖的关学曾两年后即出师，并开始在庙会、茶社等处演唱，京城的天桥、隆福寺、鼓楼市场等地都留下了他的身影。经过多次尝试，关老爷子把常德山的唱法，石金荣抓词儿、抖包袱的技巧，名家翟青山的吐字发声方法，刘宝全的“唱似说、说似唱”的技法全都糅合到一块，再加上他自己嗓音洪亮、宽厚、吐字清晰的特点，很快就自成风格，吸引了大批观众。热爱他的听众送给他一块上书“琴书泰斗”四个大字的匾，从此，“琴书泰斗”的美誉也就伴随了关学曾的一生。

saga *the Marrige of Huang and Feng*. It' s said that one time when Mr. Zhai was performing in the radio while the fellows who played instruments were absent,he had to play with the company of Yangqin. It' s out of expect that when the program was broadcast, it's very popular in audiences, and Mr.Zhai gave up the other instruments but Yangqin, so Five-tone Drum Art got another name Solo-Qin Bass Drum Art.

Mr. Guan was born in a poor Manchu family in Peking in 1922,and when he was young, little Xuezeng shared the burden with his family. He sold greengrocery and bean curd with odd odor in summer,candy-calabash in winter and delivered the painting of the God of Wealth at the end of the lunar year. Guan became interested in the Chinese Folk Art since the childhood.At 14 years old, Guan followed the famous artist Chang Deshan, Shi Jinrong to study the Solo-Qin Bass Drum Art fortunately. The talented Guan finish his apprenticeship career two years later and started to perform in temple fair and tea house in Tianqiao,the Temple of Great Felicity and Gulou Market. The technique of Chang Deshan,Shi Jinrong, Zhai Qingshan and Liu Baoquan became the resourse of

□关学曾在表演 Mr.Guan is Performing

新中国成立后，关学曾进入北京曲艺团。抗美援朝期间，关学曾两次赴朝鲜为中国人民愿军进行慰问演出，回国后又到各地巡演。在此过程中，关学曾接触到了山东琴书、徐州琴书、四川琴书、冀州琴书等地方性琴书，感到“单琴大鼓”很容易与其他琴书混淆，深感有必要对单琴大鼓进行改造。回北京后，关学曾与琴师吴长宝先生一起对唱腔、板式进行了变革，把原有的垛句发展为双垛句、大垛句，用扬琴、四胡、二胡伴奏，唱腔以声传情，表演情真意切。1951年秋天，关老爷子第一次在前门箭楼上头以“北京琴书”的名称挂牌演出，得到了曲艺界同行的认可，也奠定了关学曾作为“北京琴书”创始人的地位。改造之后的北京琴书唱词注重口语化，有时唱词加有“过口白”(演唱中加入说白)，唱腔旋律简洁，板式变化较丰富，似说似唱，听来通俗入耳、亲切感人。

关老爷子深刻意识到，只有演新唱新，才能贴近生活，贴近观众。关老曾经说:“艺无止境，老抱着师父那些玩艺儿，还不得喝西北风去！”早期琴书的曲目以长篇大书为主，关老爷子则把它改造成为以现实题材为主的短段。20世纪50年代初，关老爷子根据赵树理的《考神婆》改编的北京琴书在中央人民广播电台播出，得到了听众的好评，中篇琴书《王贵与李香香》、《王若飞在狱中》等也受到了热烈欢迎。抗美援朝期间的《火车英雄张恩忠》，三年困难时期的《父子送粮》，学雷锋时期的《伟大的战士雷锋》等都成为了经典。此外，关老爷子还整理、改编了一批优秀的传统

Guan. Mr.Guan exerted his strong suit of voice and was welcomed by all the audiences.The adorer presented him a plaque with the characters *Qin Shu Tai Dou*, which means the master of Peking Qiushu, and hence the honored title went with Guan's life.

After the PRC was founded, Mr. Guan entered Beijing Quyi Troupe and performed over the coutry. When Mr. Guan learned more about other arts,such as Shangdong Qiushu,Xuzhou Qinshu,Sichuan Qinshu and Jizhou Qinshu, he made his mind to alter Peking Qiushu. Back to Beijing, Mr. Guan and Mr.Wu Changbao transformed the aria, procedure, and accompaniment instruments.All these transformation enhanced the status of Peking Qiushu which was more popular and kind.In the autumn of 1951, Mr.Guan named the new art of Peking Qinshu. The audience accepted the new art and Mr. Guan got the great reputation of the foundation of Peking Qinshu.

Mr.Guan thought it's a must to reflect the current life, otherwise the Qinshu Art would be abandoned by the audience.So he created much production according to the situation.In 1950s, Mr.Guan performed *Query the Carlina* adapted from the novel of the writer Zhao Shuli, *Wang Gui and Li Xiangxiang, Wang Ruofei In the Prison* in the radio, which were welcomed. He also created *Zhang Enzhong, A Hero on the Train, The Father and Son Delivering Provision, Lei Feng, A Great Soldier,*etc. After the Reform and Opening Policy, Mr. Guan continued to perform for the audience and created some humour opusculum, such as *the Longevity Village*,

曲目，如《鞭打芦花》、《杨八姐游春》等。改革开放后，年逾花甲的关老爷子青春焕发，继续登台为观众演唱，创作了一些被他自己称为“五分钟艺术”的幽默小段，如《长寿村》、《礼尚往来》、《怕婆村》等。别看节目短小，可麻雀虽小，五脏俱全，小段中有人物，有情节，同样受到观众欢迎。至20世纪90年代，已七十有余的关老欣然与张艺谋导演合作，亲手完成了从作词到演唱的所有工作。琴书与电影的结合，传统与现代的结合，这是琴书诞生以来的创举，关老爷子希望借助影视作品将北京琴书发扬光大。河北三河县的青年农民王树才就是因为听到了关老爷子的这段琴书而坚定地来到北京，拜倒在关老爷子脚下，成为关老爷子的关门弟子的。

不可否认的是，目前北京琴书的发展和继承都面临困难。为了让北京琴书这一曲艺表演形式传承下去，关老爷子从1996年起就在家里办起了学习班，义务授徒，前后带出20多位徒弟，他们当中有的是专业演员，更多的是票友和琴书爱好者。目前北京琴书第二代传人包括殷长海、刘砚声、尚文和、吴林有、王树才等。

作为北京琴书的奠基人和开拓者，2006年8月，关老爷子获得了中国曲艺牡丹奖首次增设的“终身成就奖”及北京文联授予的“德艺双馨楷模”称号。2006年9月27日晚，一代“琴书泰斗”关学曾不幸在北京去世，北京琴书及关学曾其人成为了人们关注的焦点。只是对于关老爷子来说，这一切已经是“逝者如斯”的“寂寞身后事”了。

□琴书泰斗关学曾
The Master of Peking Qinshu,Guan Xuezeng

which was called Five-Minutes Art by himself. Mr. Guan cooperated with the famous Director Zhang Yimou and finished the work in the film *Keep Cool*. Mr. Guan hoped to extend the influence of Peking Qinshu in virtue of the film.A young peasant,Wang Shucai in Hebei,came to Beijing to follow Mr. Guan after enjoying the art in the film and became the last disciple of Mr.Guan.

It’s undeniable that Peking Qinshu Art have declined. So Mr. Guan ran a personal school in his own home and took in students, and there are 20 students including special actor and amateurish fans.Now the second generation have grown up, such as Yin Changhai,Liu Yansheng,Shang Wenhe,Wu Linyou,Wang Shucai.

As the founder and exploiter of Peking Qinshu, Mr.Guan was awarded the Prize of Achievement for life and the honoured title of the Model of Virtue and Art in August, in 2006. On the night of 27th September in 2006,Guan Xuezeng, the Master of Peking Qinshu passed away in Beijing. Peking Qinshu and the Master Guan were paid more attention to,but all these were nothing with the Master.

老旦李多奎与龙须沟

Laodan Player Li Duokui and Longxu Channel

提起北京天坛北门对面的龙须沟，这里曾是旧都南城有名的臭水沟，蚊蝇满天飞，脏水遍地流。解放初期，人民政府对破败不堪的龙须沟进行了整修，旧貌换新颜后，著名作家老舍先生写成了电影剧本《龙须沟》反映了这儿新旧社会的变化，并搬上银幕，从此"龙须沟"一夜之间闻名全国。

龙须沟与过去的老天桥游艺场毗邻，老北京的民俗文化、市井文化深深扎根在这片土地上，同时也孕育了一代又一代的民间艺人。远的不表，就拿早年走红京都四九城的著名京剧老旦表演艺术家李多奎先生来说吧，自幼就随父亲来京住在龙须沟鞭子巷18号。对梨园界的老戏迷、新票友来说，"铁嗓子"李多奎可是一个响当当的名字。李多奎师承罗福山，私淑龚云甫，早年曾得老旦行当祖师爷龚云甫的琴师陆五的辅佐，风格以行腔高亢圆润、韵味醇厚著称，深受戏迷和广大观众的喜爱。

不过您可能有所不知，李老先生幼年从艺时，天赋并不出众，而且一度因为嗓子"倒仓"而不得不改行拜师学习京胡。这"倒仓"一关，是梨园行中以唱文戏为主的演员必须要过的一道坎，如果这个坎儿过得顺利，成功可能近在咫尺；反之，改弦更张在所难免。"倒仓"之后，李老先生一边学习京胡，一边抓紧

There is a famous Longxu Channel, a stinky slot with lots of flies, mosquitos, and sewage water flowing all the way around in the southern part of Beijing city, at the opposite side of the north gate of the Temple of Heaven. Right after the liberation, new government started a reconstruction project on it, which changed the whole appearance of this slot. The famous writer Lao She wrote a movie script *Longxu Channel* about this . From then on, this name has got to known all over China.

Longxu Channel is just beside the Tianqiao recreational place, and people living here were all ordinary ones. This is the birth place of Beijing folk culture, and generations of folk artists are coming from here. The famous pantaloon artist, Mr. Li Duokui is one of them. He came to Beijing with his father, and living at No. 18, lash alley, Longxu Channel. Li Duokui' s master is Luo Fushan and Gong Yunfu who was the old master of Pantaloon art, and Li Duokui used to get support from Gong Yunfu's *Jinghu* player, Lu Wu. Li Duokui's voice was high and clear, quite popular among Beijing Opera fans and audiences.

It's rarely known by fans that Li Duokui was not outstanding when he started to learn Beijing Opera, and even once had to restart and learn *Jinghu* because of his voice. The change of voice

时间刻苦地吊嗓子，这一练就是十几年。每天只要五更鼓一响，李多奎便起身穿衣，从家中走出来到天坛北门里的古柏树林，伴着鸟雀儿的欢快啁啾，开始一天的踢腿、下腰、吊嗓子，日复一日，年复一年。盛夏酷暑，三九严寒，都没有动摇过李多奎练功的恒心。凭着这种永往直前、锲而不舍的精神，李多奎终于闯过了这令艺员怵头的“倒仓”关，并于25岁那年重返京剧舞台，《钓金龟》、《打龙袍》、《四郎探母》、《铡美案》等让世人再次领略了李派老旦唱腔的婉约豪放、挺拔纯正。20世纪20年代初，李多奎由老生改演老旦，30年代成为一代唱工老旦的代表性人物，至40年代已自成一家。李多奎一生为众多生、旦、净行演员配演，与高庆奎、金少山、马连良、叶盛兰、张君秋、裘盛戎等人合作，演出了大量以唱工为主的剧目，是老旦行当中继龚云甫之后影响最大的演员。李多奎嗓音宏亮宽厚，音质饱满明净，高低音均佳。在龚云甫唱腔的基础上，充分发挥了咬字真切、喷口有力的特长，加强了唱腔的力度，高腔唱得苍劲挺拔，低腔更能委婉沉着，大段唱工扎实稳健，行腔舒展大方。尤其是垛板，节奏愈快，气息愈见匀停而且字字有腔，演唱技巧高超，具有醇美酣畅的特殊韵味。

虽然李多奎先生已作古多年，但先生的李派老旦艺术，仍为广大戏迷所津津乐道。每当京剧界同仁、票友、戏迷们观看现在某些演员演唱李派代表作时，就会情不自禁地甩出一句话：“这老旦唱的味儿，连李多奎的一半儿恐怕都赶不上。”可见李多奎先生在京剧表演艺术方面的造诣有多深，影响有多广。

is a harsh problem for performers whose main skill is singing. If they get over it easily, success is right at the corner, if not, they have no choice but to change profession. When Li Duokui began to change voice, he took every chance in training his voice, and at the same time learned *Jinghu* playing. All these work lasted for over 10 years. Every morning he would get up early, and came out to the woods in the north of the Temple of Heaven, and began his training. No matter it rained and snowed, he never stopped these exercises. Finally all his effort got result, and he got over the voice change problem, and got back on stage. His performance let people hear again the outstanding character of Li style pantaloon singing. Early in 1920s, his career got started, and in 1930s, he became the icon of singing pantaloon, and established his own style in 1940s. During his performing career, he had worked with all other types of Beijing Opera performers, and cooperated with famous Beijing Opera performers like Gao Qingkui, Jin shaoshan, Ma Lianliang, Ye Shenglan, Zhang Junqiu, Qiu Shengrong, etc. He is the most influential pantaloon artist after Gong Yunfu. Li Duokui had a perfect voice, and was very good at manipulating it. His singing goes high and strong, low and clear.More quicker he sings, clearer the audience could hear.

Although Li Duokui had passed away many years, Beijing Opera fans still love to talk about his style pantaloon. When people see some of the performers show Li Duokui' s great works, they would often say:"Such a pantaloon, not even half of Li Duokui." From this word we could see his artistic feat and influences.

武生泰斗王金璐

Wusheng Player Wang Jinlu

□ 武生泰斗王金璐先生与本书作者张本瀛
Wusheng Planyer Wang Jinlu and Zhang Benying

著名京剧表演艺术家、戏曲教育家、武生泰斗王金璐老先生，是我国梨园界为数不多的国宝级艺术家之一。

王金璐1919年11月22日生于北京崇文区东珠市口一个几代居京却生活在社会最底层的城市贫民家庭。父亲曾在前门外同兴堂饭铺当小学徒，出师后也不过是为左邻右舍红白喜事张罗一些家常饭菜，偶而被请到大宅门里主厨炒菜也是收入微薄。母亲则为有钱人家缝缝补补、洗洗涮涮以补贴家用（俗称缝穷）。王金璐兄弟姊妹四人，他排行老三。由于营养不良，小金璐常常瘦得皮包骨头。

常言"老天爷饿不死瞎家雀儿"，王金璐10岁那年由干妈带着去姑妈家拜寿。一顿丰盛的饭菜后，主客谈笑之间纷纷哼起戏唱起曲儿来。常听大人闲暇

The famed Beijing Opera artist and educationist, *Wusheng* master player Wang Jinlu, is one of the most respected actor in this field.

November 22, 1919, Wang Jinlu was born in a poor family in Zhushikou, Chongwen District, Beijing. His father used to be an apprentice in Tongxing Restaurant outside Qianmen Gate, later he was just someone who helped preparing banquets in the neighborhood, sometimes got invited to be a chef, and his income was not much. His mother had to do washing and sewing for rich families to earn litle money. Wang Jinlu had 3 siblings, and he was the third child. He was very thin and weak due to malnutrition.

It' s fortunate that when he was 10 years old, his godmother brought him to her aunt' s birthday party. After a wonderful meal, people talked about Beijing Opera. Wang Jinlu used to hear adults sing, he took some water and started to sing a small piece, which made the people around quite surprised. Among the guests, there was a teacher in Beijing Opera School, named Hu Yusheng, and he said immediately after Wang Jinlu' s singing: "I think the boy has some talent in Beijing Opera." The aunt couple lived in the same alley with Hu Yusheng, and said: "If you think this child is talented, would it be possible for you to get him into your school, he

时唱上几句京戏的金璐喝了两口水，运运气拉开架势便唱《打渔杀家》：“父女打鱼在河下……”竟然将这一小段唱得抑扬顿挫、板眼清楚，让围观者颇感惊奇。偏巧这天的宾客中有一位胡玉生老先生是中华戏曲专科学校的庶务教师。胡先生听完这个一脸稚气的小男孩像模像样的演唱后，立即脱口而出：“这小子我瞧着是块唱戏的坯子。”姑父、姑妈一家与胡先生是多年同住一个院的老街坊，忙趁热打铁：“您老如果不嫌弃，瞅这孩子还成，就求您给他找个吃饭的地方，让他试试考考戏校……”古道热肠的胡先生一口应承下来。

胡先生告知王金璐，南城木厂胡同的中华戏曲专科学校正在招生。这个学校采用欧美等国办学经验，不同于传统京戏依靠科班培养戏曲人才的老模式。如打破男女授受不亲的陈腐观念，率先男女合班上课，专门开设国文、历史、英文、法文、音乐、美术、算术、体育、中国戏曲史、艺术概论、中外剧本分析、文艺理论等相关课程以丰富教学内容。校方提供专门宿舍，统一发放校服，实行规范化管理。其校董由四大名旦之一程砚秋、梨园名宿金仲荪和著名戏剧艺术家焦菊隐三位先生共同组成。

步入戏校学习后，王金璐与沈金波、冯金芙等人同班，开始行当分得并不细，为的是让学生得到较全面的摔打，当年在校生不论何人，均从最初的跑龙套开始。直到第二年，他才被划归以习老生行当为主，开蒙老师为陈少武、王荣山、蔡荣贵、鲍吉祥等梨园前辈。在陈先生亲授的第一出戏《渭水河》

□武生宗师杨小楼
The Master of *Wusheng*, Yang Xiaolou

could have some place to feed himself." Hu Yusheng kindly agreed.

Mr. Hu told Wang Jinlu that the Beijing Opera school located in wood mill alley, southern city, was taking in students at that time. The great difference between the new school and the old is that they adopted dissimilar methods in training. In the old school there used the old methods of traditional Beijing Opera. The new school not only took in boys and girls, but also adopted the way of western schooling, setting up new subjects such as Chinese, History, English, French, Music, Painting, Mathematics, Physical Education, History of Beijing Opera, Art Conspectus, Chinese and Foreign Drama Script Analysis, Cultural Theory, etc. The school provided dormitories, uniforms, and practiced in a standardized management. The board of directors consisted of Cheng Yanqiu, Jin Zhongsun and famous drama artist Jiao Juyin.

After he got into school, Wang Jinlu was in the same class with Shen Jinbo, Feng Jinfu, Li Jinhong and Zhao Jinrong. They were not classified into a specific part,because they need a comprehensive training. Till the second year in school,

中，王金璐前演周文王后饰姜太公。调皮又倔犟的他在经历"打罚"、"打戏"的苦熬之后，终于悟出一些做人从艺的门道，那就是不过分依赖别人。"艺多不压身"的观念在王金璐的心中深深地扎了根。

1932年5月14日是王金璐终生难忘的日子，这一天他在开明戏院首次登台演出《渭水河》，饰演周文王一角。头一回挑台演正戏，但他愣是以初生牛犊不怕虎的心态，恰当地把握了剧中角色的火候，受到观众的一致好评。不久出演《汜水关》中的杨滚和文戏《无底洞》中的托塔李天王，《龙虎斗》中的赵匡胤及《阳平关》中的黄忠等角色，表演很是到位，连轻易不夸徒弟的严师陈少武先生也有了笑脸。后由陈少武先生牵线，王金璐再度受业于昆曲名家曹心泉和著名老旦文亮臣。14岁那年，在焦菊隐、程砚秋、金仲苏等戏校校董的热情引荐下，深受前辈艺术家器重的王金璐，有幸拜在马连良先生门下。小金璐聪明伶俐，备受马先生喜欢，成为为数不多的马派入室弟子，由马先生口传亲授代表作《四进士》、《空城计》、《借东风》等剧目。

王金璐并不满足于京戏中的单一行当，他在文武老生、老旦、红生、小生的基础上又博采众家之长，于15岁那年根据自身条件将以后艺术发展的侧重面定位在专习武生，经名扬清末民初武生行当的一代宗师黄月山、杨小楼的得意门生丁永利和李洪春二先生的精心雕琢，王金璐终得杨派武生的硬功夫。王金璐在20世纪30年代一亮相立即引起

Wang Jinlu was classified as mainly *Laosheng* character. His teachers at the beginning was Chen Shaowu, Wang Rongshan, Cai Ronggui and Bao Jixiang, all old masters in Beijing Opera. In the first drama *Weishui River* that Chen Shaowu taught him, Wang Jinlu acted both Emperor Wenwang and Minister Jiang Ziya. Wang Jinlu was naughty and stubborn. After quite some punishments, he learned some theories in life and acting. He should not rely too much on others, and must learn as much skill as possible.

14th of May, 1932, it was a day Wang Jinlu would never forget. It was the first time he formally got on stage in Kaiming Theatre and performed as Emperor Wenwang in *Weishui River*. He managed the right acting, and was highly praised by audiences. Later on, he acted as Yang Gun in *Sishui Pass*, God Li in *Endless Cave*, Emperor Zhao Kuangyin in *Fierce Conflict*, and Huang Zhong in *Yangping Pass*. His acting was outstanding, even his master Chen Shaowu felt satisfied. Chen Shaowu introduced him to learn from Kun Opera master Cao Xinquan and famous female character actor Wen Liangchen. When he was 14 years old, with the schools board of director' s recommendation, Wang Jinlu fortunately became the student of Master Ma Lianliang. This master was quite happy about him, and taught him personally some of his best performed programs.

Wang Jinlu was not satisfied with just learning a particular part in Beijing Opera, and he also tried to learn more from other parts. When he was 15, he put emphasis on *Wusheng*. With the training of master Ding Yongli and Li Hongchun, he

轰动，马不停蹄在北京各大戏园子分别演出《铁笼山》、《挑滑车》、《长板坡》、《林冲夜奔》、《八大锤》、《状元印》、《恶虎村》等高难度的武生经典剧目，让广大观众再度观赏到了难得一见的纯正地道的杨派大武生的风格戏，从而被当年的热情戏迷称之为少年武生的英秀，在1937年北平《立言报》主持的童伶竞选中一举问鼎生部冠军。1939年秋自中华戏曲职业专科学校毕业后，学戏初成的王金璐在众多老艺术家的精心栽培下，得以和前辈艺术家们同台演出，技艺精进。如与著名黑头“金霸王”金少山在中和剧场联袂演出《二进宫》，与“活张飞”侯喜瑞在吉祥戏院合作《战宛城》，另外还和当红须生奚啸伯、一代名旦于连泉等人都合作过。

抗战胜利前后，德才艺俱佳的王金璐还应恩师焦菊隐、著名剧作家翁偶虹之邀，出演由他们导演的《白虹贯日》、《桃花扇》及《铸情记》。20世纪50年代初，王金璐加入华东戏曲研究院实验京剧团（上海京剧院前身），与海派表演艺术大师“麒麟童”周信芳老先生合作演出《十五贯》、《战长沙》等多部剧目，为麒派艺术的发扬光大作出了可贵的贡献。由先生单独挑台出演的大轴戏《挑滑车》，在1954年华东戏曲观摩演出大会上荣膺演员一等奖。作为国际间文化交流的使者，王金璐出访前苏联各加盟共和国。把中国传统京剧的优秀剧目《雁荡山》、《双射雁》、《两将军》等奉献给外宾，将国粹璀灿迷人的艺术魅力展示于外国朋友面前，受到极其热烈的欢迎，由先生主演的上述经典剧目被白俄

□长靠武生 *Wusheng*

finally managed the true skill of Yang style. In the 1930s, Wang Jinlu made his fame in his show. He acted all the highly skilled *Wusheng* programs around all the big theatres in Beijing, and provided the audiences the real charm of Yang School *Wusheng*. He was considered the best young *Wusheng* actor by enthusiastic fans. In the young Beijing Opera actors election, held by Beijing's *Li Yan Daily* in 1937, he was the champion. In 1939, he graduated from Beijing Opera Professional School. With the support of all the old artists, he got the chance to perform with them. He had performed with the famous Jin Shaoshan and Hou Xirui. Xi Xiaobo and Yu Lianquan also cooperated with him.

After the Anti-Japanese War, Wang Jinlu was invited to perform in his master Jiao Juyin and dramatist Weng Ouhong directed program, *Baihong Guanri, Peach blossom Fan* and *Zhu Qing Ji*. Early 1950s, he got into the Beijing Opera group of Huadong Drama Research Institute, and worked with the master Zhou Xinfang in programs like *15 Guan, Fight in Changsha*, etc. He made quite some contribution to *Qi* Style art. He also performed one program called *Tiao Huache* mainly by himself, which claimed the first award in drama performance convention of 1954. Wang Jinlu also brought his art abroad. He visited states of the Former Soviet

罗斯政府授予最高荣誉奖。

1958年初，王金璐又被有关方面请出，授命援建京剧力量薄弱的陕西省京剧团。来到西安后，由先生担纲主演的《七侠五义》一炮打响，创下了连续演出客满近两年的纪录。正在他欲施展更大的抱负时，却不幸在1961年夏季一次演出中腰受重伤，不得不暂时告别舞台，而这一离开就是18年。在此期间，王金璐克服种种困难，以惊人的毅力战胜身体的伤痛，坚持练功健身，博览各类书刊用以提高理论素养，终于于1978年重返阔别多年的舞台，同时应邀到中国戏曲学院担任教书育人的重任。

王老几十年来供职于中国戏曲学院表演系，他以教书育人为已任，为戏曲人才的培养供献毕生之力。老先生为人心胸宽广，豁达开朗，虽说已步入耄耋之年，身子骨儿仍相当结实。王老一辈子坚持习武练功不辍，风雨无阻，在边教、边导、边演的过程中，王老老当益壮，孜孜以求，展示了自己对京剧艺术的不懈追求。

Union, and let people there enjoy the Chinese artistic show. He was welcomed by local people, and awarded by Byelorussia government with the highest honor award.

Early in 1958, he was asked to help establish the Beijing Opera Troupe of Shanxi. After he arrived in Xi' an, the new program he performed named *Qi Xia Wu Yi* made a surprising success, and there were no tickets left for 2 years, which also made a record. Unfortunately, he was badly hurt in a show in the summer of 1961, and had to leave the stage temperarily, and this leave lasted for 18 years. During this time, he kept training and reading all kinds of books. All these efforts helped him get back on stage in 1978, and he was employed as a teacher in Beijing Opera College in the same year.

Wang Jinlu have worked in Performance Dept. of Beijing Opera College for decades, and dedicated his life to training new talents. Wang Jinlu was an old optimist with a strong body. He never stopped his training all his life. During his training and teaching, he would go even further in Beijing Opera.

名丑张春华

Famous Clown Player Zhang Chunhua

□ 名丑张春华先生
Famous Clown Player Zhang Chunhua

在京剧新老戏迷中，只要一提名丑张春华，立马儿便会想到张春华的拿手好戏——《三岔口》、《打瓜园》、《杨香武三盗九龙杯》等一批以武丑为主角的京剧经典剧目。

张春华老先生1924年生于老天津卫。为家境所迫，9岁时正式到天津天华景稽古社学习京戏。1941年，因主演外国故事京剧《侠盗罗宾汉》初现峥嵘。1944年出科后便来到北京寻求发展，经梨园行的朋友牵线，拜著名京剧武丑表演艺术家叶盛章先生为师，后成为叶盛章先生的主要传人，经常在天津、北京等地演出。1944年与贺玉钦等人合作在上海天蟾舞台挑大梁，1948年与张云溪先生合组云华社。在这期间，张春华凭着他主演的《雁翎甲》、《酒丐》、《巧连环》等多出精彩剧目活跃在京、沪京剧舞台上，以白口脆快、开打火爆的高超技艺取胜。

While mentioning the famous clown player Zhang Chunhua, the traditional Peking Opera plays, like *At the Crossroads*, *Fighting at a Melon Garden*, *Yang Xiangwu Steals the Nine-dragon Cup*, occur to his fans at once.

Zhang Chunhua was born in Tianjin in 1924. He was forced to go to Tianhuajingjigushe Troupe to learn Peking Opea by his poor family. In 1941, he acted the leading role in the foreign story play *Robin Hood* and made a great success. In 1944, he went to Beijing to seek a new development. With friends' help, he formally acknowledged the famous warrior clown perform artist Ye Shengzhang as his teacher and began to learn from him. Later, he became the chief disciple of Ye Shengzhang and performed in Beijing and Tianjin from time to time.

In 1944, he and He Yuqian began to lead performance on the stage of Tianchan in Shanghai. Later, in 1948, he cooperated with Zhang Yunxi and founded Yunhuashe Troupe. During this period, Zhang Chunhua led the play *Wild Goose Plume Armour, Wine Beggar, Interlocking Stratagems.* And he spoke the dialogue part both clearly and quickly, and his marshal arts performance in the opera was superb. In 1950, he played in the opera *Taking the Zhu Family Village by Strategy* and *Jianghan Fisherman's*

1950年在京剧《三打祝家庄》、《江汉渔歌》中担任重要角色。1955年中国京剧院二团成立，张春华与张云溪、李宗义、云燕铭等主要演员先后联袂排演了《猎虎记》、《高亮赶水》、《九龙杯》、《三盗令》、《大破铜网阵》等优秀京剧剧目。张老还曾多次随团应邀出国访问演出。

在所演的戏曲中，张春华先生遵循技术动作为内容服务这一宗旨，擅长武打动作设计。京剧行内有句老话，"曲不离口，拳不离手"，它非常形象地说明了京剧艺术的学习没有任何捷径可言。京剧艺术分为生、旦、净、丑几个行当，丑行又可细分为"文丑"和"武丑"，文丑与生、旦配戏，武丑与武生联手献艺。张春华老先生以演武丑为主，同时兼演文丑。但懂行的人都深知，不论是讲究作工、念白的文丑还是讲究武功技艺的武

□1984年在香港演《火焰山》剧照
The Photo of Zhang Chunhua in *Flame Mountain*,1984,Hongkong

Song. In 1955, the Second troupe for Chinese Peking Opera Theatre was set up. As its major actors, Zhang Chunhua, Zhang Yunxi, Li Zhongyi and Yun Yanming rehearsed *Hunting the Tiger, Gaoliang Catches up with Water, Yang Xiangwu Steals the Nine-dragon Cup, Stealing Mukaling* and *Breaking down Copper-netted Trap* and so on. Zhang Chunhua had also been invited to perform overseas for many times.

Zhang Chunhua believes that all technic should always serves the content. He is adept at designing the marshal art movement. And there are no shortcut during learning Peking Opera but practising more. In Peking Opera, the four main roles are *Sheng*(male role), *Dan*(female role), *Jing* (face-painted male role) and *Chou*(clown). *Sheng* is a main role including the character of an old or middle-aged gentleman wearing a beard and long mustache, namely *Laosheng*, and the character of a young man without beard and mustache, namely *Xiaosheng*. Those specializing in acrobatics are called *Wusheng*. And *Chou* can be subdivided into those specializing in acrobatics, namely *Wuchou* and those in civil plays, namely *Wenchou*. *Wenchou* acts with *Sheng* and *Dan* while *Wuchou* acts with *Wusheng*.

Zhang Chunhua is a outstanding *Wuchou*, but he acts as *Wenchou* sometimes. Whether *Wenchou* attaching great attention to acting, dialogue and monologue or Wuchou with consummate skill in acrobatics, perfect skill is a must for the clown actor. In Peking Opera, clown or comic role, often paints his face and behaves or speaks comically as negative role or, sometimes, as positive role. Some have a stentorian voice, some are

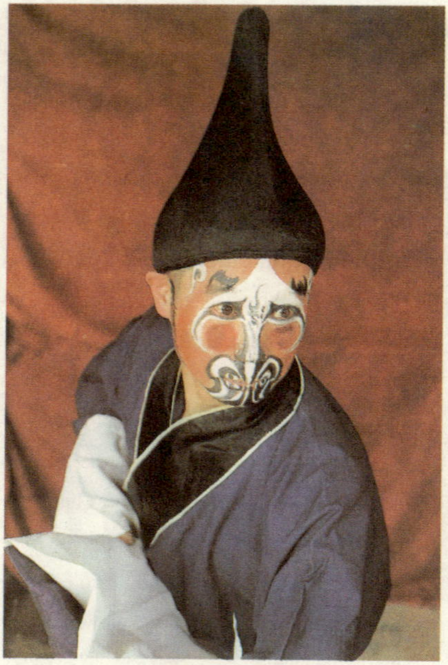

□武丑形象 The Image of *Wuchou*

丑，都要求演员必须具备扎扎实实的技巧。丑角常常以生动诙谐的形象出现，或嗓音宏亮，或滑稽幽默，或武艺高强，是一出大戏中不可缺少的角色，同样可以令人眼花缭乱。在中国京剧院，张春华先生和已故著名武生演员张云溪的合作演出长达50年，这其间所下的苦功可以想见。张老言称，每天少吃一顿饭可以，但绝不可一日不练功。人吃五谷杂粮难免有个头疼脑热的小病，可他觉得这些都实在算不了什么，也从来没有因此而放弃练功。张老几十年如一日练功不辍，因此人们就在以吃功夫见长的《三岔口》、《打瓜园》、《时迁偷鸡》以及与老生相配的《秋江》等经典剧目中观赏到了张春华老先生轻灵、绵软、松弛、舒展俱佳的"童子功"。张老常以一句剧坛行话自勉，即

funny and humorous. Others excel at acrobatics. So clown actor is indispensable in an entire opera show, who can produce dazzling effect. In Chinese Peking Opera Theatre, Zhang Chunhua had cooperated with a deceased actor, famous *Wusheng* player Zhang Yunxi for 50 year. The painstaking effort can be imagined. Mr. Zhang said, "One can miss a meal one day, but can not give up practising one day." Even he was ill, he still sticked to practising. And he kept practising for several decades, so in the plays *At the Crossroads, Fight at a Melon Garden* and *Shi Qian Steals the Cock* as well as *Qiu Jiang*, people could appreciate his "Tongzigong" with great litheness and laxity. Mr. Zhang often urges himself with such words, " A short performance on the stage needs several years' practice. To win the fans or audience, the quality of the performance must be very high, or else people won't acknowledge the seniority of you. "

Zhang Chunhua has been a popular clown actor among numerous Peking Opera fans for several decades. On the Eve of Chinese Spring Festival of 1955, his fans queued for a night to buy tickets for the opera *At the Crossroads* despite the cold in front of the gate of Chinese Peking Opera Theater. Unfortunately, Mr. Zhang caught a serious cold and fever. And the body temperature was as high as 40 centigrade. The leaders of the theater asked him to put off the performance, but Mr. Zhang refused to do. During his performance, his broadsword fell off his hand because he was too week to hold it. But none of the audience booed him. While answering the curtain call, Zhang Yunxi told the truth to

"台上运用自如的一分钟，离不开台下三年功。好戏要想赢得戏迷和观众，惟有靠实实在在的表演质量，否则人家决不会买你的账"。

几十年来张春华先生一直是一位深受广大戏迷喜爱的京剧名丑儿。1955年大年三十晚上，在中国大戏院门口一些痴迷的观众朋友冒着冬日的严寒，提着小板凳，硬是排了一夜的队买票，图的就是看初一主演的剧目《三岔口》。不巧的是，张老患感冒发烧40度，京剧院领导征询是否变更一下时间演出，张老一口回绝，坚持如期定时开锣。演出当中，由于之前一直在发烧，所以手没劲儿，刀有些攥不住，结果耍的时候一下子掉在台上，但观众中却没有一个喝倒彩儿的。当戏终谢幕时，京剧院遂将张老患病发烧但坚持如期演出的情况告知观众，迎来了戏迷经久不息的热烈掌声。许多年来，正是戏迷的大力支持、观众的热切关爱鞭策和激励着张老演好每一出剧目。张春华先生坚持无论演哪出戏，始终以饱满的激情塑造好每一个人物，不会有一丝一毫的懈怠情绪，张老认为这是一个演员必须具备的艺德。

张春华老先生不顾自己年事已高，先后收上海京剧院的严庆谷、天津京剧院的石小亮、北京京剧院的年金鹏等年轻人为徒，倾心传艺。与此同时张老还应邀为中国戏曲学院的研究生授课，尽其所能地让京剧丑行儿有合适的接班人接班，为弘扬光大丑角艺术贡献一份力量。

□张春华在《杨香武三盗九龙杯》中剧照

Zhang Chunhua in the Play *Yang Xiangwu Stole Nine-Dragon Cup Three Times*

the audience, and the latter responded Zhang Chunhua with long and ardent applause. For so many years, it was the support and careness from his fans and audience that urged Zhang Chunhua to perform perfectly at each opera. And he always plays the charaters with full emotion, as which is a moral character every actor should have.

Despite his age, Zhang Chunhua accepted Yan Qinggu from Shanghai Peking Opera Troupe, Shi Xiaoliang from Tianjing Peking Opera Troupe and Nian Jinpeng from Peking Opera Troupe of Beijing as his disciples and passed down his feat. Meanwhile, Mr. Zhang is also invited to give lessons to the graduate students of Chinese Opera College. He has devoted himself to the cause of trainingg successors and carrying forwards the clown art.

琴师姜凤山

Huqin Player Jiang Fengshan

□ 琴师姜凤山与周总理在一起

Huqin Player Jiang Fengshan and the Prime Minister Zhou

京剧四大名旦之首梅兰芳先生在其长达60余年的辉煌艺术生涯中，曾对菊坛的青衣、旦角行当在唱腔、念白、舞蹈、音乐、服装、化妆等诸多方面进行了独具匠心的探索和创新，从而形成了其独特高雅、自成一体的艺术风格，在海内外影响尤为广泛，世人称为“梅派”。但回首梅派表演艺术辉煌灿烂的形成和发展过程，会发现背后凝聚着不少幕后英雄的聪明才智和无私的贡献，正是他们甘当绿叶的“一棵菜精神”（梨园行内对精诚团结在核心角色周围的行为的专称术语），才使梅大师全身心地把一个个艺术形象性格刻划得鲜明生动、入木三分。其中伴随梅先生从艺多年的著名琴师姜凤山老先生，就是幕后英雄之一。

Mei Lanfang, one of the Four Great Famous Opera Female Roles, was the great master of Chinese drama art. During his stage career over half a century, he constantly explored the singing, recitation, dancing, music, make-ups and costumes, and turned the Peking Opera into a colorful, comprehensive art of the highest stage effects. As a result, he had a wide repertoire, formed his own original style and developed the unanimously accepted Mei School Art with unique characteristics and subtle dignity. He was accepted worldwide and applauded as a great artist and the embodiment of beauty. However, behind the development of Mei school performing art, there were many obscure people who dedicated their wisdom to the art of Mei Lanfang. It was under their support and cooperation that Mr. Mei could create many lively and unforgettable artistic images with heart and soul. And the famous Jinghu player Jiang Fengshan was among these people, who accompanied Mei Lanfang for many years.

Jiang Fengshan, who accompanied for four generations of Mei family, was one of Four Famous Jinghu Players. The other three were Huang Tianlin, He Shunxin and Chi Tianbiao respectively. Jiang Fengshan was born in a poor family in Huashi, Chongwen District,Beijing in

姜凤山是为梅家四代人都操过琴的梨园京胡四大金刚之一（另外三位分别是黄天麟、何顺信、迟天标）。姜凤山是地地道道皇城脚下的北京人，1923年生于南城崇文区花市一个城市贫民家庭。父亲是个安分守己以修理眼镜为生的手工匠人，他对儿子的期望值并不太高，惟一的希望是自己的后代能跟着他学会这门手艺，“长大有口子饭吃”。哪知，慢慢长大的小凤山对父亲的一番用心良苦不以为然，倔强的他无论大人如何苦口婆心地劝说，就是坚决不肯子承父业，一门心思要学京戏争取日后唱红成为“名角儿”。看到铁下心来执意要学戏的儿子态度坚决，父亲就勉强同意小凤山到戏班子去学戏。

姜凤山8岁时由家人带着来到位于城南的中华戏曲专科学校考场。经过考官的一番例行询问，试唱几段戏之后，眉清目秀、身材适中的姜凤山被戏校老师挑上了。当年校方根据他的个人条件安排他学习小生行当。但是在此之前，

□梅兰芳教子学艺，王少卿（右）操琴

Wang Shaoqing playing Huqin while Mei Langfang was teaching Mei Baojiu

1923. His father was a glasses repairman and he only hoped his son could learn his repair skill to make his living when he grew up. However, Jiang Fengshan neglected the father's exoect and insisted on learning Peking Opera whatever his parents tried to persuade him. And he had his own dream, that is, to become a popular opera player. Later, for his firm attitude, his father conceded to send him to opera troupe.

At the age of eight, Jiang Fengshan came to Chinese Opera School with his family. After a routine enquiry and singing several sections of opera, Jiang Fengshan with delicate features and moderate stature passed the examination. According to his condition, he was arranged to learn *Xiaosheng* role. But, before this, Jiang Fengshan had been fond of *Heitou* role because he thought whatever *Heitou* role or *Wu'erhua* role was masculine by their acting, singing and recitation. Jiang Fengshan didn't accept the arrangement of the school, so he missed the opportunity of learning opera further at the school.

Before long, Jiang Fengshan got a chance to learn opera in Beijing Wenlin Troupe through a relative's introduction. He stayed there for four years until Wenlin Troupe went bankrupt because of poor management, and its members were merged into Fuliancheng Troupe, an old-type opera school. The owner asked Jiang Fengshan to change the role from *Heitou* to *Qingyi* or *Huadan* which he disliked. Eventually, Jiang Fengshan didn't consent with the owner's order and went over to Fuqingshe Troupe. Through the recommendation of Guang Hongbin, a disciple of "Living Zhangfei" Hou Xirui,

小凤山却一直喜欢京剧中的黑头行当，觉得唱黑头或演武二花一类的角色从人物作派、行腔、念白等更有铿锵伟岸的气势，更像个真正顶天立地的男子汉。因此，姜凤山没有接受校方的安排，也就错过了进入戏校学习深造的机会。

之后不久，经热心的远房亲戚牵线搭桥，姜凤山又来到京城文林社学戏，这一学就是四年光景，后来文林社因经营不善破产散伙，原班人马并入“富连成”科班。这回科班的班主让学黑头已有一定水准的姜凤山改攻青衣、花旦行当，姜凤山最终还是没有听从，万不得已来到了另外一家戏班子“福庆社”搭班唱戏。在这一节骨眼上，姜通过在梨园界有“活张飞”美誉的梨园前辈侯喜瑞的入室弟子关洪斌举荐，跟侯老学习了一阵京剧净行，随后拜京剧铜锤名家张鑫奎为师专攻文武花脸，这一学又是3个年头，从艺方式为边学边演，业内人士称之“带艺演戏”。至1933年时，学艺历尽坎坷的姜凤山差点儿又被黑心戏班子的班主给卖到外地，紧急关头多亏梅兰芳先生等一些侠义人士出面打点了不少钱财，才算平息了事。迫于生计的姜凤山还在名旦尚小云创立的“荣春

□ 琴师姜凤山　Huqin Player Jiang Fengshan

Jiang Fengshan followed Hou to learn the *Jing* role, then he followed the famous *Tongchui* player Zhang Xinkui for another three years. At the same time he also performed on stage, which is a very popular way at that time. By 1933, another frustration hit Jiang Fengshan. A troupe intended to sell him to other place. Jiang Fengshan was rescued because Mei Lanfang and other people gave much money to the owner. Under living pressure, Jiang Fengshan also joined Rongchun Troupe founded by famous *Dan* player Shang Xiaoyun.The troupe was led by the *Jing* player Lei Xifu, cooperating with Lei Zhendong and Shi Huibao to perform the excellent traditional plays, such as *Catching and Releasing Cao Cao(Zhuo Fang Cao)*, *Saving Song Jiang from Jiangzhou(Nao Jiangzhou)* and *Attacking Wancheng(Zhan Wancheng)*.

In the old society, to make a living Peking Opera players had to go to several opera theatres to perform throughout a day. As time went on, many actors couldn’t continue performing because of exhaustion and lack of the knowledge about protecting their throat. Young Jiang Fengshan didn’t escape the bad luck. But there is always a way out. Jiang Fengshan had been learning Jinghu accompaniment while learning opera. So at the age of 14, when he couldn’t perform on the stage, he began to accompany for Ma Decheng, his adoptive father.

There was an unwritten rule in the circle of opera performance.It was however well you sang or played Huqin, you would be regarded as a *Piaoyou* or an amateur who couldn’t go to elegant places. When he was 18 years old, Jiang

□姜凤山先生与陈立夫先生合影
Mr.Jiang and Chen Lifu,a Senior Kuomintang Member

社”以及净行前辈雷喜福挑班的戏班子里搭班唱戏，与雷振东、时慧宝等人联手上演了《捉放曹》、《闹江州》、《战宛城》等优秀的传统剧目。

旧社会京剧艺人为了养家糊口只能拼命“赶包”(意思为：一天内到几个戏园子之间轮番演戏)，久而久之不少演员疲惫不堪，加上不懂得科学保护嗓子，少年姜凤山嗓子倒仓，无法继续唱戏。有道是“天无绝人之路”，学戏唱戏之余的姜凤山，还一直将学习京胡伴奏作为“艺多不压身”的另一功夫加以操练，于是刚刚14岁的姜凤山，在不能唱戏的同时就开始为其义父马德成老先生操琴吊嗓子。

在过去演艺圈子里有条不成文的老规矩，甭管你戏唱得有多好、胡琴拉得有多棒，如果不正式磕头拜师于这个行当的权威人士，那么圈子内外永远把你当票友看。姜凤山在18岁那年经朋友沈子厚帮忙得以结识杜奎三。拜杜奎三为师后，姜凤山在梨园大多以操琴为主，中间偶尔也因救场而临时客串一下某些角色。像随京剧四大须生之一马连良先生创立的扶风社戏班子到上海、天津等地演出，姜凤山作

Fengshan got to know Du Kuishan, a disciple of Xu Lanyan (Mei Lang's uncle and first Jinghu accompaniment player). He began his accompaniment career after formally acknowledging Du Kuishan as his teacher. Occasionally, he would perform as stage-vacancy-filling actor. The Fufengshe Troupe, founded by Ma Lianliang, one of the Four *Xusheng* Players, went to Shanghai and Tianjin for performance, and Jiang Fengshan accompanied for Mr. Ma as a Jinghu and Erhu player in the opera F*our Successful Candidates of the Imperial Examination*, *Borrowing East Wind* and *Ruse of Empty City*. Jiang Fengshan sometimes accompanied for other performers such as famous *Laosheng* player Tan Fuying and Jin Boyin as well as Zhang Junqiu, Li Shifang and Song Dezhu, three of the Four Junior Famous *Dan* Players. Around 1948, because of the recommendation of Yu Yongli, the older brother of popular *Dan* player Xiaochuihua, Yu Lianquan, Jiang Fengshan became Peking Opera master Mei Lanfang's Huqin player. From then on, the two families developed friendship spanning two or more generations.During the Anti-Japanese War(1937-1945), Mei Lanfang maintained his beard and mustache, and refused to perform for the Japanese invasion army. And he didn't give any performance during the eight years.

In the early years after the founding of the People's Republic of China, Jiang Fengshan was invited to Mei Lanfang's residence in Huguo Temple as the Huqin player and to help Mr. Mei exercise his voice to resume his stage career. Hence, every day, they practised under the Chinese flowering crabapple

为乐队中主操京二胡、京胡的琴师，先后为马老板主演的传统剧目《四进士》、《借东风》、《空城计》等戏伴奏。有时又在其他名角儿如著名老生谭富英、金伯吟，四小名旦中的张君秋，李世芳、宋德珠等人表演的剧目中操琴。1948年前后，由这一时期的当红名旦“筱翠花”（真名：于连泉）的哥哥于永利热情推荐，姜凤山为在抗战期间拒绝为日本人演出而蓄须明志达数年的一代京剧大师梅兰芳担任琴师，姜老爷子开始了与梅家几代人之间的交往。

新中国建立初期，姜凤山作为专门为梅先生吊嗓子的琴师被日日请至护国寺的家中，帮梅兰芳尽快吊出唱青衣的小嗓儿以重返梨园。从此，梅兰芳家四合院内的海棠树、苹果树下，几乎天天都可听到大师在姜凤山所操京胡的悠扬曲调中咿咿呀呀的吊嗓子声音。为了使

□ 姜凤山老先生与梅葆玖在后台试嗓

Jiang Fengshan and the Son of Mei Lanfang, Mei Baojiu

trees and apple trees, and Mei Lanfang' s singing and Jinghu' s melodious tune could be heard from Mr. Mei' s Quadrangle. To get a better result, Jiang Fengshan adopted a step-by-step way. Every time he tuned higher a little and didn' t tell Mr. Mei in advance. As a result, it only took Mei Lanfang half a year to resume his voice for *Qingyi* role, which shook the world.

The news Mei Lanfang resuming his stage career brought great happniess to his fans. They lost no time in telling the good news to each other and rushed to opera theatres to watch Mei school performance, such as *Drunken Beauty*, *Luoshen, the Goddess of Heaven Scatters Flowers* and *Overland Parts with His Favorite Concubine*. It was well-known that Mei Lanfang had three Huqin players in his life, Xu Lanyuan, Wang Shaoqing and Jiang Fengshan respectively. Because of old age and poor health, Xu Lanyuan, Mei Lanfang's uncle and the first Huqin player, retired as early as before 1949. The second Huqin player was Wang Shaoqing, whose father was famous *Laosheng* player Wang Fengqing and his uncle, *Tongtian Jiaozhu* Wang Yaoqing. And he stayed in Mei's troupe longer than the other two. But due to poor health, he could not go on circuit performance with Mei Lanfang. Therefore, when Mei Lanfang visited the former Soviet Union, Japan, European countries as well as the Chinese People's Volunteer Army (PVA) in Korea, the first Jinghu player of his band was always Jiang Fengshan. During this period, Jiang Fengshan became the one who exchanged views with Mei Lanfang about performance most frequently. Because Jiang Fengshan had the experience of

吊音效果更佳且少走一些弯路，曾唱过戏的姜老采用循序渐进的吊嗓子方式，每次只调高一点但又不让梅先生事先知晓，以避免其因预先了解而紧张。结果用这样的方法练就下来果然效果不错，只一年半左右，连梅兰芳自己均未感觉多么费心吃力，嗓儿竟然神奇地顺利出来了。这让不少圈内外的人士惊奇不已。

梅兰芳先生复出梨园的消息，让憋闷许久的“梅派”戏迷高兴极了，人们互相奔走相告，争先到京城各大戏园子里一睹“梅派”《贵妃醉酒》、《洛神》、《天女散花》、《霸王别姬》等一系列优秀经典剧目的风采。众所周知为梅兰芳先生一生操琴伴奏的共有三位琴师，即徐兰沅、王少卿、姜凤山，其中梅先生的姨父徐兰沅老先生在解放前就因年事已高身体不太好而早已颐养天年。随后接班的王少卿是在梨园界有通天教主美誉的王瑶卿之侄，其父是京剧老生名家、人称凤二爷的王凤卿，他随梅老板的梅家戏班子年头最长。但王少卿先生身体状况也不佳，不便随梅兰芳出行。有鉴于此，在梅兰芳先生出访前苏联、日本、欧洲和慰问在朝鲜的中国人民志愿军时，随行担任乐队中首席京胡琴师的是姜凤山。这期间，有唱戏经历并担任操琴伴奏的姜凤山无疑就成为与梅兰芳先生就演戏问题切蹉最多的人之一，他们在艺术上经常不谋而合，而且姜老爷子还能不时地提出一些令梅先生也点头称道的好点子。

梅兰芳先生晚年曾在郑州应邀观看由马金凤主演的河南豫剧《穆桂英挂帅》，深受启发，回京后决定将其移植成

performance on the stage, they often had the same idea without previous consultation. And from time to time, Mr. Jiang could bring forward good ideas which were praised by Mr. Mei.

In his late years, after watching Henan Opera *Mu Guiying Takes Command* with Ma Jinfeng acting its leading role, Mei Lanfang was inspired and decided to adapt it into Peking Opera. He and other members worked day after night and just more than two months later, the Peking Opera *Mu Guiying Takes Command* took shape. As one of the main designers, Jiang Fengshan and the band made remarkable contribution to the sing or melodies, the spoken part, the rest and beat of music(Banshi) and the tune of Jinghu in this opera. The opera had been successively presented for 16 times in Beijing and there was not any vacant seat each time. It was the close cooperation among Mei Lanfang, the Huqin player and the drum player that made this opera set such a high ticket office record.

As the senior art director for Peking Opera Troupe of Beijing, Jiang Fengshan attached great attention in cultivating the successor of Mei school art, along with Mei Baojiu, the son of Mei Lanfang. Despite his age, Jiang Fengshan went to the troupe every month to explain the opera and demonstrate for the young performers from the basic skills such as gait to the expression in eyes, pronunciation, tune, and the cascading sleeve(Shuixiu). Mr. Jiang demonstrated very carefully so that the young performers could understand the true Mei school art rather than form. For thirty years, he and Mei Baojiu taught by personal example as well as verbal instruction.

京剧进行演出。梅兰芳先生与剧团里的其他主要演职员夜以继日通力合作，结果只用了两个多月的时间，就将这部规模宏大的杰作设计了出来。作为这出戏中唱腔、道白、板式、京胡曲调主要设计者之一的姜凤山老先生和乐队的贡献功不可没。正是梅兰芳先生和琴师、鼓师三方的鼎力协作才创下了该戏在北京连续上演十六场，场场爆满、座无虚席的高票房纪录。

作为北京京剧院梅兰芳京剧团元老级的艺术指导，姜凤山老爷子现已将主要精力放在与梅兰芳之子梅葆玖等人携手、培养深受观众喜爱的“梅派艺术”接班人的问题上。他不顾年事已高，每个月都要到剧团里为新人说戏、讲戏，从走台步等基本功到眼神、吐字、行腔、水袖等京戏的一招一式，老爷子示范起来都一丝不苟，目的就是要让更多的年轻演员学“梅派”不要学成“花架子”，而是真正领会梅大师系列经典剧目人物的神韵和表演技巧。姜老的努力耕耘终于结出了累累果实，在姜老和梅葆玖先生近三十年来的言传身教中，一批批海内外优秀的“梅派”青衣演员脱颖而出。如早已崭露头角的“梅派”再传弟子香港人董圆圆、台湾国剧社的魏海敏女士、中国京剧院的当红演员李胜素等年轻“梅派”青衣，均时常献艺于国内外的舞台上，使广大观众能再度欣赏到了极富艺术魅力的京剧“梅派艺术”的风韵。特别是近些年来，经姜凤山老先生、梅葆玖等其他戏曲专家的共同努力和深入挖掘，终于把梅兰芳先生几十年前一直未能彻底完成的优秀剧目《洛神赋》搬上

□《穆桂英挂帅》
Mu Guiying Takes Command

Jiang Fengshan's hard work had been paid off. Many excellent Mei school *Qinyi* players, both domestic and overseas, have come forth. For example, Dong Yuanyuan from Hongkong, Wei Haimin from Tianwan Peking Opera Troupe, and Li Shengsu from Chinese Peking Opera Theatre, often performed on domestic and overseas stages, and afforded numerous audience the opportunity to enjoy the charm of Mei school art. Through the concerted effort and further exploration from Jiang Fengshan, Mei Baojiu and other Peking Opera experts, Mei Lanfang's incomplete play, *An Ode to the Goddess of the Luo River*, was staged at last with the leading player, Ye school *Xiaosheng*, Ye Shaolan and Mei school *Qingyi*, Dong Yuanyuan. The incredible plot, fascinating character conflict, clear and elegant singing and performance, and magnificent lighting and setting, all these had produced a dreamlike audio and video art effect and made the audience immersed in the wonderful singing completely.

了梨园舞台。剧中故事情节跌宕起伏，人物冲突引人入胜，唱腔和表演堪称清丽优美，灯光布景华丽考究，营造出了一幅如梦幻般的视觉、听觉艺术效果，使人完全沉浸在叶派小生叶少兰、梅派青衣董圆圆那无比美妙的演唱之中。

姜凤山老先生本行是操京胡，戏迷们大多知道他是梨园界现为数不多的几位仍健在的泰斗级的京胡琴师，光拜老爷子为师的入室弟子就达30人之多，没有履行仪式的徒弟连他本人也记不清有多少了。其中有些人在社会上已具有相当的知名度，如北京京剧院优秀老旦演员赵葆秀的琴师燕守平先生、王福龙先生，梅葆玖先生的琴师舒健先生，上海京剧院著名京剧表演艺术家童祥苓先生的琴师陈正伟先生等人都出自其门下。20世纪90年代初，应台湾方面的邀请，姜凤山老先生随北京京剧院三次赴台访问演出。作为文化交流的主要内容之一，姜凤山老先生还特地为酷爱京剧的老票友张学良将军操琴助兴，就京剧流派、振兴京戏等艺术方面的问题与国民党元老陈立夫老先生进行了热情探讨。

姜老家住在劲松西街一幢旧式楼房里，屋内的陈设简洁明快，墙壁上悬挂着一幅幅姜老爷子不同年代从艺操琴的艺术照片。透过这些像片，可以看到一位老艺术家所走过的艺术之路。姜老爷子与梅家的世交堪称中华民族艺术界里尊情重谊、肝胆相照的杰出典范。

Jiang Fengshan is one of the few senior Jinghu players in Theater Garden cirle. He has no less than 30 formal disciples and countless informal ones. Some of them has enjoyed high popularity, such as Yan Shouping and Wang Fulong, Huqin players for Zhao Baoxiu (outstanding *Old Dan* player, Peking Opera House of Beijing); Shu Jian, Huqin player for Mei Baojiu; and Chen Zhengwei, Huqin player for famous Peking Opera perform artist Tong Xiangling. In the early years of 1990s, under the invitation of Taiwan, Peking Opera Troupe of Beijing had been to Taiwan for performance tour three times. And Jiang Fengshan was one of the members. As one major part of culture exchange, Jiang Fengshan particularly accompanied for Gen.Zhang Xueliang, an old *Piaoyou* who was very fond of Peking Opera almost a hundred years old. He also made a hot discussion with Chen Lifu, a senior Kuomintang member, about the different schools of Peking Opera and how to develop the opera.

Today, Mr. Jiang lives in an old style building, Jinsong West Street, Chaoyang District. Decorated simply. There are many Jiangfengshan' s art photographs in different ages on the wall. Through these photos, we can find the art track that this old artist has left. And the friendship between Mr. Jiang and Mei family is an excellent model of cherishing friendship and being royal to each other in Chinese national art circle.

新凤霞与万胜轩

Xin Fengxia and Wanshengxuan Theater

□ 万胜轩旧址 The Relic of Wansheng Theater

地地道道的老北京人，都知道过去的宣南老天桥平民游艺场，因为它一度是许多京城老百姓的娱乐场所。但是如果忽然冷不丁地问这样一个问题：“听说老天桥过去有个叫万胜轩的小戏园子，已故著名评剧表演艺术家新凤霞早年没出名以前，曾在这里演出过评剧《小二黑结婚》、《李三娘》等剧目，您知道吗?”这个来自犄角旮旯的问题，十有八九可能把老北京也给问愣。今天我们其他问题一概不论，只表新凤霞与著名京味儿文学家老舍先生相识于老天桥万胜轩的一段鲜为人知的往事。

当年的万胜轩小戏园子条件十分简陋，土坯戏台上面搭个芦苇席棚，既不能为演员挡风，也不能遮雨，远道而来的观众则在露天地里的大条板凳上就坐看戏。1949年，新凤霞和家人迫于生计，从徐州、唐山、天津等地，一路辗

Native-born Beijingers all know the old carnie of Tianqiao outside the South of Xuanwu Gate because it was a recreational place for ordinary people. But if they are asked with such a question,“I heard there used to be a little theatre called Wansheng Theater, and the Ping Opera artist Xin Fengxia who has passed away now used to put on show there before she got her fame, such as shows like *Little Erhei’s Marriage* and *Ma’am Li San*, do you know about these?” Such an odd question would probably beat most of them. There are a lot to say, but here we would only tell the story about how the famous Beijing style litterateur Lao She got to know Xin Fengxia, the famous Ping Opera artist, at the Wanshengxuan.

The old Wansheng Theatre was a simple earth-brick stage with a shed over. It couldn’t keep the wind and rain out and audiences could only be seated on the long benches while enjoying shows. Ping Opera was very popular in Beijing, Tianjin, North and Northeast China with a history of more than 70 years. In 1949, Xin Fengxia and her family moved from Xuzhou, Tangshan, Tianjin to this place, in order to make a living. Right after putting up the first show, she gained applause with her clear and beautiful moving voice. Xin Fengxia did her best with several good shows

转来到这里落户卖艺。新凤霞当年在万胜轩小戏台甫一亮相，就以其清脆、婉转、动听、极富感染力的评剧疙瘩腔，引起台下评剧戏迷的热烈掌声。新凤霞也拿出了自己的浑身解数，将几出拿手好戏如《小二黑结婚》、《白毛女》、《李四娘》奉献给了京城的平民百姓，很快就在这儿站稳了脚。新凤霞在天桥游艺场万胜轩小戏台唱评剧一炮走红的消息，很快传遍北京四九城，短期内便吸引了不少评剧戏迷。天桥一家客栈为了招揽生意，甚至在旅店的显著位置挂上了新凤霞的大幅照片，与照片相配的是六句极富诱惑力的广告："新凤霞唱戏在万胜轩，一毛钱就能看上一整天，请您来住我们兴盛店，大通铺卫生舒坦保平安，兴盛店离万胜轩不太远，看戏回来还能省车钱。"

一天，刚从国外回到北京定居的老舍先生在赵树理等人的陪同下，也来到了天桥万胜轩戏园子，和其他观众一样坐在大条板凳上有滋地味地欣赏新凤霞表演的评剧，而且一看就是两三出。老舍先生是个地地道道的北京通，更是北京方言的大师。戏刚一演完，顶礼帽、戴

like *Xiao Erhei' s Marriage*, *White Hair Lady*, and was immediately accepted by the Beijing ordinary people. The news that Xin Fengxia was putting up shows in Wansheng Theater soon spread out in Beijing, and lots of Ping Opera fans came to see her. A little hotel has even put out an enlarged picture of Xin Fengxia in a prominent place, and there was an advertisement beside it, saying "Xin Fengxia is giving show at Wansheng Theater, 10 cents for a whole day, please come to live in our place, with clean and comfortable beds, convenient transportation for seeing the show".

One winter day, Lao She who just returned to Beijing from abroad came with Zhao Shuli, the famous novelist and leading figure of modern Chinese literature, to Wansheng Theatre. He got seated on a bench like common audience and enjoyed Xin Fengxia's performance. Lao She knew Beijing very well and was a Beijing dialect master. After the show, Lao She came onto the stage, and congratulated to all the performers and musicians. He shook hands with Xin Fengxia and said humourously: "Are you Xin Fengxia? So you are a new performer of the new country with the new

□《刘巧儿》剧照
The Photo of *Liu Qiao' r*

□ 新式戏棚万盛轩
The Fashion Theater, Wanshenxuan

着眼镜、拄着拐杖的老舍先生就主动走上台去，双手抱拳向所有演员和乐师表示由衷的祝贺，并握着戏中主角新凤霞的手幽默地说："你是新凤霞吗?新社会的新演员，又唱出评剧的新腔新调儿，你占了好几个新呀……"当得知自幼从艺的新凤霞不识几个字时，老舍先生严肃而又不失亲切地说："这可不行啊！要先从一二三四等最简单的东西学起，要随时想着学，抓紧学，有了文化才能提高演唱艺术。以后不演戏了，拿起笔来能写，当作家，当先生。"最后老舍先生还风趣地说："天桥儿是个好玩的地方儿，藏龙卧虎哇！七行八作都是有能耐的人……"正当演员们忙着搬道具准备下一场戏的时候，老舍先生悄没声儿地从外边买来了一大把冰糖葫芦，随之送给每一位在场的演职员。当时时值寒冬腊月，大家围着煤火炉子，边吃边聊。陪同老舍先生看戏的赵树理笑着介绍说："老舍先生刚刚从国外回来，他把祖国比作一个温暖的火炉呀。"

在以后的岁月中，老舍先生为了解和吸收北京民间艺术的营养，又先后数次来到北京市井文化的发源地天桥。而且每次来，总是不言不语地选择到万胜轩小戏园子，专注地听新凤霞唱评剧。也许是缘分吧，新凤霞也很喜欢向老舍先生请教各类问题，先生尽其所知一一作答。在繁忙紧张的写作之余，老舍先生有时遛弯儿就来到新凤霞家住的小小院落，到家中嘘寒问暖，共同切磋评剧，探讨艺术等。随着交往的日益增多，彼此成为了推心置腹的好朋友。

新凤霞没几年就到了女大当婚的芳

way of performing Ping Opera, you' ve got quite some news, right?" When he got to know that Xin Fengxia was illiterate, he talked to her seriously and affectionately: "You have to improve, start from the very beginning, learn whenever possible, you can improve your skill only if you are educated. Even later on you do not act, you could write things, becoming a writer, a teacher." Finally he said, "Tianqiao is a great place, with lots of talented people, in all kinds of professions." When performers prepared the stage for the next show, Lao She went out and bought many local snacks, and ate with the performers around the furnace. Zhao Shuli told them in a smile:"Master Lao She just came back from overseas, he think our homeland is just like a warm furnace."

In the following years, Lao She has been back to Tiaoqiao area, the cradle land of Beijing folk art, for serveal times. Whenever he came, he would quietly sit in the Wansheng Theatre and enjoy Xin Fengxia's performance in full attention. Xin Fengxia also liked to ask him all kinds of question, and Lao She would provide answers as much as he knew. He would drop by Xin Fengxia's little courtyard, chatting about

□新凤霞与吴祖光
Xin Fengxia and Wu Zuguang

龄，不少热心的人都愿为新凤霞张罗人生大事。此时新凤霞与相依为命的二姨共同生活在北京天桥的一处院落中，老舍去过几次她家，朋友之间真诚相待，互不隔心。二姨深知老舍的为人，凤霞更是打心眼里信赖文质彬彬的老舍先生，娘儿俩不谋而合地都愿意在婚姻大事上，请老舍先生拿主意。于是心细的新凤霞将自己的择偶想法，先向老舍先生交底："希望选择一个在艺术上能帮助我，文化知识上能教导我的人，岁数如果大些也行……"老舍先生听完凤霞的想法后，接连说出了几个人的名字，其中就有大名鼎鼎的著名剧作家吴祖光。新凤霞闻听吴祖光的名字后，腼腆羞涩地低声说："吴祖光这个人我有印象，在解放前我就演过他写的话剧《风雪夜归人》。"老舍先生脸上露出了笑容，紧接着很恳切地说："吴祖光是我抗战时期的好朋友，他为人厚道正直，又特别有才华……"不久，经过老舍先生这个红媒牵线，这对有情人经过一段时间的交往与了解，终于水到渠成喜结连理。在以后的几十年中，不论经历了多少风云变幻，老舍先生一家始终是吴祖光新凤霞夫妇可以信赖的好朋友。

评剧名家新凤霞当年成名时的万胜轩小戏园子，于20世纪60年代初经过改建，如今已成为万胜轩剧场。经过几十年的风风雨雨，这座文物级的剧场仍然矗立在天桥北纬路上。

Ping Opera and discussing art. They became good friends.

Several years passed, Xin Fengxia has reached the age of getting married, and many people were willing to help her. At that time, Xin Fengxia lived with her auntie in a courtyard at Tianqiao area. Lao She have visited her residence for several times. Both her auntie and she knew Lao She was a gentleman and they relied on him to make decisions on her marriage. Xin Fengxia told Lao She her ideal partner: "Should be someone who could help me in art, someone who could teach me, older is acceptable." Lao She picked out some names, and one of them was Wu Zuguang, the famous dramatist. When his name was mentioned, Xin Fengxia said in a shy voice:"I know him, I played his drama *Coming back in a Blizzard Night* before the liberation." Lao She smiled and said in a warm voice:"Wu Zuguang is a good friend of mine, and we met in the Second World War. He is an out-straight and especially talented person." With Lao She's help, the two persons got to know each other, and finally got married. The new couple have always taken Lao She as their trustworthy friend.

The little show place that Xin Fengxia got famous was rebuilt in early 1960s, now it has become the Wansheng Theatre. After all these years, this historical site is still standing on the Beiwei Road of Tianqiao area.

图书在版编目（CIP）数据

北京杂谈／张本瀛著. —北京：中国建筑工业出版社，2006
（老北京的故事）
ISBN 978-7-112-08794-5

Ⅰ.北… Ⅱ.张… Ⅲ.北京市—概况 Ⅳ.K921

中国版本图书馆 CIP 数据核字 (2006) 第 116871 号

责任编辑：张幼平
责任校对：梁珊珊

老北京的故事 THE OLD STORY OF BEIJING
北京杂谈 Beijing By-talk

张本瀛　著 Written by Zhang Benying
李有光　译 Translated by Li Youguang
胡伟雄　金　菊　校 Proofread by Hu Weixiong,Jin Ju
*
中国建筑工业出版社 出版、发行（北京西郊百万庄）
各地新华书店、建筑书店经销
北京方舟正佳图文设计有限公司制版
北京中科印刷有限公司印刷
*
开本：880 × 1230 毫米　1/32
印张：6　字数：228 千字
版次：2008 年 3 月第一版
印次：2008 年 3 月第一次印刷
印数：2500 册
定价：39.00 元
ISBN 978-7-112-08794-5
(15458)